THE

OBJECT

STARES

BACK

ALSO BY JAMES ELKINS

The Poetics of Perspective

On the

Nature

of Seeing

A HARVEST BOOK
HARCOURT BRACE & COMPANY
San Diego   New York   London

THE
OBJECT
STARES
BACK

James Elkins

This Harvest edition published by arrangement
with Simon & Schuster, Inc.

Library of Congress Cataloging-in-Publication Data
Elkins, James, 1955–
The object stares back: on the nature of seeing/James Elkins.
p.   cm.—(A Harvest book)
Originally published: New York: Simon & Schuster, c1996.
Includes bibliographical references and index.
ISBN 0-15-600497-6
1. Visual perception. 2. Vision. 3. Visual communication   I. Title.
[BF241.E45   1998]
152.14—dc21   97-15949

Text set in Bembo
Designed by Karolina Harris
Printed in the United States of America

First Harvest edition 1997

A C E F D B

*Special thanks to my literary agent, Patricia Van der Leun:
her insights gave this book its form.*

For the

inconstant memory

of a face

that I will never

see again

Contents

Introduction

A T first, it appears that nothing could be easier than seeing. We just point our eyes where we want them to go, and gather in whatever there is to see. Nothing could be less in need of explanation. The world is flooded with light, and everything is available to be seen. We can see people, pictures, landscapes, and whatever else we need to see, and with the help of science we can see galaxies and viruses and the insides of our own bodies. Seeing does not interfere with the world or take anything from it, and it does not hurt or damage anything. Seeing is detached and efficient and rational. Unlike the stomach or the heart, eyes are our own to command: they obey every desire and thought.

E A C H one of those ideas is completely wrong. The truth is more difficult: seeing is irrational, inconsistent, and undependable. It is immensely troubled, cousin to blindness and sexuality, and caught up in the threads of the unconscious. Our eyes are not ours to command; they roam where they will and then tell us they have only been where we have sent them. No matter how hard we look, we see very little of what we look at. If we imagine the eyes as navigational devices, we do so in order *not* to come to terms with what seeing really is. Seeing is like hunting and like dreaming, and even like falling in love. It is entangled in the passions—jealousy, violence, possessiveness; and it is soaked in affect—in pleasure and displeasure, and in pain. Ultimately, seeing alters the thing that is seen and transforms the seer. Seeing is metamorphosis, not mechanism.

This is a book about the nature of sight, and whether it is possible to understand what the eyes are about. The first chapter introduces the problems that beset vision, especially the strange connection that links the observer with the observed. The second chapter pursues that relation into an odd realm where objects have eyes and can stare back. That idea begins, I think, in childish fears. There's an uncanny feeling when a darkened doorway becomes a roomful of eyes and every shadow seems to grow a face. That fear, left over from some ancient instincts, is with us every day in an attenuated form. Each object has a presence—a being and a face of its own—and if we take that seriously (not as a vague intuition but as a fact of vision), then the world is full of eyes. Seeing is being seen, and the world is so crowded with things that see and stare that we can stand to be aware of only a tiny fraction of them: more would overwhelm us. Chapter 2 paints a picture of that world and populates it with seeing eyes, unseen eyes, and unseeing eyes, on humans, on objects, and especially on butterfly wings.

As the book progresses it turns more to the problem of what cannot be seen. Chapter 3 is about the inconstancy of vision and our helplessness to control how we see the world. There are things we don't see, even when we are looking straight at them, and other things we stare at obsessively, so that we are blind to everything else. Some things can never be clearly seen, no matter how much we may want to see them: the sun will blind us (or so it seems), and it may not be possible to see the moment of death. Thinking about things that are hard to see also shows us how we ordinarily see, and how every scene is punctured with unacceptable objects. Vision skips them, like a man stepping over half-buried mines.

The next chapters explore two of the most important kinds of visible objects: bodies and faces. Bodies of any sort (even microscopic ones) have an intense fascination all their own. In daily life, as each new scene presents itself, we tend to look first at bodies and only afterward let our eyes take in whatever else is there. It may be that the unthinking search for bodies is the most fundamental operation of vision and that, even when there are no bodies present, we continue to understand the world in terms of bodily forms, textures, or metaphors. Chapter 4 is about bodies, especially their insides—the parts we cannot see, and fear the most because they herald death.

Next to bodies, faces are most crucial. Faces are so elementary, so immured in what it means to be human, that it can be nearly impossible to understand what they mean to us. In the ordinary way of speaking, a face is something that has eyes, a mouth, and some other orifices and sits atop a body. But that kind of clinical definition cannot be enough, because faces have such a persistent fascination for our eyes. How do we look at faces? What are faces most like? How do we remember them? And most important, what happens if we are unsure whether we are looking at a face at all? The fifth chapter pursues these questions and proposes that faces are different from all other visible objects in that they represent the idea of the mind.

Many examples in this book have to do with failing to see, and the final chapter explores one of the deepest strata of vision, the complicity between blindness and sight. Recent medical experiments have shown that a great deal of vision is unconscious: we are blind to certain things and blind to our blindness. Those twin blindnesses are necessary for ordinary seeing: we need to be continuously partially blind in order to see. In the end, blindnesses are the constant companions of seeing and even the very condition of seeing itself.

T H E thoughts that led to this book have taken me far outside the field in which I am trained, the history and theory of art. Even so, I often start on a problem by thinking about paintings and other kinds of pictures. Some of what art historians say comes from psychoanalysis and philosophy, and I have drawn freely from those fields. The book also makes connections with some psychology and neuroanatomy of vision, with biological studies of vision in animals, and with technological research on machine vision. Other disciplines are engaged with vision, but perhaps the most important is creative art, since artists have been making exact statements about the ways the world appears since long before vision was ever an academic question. For that reason, pictures are a central subject of this book, both as history and as studio experience.

The art historian Erwin Panofsky once spoke of the Renaissance as the time of "decompartmentalization." It's a gangly word, but it's apt for the breaking of barriers that was typical of some Renaissance thought. (Yet Leonardo da Vinci, the exemplary Renaissance man, did not always break down the compartments of knowledge. As often as not, he built them up by developing each field to new heights.) Decompartmentalization makes sense when a number of different specialties are working on the same subject, but separately from one another. In this case, psychoanalysis, neurophysiology, phenomenology, existentialism, experimental and clinical psychology, painting, art history, medicine, and strains of poststructuralism are all at work on questions of how we see, and it does not always help to keep them distinct. I have mingled those disciplines in this book, though this is not the kind of text where theories can be argued at length with the one-track determination of a monograph. For those who want to go further, readings are gathered at the end of the book—but because this is a synthetic effort, there is no book that covers the same material, no introductory reader's guide to visual theory.

Even though this book presumes no special knowledge, it is not a popularization of existing ideas. Ordinarily I do not think it's a particularly good idea to write a popular account of some science or art. Especially in the sciences, popularization means bowdlerization, because what is exact about the exact sciences is their equations, and without them an explanation is at best a translation into a new language. Stephen Hawking's history of time and James Gleick's chaos, for example, are not just simpler versions of the original sciences but entirely different enterprises that make different claims and lead to different questions. The same may be said of omitting the jargon that makes some texts in the humanities opaque: when that is done, the subject itself changes, and a readable version of Martin Heidegger or Jacques Lacan is different in kind from the original. Jargon, contrary to the usual opinion, cannot be stripped away in favor of good writing. So I would not have written this book if it were only a matter of re-presenting ideas that were already known in their respective fields. Instead, what I have tried to do is write an interdisciplinary account of vision, keeping to the common ground of ordinary language in order to be able to speak differently. Vision is too close to our lives to be left languishing in its opaque disciplines.

One

"Just Looking"

W H A T is the simplest—the absolute minimum—that can be said about seeing? That the eye opens and the light comes in. What is the least that vision can accomplish, the easiest task for the eyes? It is seeing without thinking of seeing: seeing without strain, not squinting at a sharp light or peering intently into a darkness or trying to focus on something a finger's breadth away, but merely seeing, in a passive, unthinking way. In a word: just looking.

And when does that happen? Normally, almost all the time: seeing happens without our noticing that we are seeing. There are, of course, those bewildered moments in the early morning when your eyes are trying to remember how to see and you have to help them find their focus. Eyes just opened after a heavy sleep are bleary, and clogged with the thoughts of the night. They are unfocused and unwilling. The first look in a mirror may reveal not a face but a cottony blur bathed in garish fluorescent light. Only later and with effort does the face congeal into an approximate focus and reflect a more or less acceptable human shape. And at the end of a long day, it all happens in reverse: late at night the words in a book start to slur and waver, until black-and-white becomes gray, gray darkens into black, and the eyes close over what remains of the page. These are daily problems with seeing, and they do not require much attention—not more than one or two minutes a day.

The same happens on a much larger scale over the course of a lifetime. To infants, the world is said to be a great glowing confusion, a bewilderment with no beginning or end. In old age the world can become infuriatingly inexact, and it can refuse to snap back into focus. As the eyes weaken and slowly give way, the world and the people in it dim and recede and finally die along with the eyes in an opaque gloom. In that respect, each day rehearses the progress of the eyes from birth to death.

Still, this daily drama of the eyes, which foreshadows the darknesses of old age, is only a minuscule portion of the daily ration of sight. Normally we open our eyes and see, and it is as easy as breathing. Even people with thick glasses spend many hours forgetting how oddly they are forced to view the world. Ordinarily, just looking is just what the eyes do: they open, they see the world, they close.

But vision, I think, is more like the moments of anxious squinting than the years of effortless seeing. Looking at the world is not a matter of raising the eyelids and turning the eyes in their sockets; or, to say it more exactly, that idea is a lie we tell in order to make sense of ourselves. In hopes of overturning that fiction as forcibly and quickly as possible, I have arranged this first chapter as a kind of point-by-point refutation of "just looking." It is a skeptical exercise, and it opens the door to a wider and deeper account.

The first thing to be said is that this informal notion of just looking will not do, since the eyes never merely accept light. Instead, there is force to the light: it pushes its way into our eyes; and conversely, there is force to the eyes: they push their way into the world. The phrase "just looking" is a point of departure, and later I will use a more formal sentence to describe seeing: "The observer looks at the object." That sentence—that version of the fiction—condenses the three irreducible elements of vision: the subject, the act of seeing, and the object that is seen. It looks as sturdy as a description of seeing could be. Yet it also comes apart: first, because looking is suspect, and then, because it is built on the very simple but mistaken idea that the observer and the object are two different things. In the end, I think, the sentence itself is a kind of hopeless nonsense: there is no such thing as an observer looking at an object, if seeing means a self looking out at a world.

(One word about vocabulary. "Vision" usually means the anatomical action of the eyes, and "sight" refers to all the wider senses of seeing, from suspicion to unconscious desires. I follow that distinction in a haphazard way because I think that, the more neurological evidence is taken into account, the harder it is to separate anatomy from history, manners, or psychology.)

L E T me begin with another daily example. Sometimes, when I'm shopping, I pause a little too long in front of a counter. A salesperson leans my way and says, "May I help you?"

And I reply, "No, just looking."

I wonder at that question. How did she know just when to ask? Was it something in the way I was standing? Was I lingering, as if I couldn't quite leave? Maybe I looked a little dazed, as if I weren't really concentrating. Probably, though, I looked as if I had been caught: hooked by the object in the display case. Some objects have an irresistible effect, as if we were tied to them by little wires. It could be that the salesperson had been watching me from a distance, the way some spiders hide at the edge of the web until a moth becomes so tangled that it's safe to approach. When the salesperson saw I was half caught, she came a little nearer and asked her question.

The threads that tie us to objects are invisibly fine, and normally we scarcely notice their little tugs and pulls. But the webs of vision are there nonetheless. All those familiar gestures of shoppers—bending forward for a closer look and then straightening up, raising the eyebrows, tilting the head to one side, stepping back to think, shifting weight from one foot to the other, crossing the arms, sighing, scratching the head—those are signs that they are already caught in the web.

Thinking of things this way, I begin to wonder if shopping isn't like being hunted. Instead of saying I am the one doing the looking, it seems better to say that objects are all trying to catch my eye, and their gleams and glints are the hooks that snare me. A harmless display case of watches becomes a forest of traps, a dangerous place for my eyes. Every shining dial and silver band is a barb, a tiny catch just the size of my eye. Perhaps shoppers are like fish who like to swim in waters full of hooks.

At the same time, shopping is also hunting. After all, I am the one who decides to go shopping, and normally I'm on the lookout for something in particular: I'm hunting for it and trying to pick it out of the thousands of objects that I do not want. If I can find the one perfect watch, it's because I know what I'm looking for, and I can tell a good watch from imitations and distinguish styles that are very close to one another. In this way of looking at things, the watches are all camouflaged: each is almost identical to the next, and the one I want is somewhere among them. Like a leopard hunting in the jungle, I can look at a tangle of leaves, vines, and flickering lights and pick out just half of the pupil of a frightened deer.

J U S T looking is just hunting, but it is not quite right to say it is *only* hunting. There is also something quietly hypnotic about just looking, something less like hunting and more like dreaming. It is as if the looker were Gulliver, tied to the beach by the Lilliputians but still dreaming he's in England having a nice time, perhaps out for a stroll, but beginning to notice in some dull way that it's hard to move—it's inexplicably difficult to just *walk* down that street in London, to reach out and turn that doorknob—and then waking up and discovering himself in a much worse nightmare. But unlike Gulliver, I never really wake up. Just looking is like dreaming, but dreaming fitfully, tossing and turning and not knowing quite what's happening.

And the dream also gives pleasure. The shoppers who struggle, and then let themselves become even more entangled, and then struggle again, are often hoping to lose. They want to be caught— that's part of the game of shopping—and they let themselves be swathed in threads. When I am entranced by something, I tend to forget everything else. I lose track of where I am, what I'm doing there, and how much time I have before my next appointment. If there are people waiting in line behind me, I forget them. For a while I am harmlessly hypnotized, and the world falls away, leaving me in a silent, empty place, alone with the object.

So just looking is like hunting or being hunted, but it is also kin to hypnosis, nightmares, and dreams. Those meanings draw near to yet another, because there is also a deep parallel between looking and loving. Sometimes falling in love really feels like falling, as if you have no control, always tilting forward like that first step parachutists take out of a plane. Then you may be genuinely helpless, at the mercy of the person who has caught your eye. Saying that someone is caught or is swept off her feet or falls for someone are all ways of describing the work of the invisible strands. On other occasions love is all a calculated pursuit. Some people spend their lives searching like detectives among all the faces and bodies they can find. The snares and visual wires are laid thick between their eyes and the eyes of the people they love. But as lovers say, it's not always so easy to know who catches whom, and looking happens in both directions. There might be a good definition of love here: love as the moment when the prey becomes another hunter, so that both people are hunters and hunted at once. It wouldn't be enough that I hunt you and you hunt me in return—love would be the state in which I hunt a hunter or fall prey to prey.

It's strange that love stories begin to fill my mind when I meant to think only about looking, and that is what I want to say about that phrase "just looking." It is not possible; there is no such moment. All seeing is heated. It must always involve force and desire and intent. Even when I think I am *least* interested, I am already on the prowl. It doesn't matter what I'm looking at—a watch, a shiny hook; "just looking" is a lie. I am always looking *out,* looking *for,* even just looking *around*. Even the mildest looking—for example, right now, as I sit typing these words, glancing at my hands and up at the screen, looking over at my empty coffee cup—even this weightless looking is *directed*. I need to hit the right key and find the right word. I need to see the words on the screen, and at the moment I would like to see a full cup of coffee. There is no looking that is not also directed at something, aimed at some purpose. Looking is looking *at* or *for* or just *away*. Everything that the eye falls on has some momentary interest and possible use.

The proof of this is the way that absentminded looking becomes contaminated with stray thoughts. If I'm just looking around while thinking of something else, every object that comes into focus will remind me of my life: the calendar reminds me I haven't changed it this week; the old file folders remind me of work not yet done; the black architect's lamp reminds me I don't like architect's lamps; the coffee cup reminds me again that I am thirsty. Even when I am not thinking of the use of objects, they remind me of use. And there is a curious thing here that easily passes unnoticed: I do not focus on anything that is not connected in some way with my own desires and actions. I fail to see the stretches of wall between the lamp and the coffee cup, or the manila paper of the file folders, or the black plastic calendar holder. My eyes can understand only desire and possession. Anything else is meaningless and therefore invisible.

When I say, "Just looking," I mean I am searching, I have my "eye out" for something. Looking is hoping, desiring, never just taking in light, never merely collecting patterns and data. Looking is possessing or the desire to possess—we eat food, we own objects, and we "possess" bodies—and there is no looking without thoughts of using, possessing, repossessing, owning, fixing, appropriating, keeping, remembering and commemorating, cherishing, borrowing, and stealing. I cannot look at *anything*—any object, any person—without the shadow of the thought of possessing that thing. Those appetites don't just accompany looking: they are looking itself.

ORDINARILY we are convinced otherwise. Aren't there moments of pure seeing, when I'm not trying to find anything in particular? Even if desire infects seeing, can't there be times when I am in remission from the incessant urging of desire? Is looking always also shopping and hunting and loving and dreaming, never blank, affectless seeing? As I write these lines, I'm sitting at a desk that faces a blank wall. I like it that way because it offers no distraction, but sometimes I turn my head to my left, where there's a panorama of the city. Today is a particularly beautiful summer afternoon with a bright hazy sky. The trees are sheets of green broken by buildings, and there's a lake scattered with white sails. My eyes love this scene, and I keep looking away from the computer and letting my gaze drift through the trees and the heavy air and then out onto the distant lake. Could there be anything tense about this? Is this still a kind of hunger? I think it may be, since I also look out there when I find myself at a loss for a word or an idea. Writing is hard, and when my concentration is broken it needs to be healed by bathing in the soft, meaningless landscape. That unselfish, abstracted, empty moment I spend looking at sailboats and thinking of nothing is really an oasis for my eyes, a source of nourishment that lets me continue my pursuit of words. It only seems to be a senseless pleasure. It's more like a quick drink of water during a speech or a gasp of air after a long dive. I would almost say that the moments I spend looking at the view are not looking at all: they are the gasps between looking, the balm that lets me use my eyes as pitilessly as I can. Seeing is incessant searching from the first moments we can focus our blurry infant eyes all the way to the closing second when we last see the world.

Usually an afternoon in an art museum is a way to relax and enjoy a little leisure. We may even lull ourselves into believing we are there for purely aesthetic reasons, just to bask in the colors and to remain impassive. I'd like to think that's true, anyway: that I could lose myself in the pictures and be finally freed of the pressing little urges and necessities of ordinary living.

But another part of me knows it is not so. For one thing, I can sense that I'm relaxing in order to work after I've left the museum. The paintings offer the same softness as the view out of my window. They're like erasers moving over a crowded blackboard: the clutter is gone, leaving a beautiful emptiness—but the entire purpose of erasing the blackboard is to do *more work* and to get at it right away, as soon as the confusion is cleared. It's no different for me, even though I am trained as an art historian, and so a museum is a place I go to work. Paintings still have that effect—they are ways of thinking about something *other* than what I am. And if I attend to my seeing carefully enough, I will note all the signs of possession creeping under the veneer of disinterested enjoyment. In front of an imposing portrait of Napoleon I begin to feel a little edgy, and I may find my eyes straying from his face to his epaulets or his buttonholes, just like an intimidated clerk who can't look his master in the eye. In front of a painting of a nude I may start to feel uncomfortable, thinking about how I might be caught staring; or else my mind may begin to swim with thoughts of smooth skin and warmth. In front of a still life, I may—if I listen to my thoughts closely enough— begin to hear a faint voice urging me to eat, as if I could pick up the knife that the painter has carefully left on the table and begin buttering some bread. These are the almost inaudible urgings of my possessive eyes, trying to work the way they would with real-life objects and knowing they shouldn't and can't. One of the most interesting properties of pictures is the way they provoke this stifled dialogue, how they hold out the possibility of disinterested seeing while offering the eyes so much. My eyes and mind and body and fingertips all respond to the picture, or rather they *want* to respond, and the picture keeps stopping them, shutting them down and trying to keep them quiet. So even a museum is a place where seeing is possession, or the hope or memory of it. I can't "just look" in a museum any more than I can in a store, and it's worse in a museum because I can't touch, I can't hold, I can't own—in short, I can't complete the urge that seeing starts.

Even so, it would be wrong to insist too much on any of this, because we get along in the world by pretending, or perhaps I should say deeply believing, that vision is passive. In a word, we sometimes think that artworks provoke "disinterested interest": we are engaged, but we don't *want* anything but ocular pleasure. I would say that those who defend that idea may *need* to see artworks in that way: they may need to think that the work provides a privileged kind of seeing, released from the unpoetic urges of biology. And in a way that's a sensible attitude, since it lets them get on with the business of seeing without being tied down to metaphors of spider's webs and helpless moths. I can't see the way I normally do if I'm constantly thinking of how each harmless glance is tangled in some sticky web of unthought urges.

Seeing is effortless and mercurial, or so it seems, and it appears we prefer it that way. But we cannot permanently forget the harshness and pressure of seeing. Seeing is at the very root of our way of getting along in the world, and a single look can have all the force of hatred and violence that may end up being expressed in more brutal ways. Consider, for instance, a particularly harsh example of seeing, one that bears evidence of the intimate connection between the habitual incessant searching of seeing and some less pleasant thoughts, especially unhappiness, displeasure, violence, and pain. The example comes from La Salpêtrière, a Parisian hospital. In the nineteenth and early twentieth century, the doctors at La Salpêtrière published a journal that was mostly concerned with the appearances of patients. They wondered, for instance, how a hysterical patient looks. Does hysteria give a person a particular face? Does it produce certain gestures, certain typical poses? Does a melancholic have an identifiable expression? Is there such a thing as a wandering Jew, and if so, how might one appear? What happens to someone who spends her entire life in bed? What does it look like to have a belly so fat it scrapes the floor? The doctors who worked at La Salpêtrière were interested in neurological pathologies, and they tried to understand them by photographing the patients' gestures, their poses, expressions, mannerisms, "irritable signs," and twitches.

One article exhibits a photograph of a eunuch (figure 1). The face is impassive or perhaps resigned. It is a tired face, and the eyes are gently shut, as if to close out the world and "dissolve the skin and the name," as the novelist Harold Brodkey puts it. At first the body seems posed, as if the eunuch meant to show off some feminine grace, and then we see the inwardness of it, how the arms enclose the body without hiding it, how the legs are relaxed and frail.

The accompanying text tells a sad story about a forty-year-old man, habitually stoned on hashish, who declared he was going to marry a princess and raise a family. With the princess, he thought, he would have an orgasm and an ejaculation. He had once been manic-depressive, but recently he had "entered into a period of continuous calm." The text is written by a doctor and it is not unsympathetic. But these stories are followed by a brutal medical assessment. "Rectal examination revealed a normal prostate," the

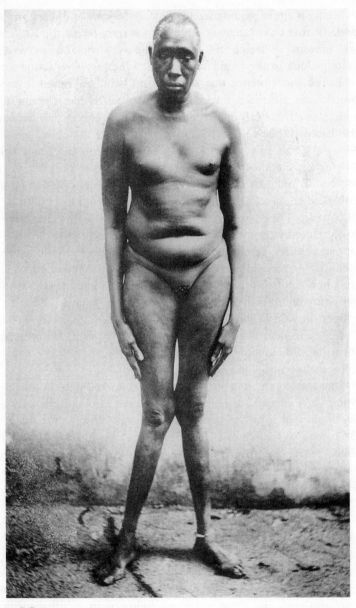

■ FIGURE 1

doctor writes, meaning nothing less than that he had inserted a finger into the subject's rectum. Ejaculations in such cases are possible, the doctor explains, by the expulsion of nonspermatic secretions. The orgasms are to be understood as wishful thinking based on the sensations produced by irritating the mucous membrane around the urethra.

The whole diagnosis is impersonal, and it is done in a particularly medical fashion: the body is a hard fact, and even the strongest fantasy cannot make it into something else. The doctor's entire manner is professionally impeccable—which is to say it is horrible, invasive and brutish. The eunuch, who is already once removed from us in the photograph, is brought a little nearer by the story of his imaginary wedding and then thrown back away from us by the medical account of his body. The photograph is the harshest of all: it penetrates his privacy with an insistent, intense thrust that cannot be rejected.

This is the violent side of seeing, where the mere act of looking —an act that can also be the gentlest, least invasive way to make contact with the world—becomes so forceful that it turns a human being into a naked, shivering example of a medical condition. However nourishing and eloquent the eunuch's intimate thoughts might have been, whatever qualities his life might have had, they are lost forever. In their place we inherit this document: part of it a clipped medical narrative and part a wordless photograph. This seeing is aggressive: it distorts what it looks at, and it turns a person into an object in order to let us stare at it without feeling ashamed. Here seeing is not only possessing (the doctor "owned" this case: he was the authority, he got to lecture about it, he had the reproduction rights to his photograph and his article); seeing is also controlling and objectifying and denigrating. In short, it is an act of violence and it creates pain.

Yet it seems to me that all seeing has this property, and even though it can be modified or diluted, it can never be eradicated. Any sequence of photographs bears out that point. Imagine a set of twenty portrait photographs newly arrived from the studio. Of the twenty, five might sport an awkward smile, several more a dumb grin, and the rest might have that portentous look that comes from trying to look serious. There's usually at least one photo that catches its subject with the eyes half closed, as if she were on the point of falling asleep. The fact that most people don't enjoy photographs of themselves is usually chalked up to vanity, as if they don't like the photographs because they think they look better. There is some truth in that, and there's a physical reason for it. Photographs clip out instants in time, and since we see in overlapping moments and usually base our sense of a person on a fluid sequence of moments and motions, a single photograph can often seem wrong. (Painters can blend moments, so that few oil portraits have the weirdness of snapshots.) But there's something else at stake as well: a photograph pushes a small part of the person forward and presents it as the whole and adequate person, and that will tend to hurt the subject's sense of herself. "I am not that exaggerated thing," she might say, "or that gangly model, that stiff mannequin, that mysterious brooding actress, that adolescent poser—and I am certainly not the punch-drunk person in that last photo." It is significant that we take vain offense at photos of ourselves but hardly notice the same problems in photos of other people. That is partly because we know our own selves so well that we are hypersensitive to partial versions of what we are. I think this incompleteness is an inbuilt property of photographs, and it is only because we see so many thousands of photographs that we lose sight of how each one is a little travesty, a peculiar caricature. It is as if all the pictures of a person were pieces of different jigsaw puzzles. Someone who had never seen that person could never force them together into a single picture, even though it would seem as if they must fit somehow, since each snapshot is an aspect of that one person. But photographs are strange connivances. Their conventions are not those of the living experience of a person —and why should they be? Instead, they are bitter, pungent, sweet, sour, and salty droplets mechanically extracted from a more fluid existence.

I'm backing away from the example of the desolate eunuch because I want to say that displeasure is something that accompanies all seeing, not just medical photographs. John Pecham, a medieval scientist who thought long and hard about seeing, came to the conclusion that in order for vision to work, it must hurt just a little. "The action of the visible object on the eye," he wrote, "is painful." He meant that light itself causes a sensation in the eye—that is, a gentle pain—that enables us to see. It is an interesting thought, this almost invisible daily pain of seeing, and I like to sense its echoes in the urges I have been describing. All seeing, I think, is painful. The eunuch would have felt real pain if he had ever seen a copy of the Parisian journal. The doctor shared some of the eunuch's pain and mixed in some of his own, and his essay continues to cause pain in everyone who sees it. The photograph is the crossroad of this pain. Every photograph is a little sting, a small hurt inflicted on its subject, but even more: every glance *hurts* in some way by freezing and condensing what's seen into something that it is not.

This may seem entirely different from my opening examples. Looking at some object for sale in a display case hardly conjures this kind of trauma. But can we really say what the difference is? If I listen very carefully, there is displeasure in every glance. Looking is not only active—it is a form of the desire to possess or be possessed —but also potentially violent. The evanescent displeasures of searching for an object or confronting some wild version of myself in a photograph are linked by imperceptible degrees to the violent hatred and sexual obsession of the photograph of the eunuch. And in an exactly mirroring fashion, the pleasure of finding the object I'm looking for or discovering some glamorous picture of myself are continuous with the temptation to succumb to the morbid fascination of the eunuch's portrait. Storms of uncontrolled violent emotion can calm themselves into the slight aversions and the faint breaths of interest that I feel in a department store. There are many ideas mingling here, and it will take the rest of this book to tease them apart. Seeing is wonderfully complicated, and people who study it—art historians, art critics, artists, cognitive psychologists, neurobiologists—are just beginning to understand what it involves. We have arrived at the point where we can say what seeing is *not:* it is not merely taking in light, color, shapes, and textures, and it is not simply a way of navigating through the world.

Sometimes the desire to possess what is seen is so intense that vision reaches outward and *creates* the objects themselves. The Parisian doctor did not need to create his eunuch, exactly; he discovered the eunuch in Tunis. His creation was limited to matters of presentation: making sure the eunuch was interviewed, examined, described, pictured, and packaged in the way he wanted. But if the desire grows large enough, it can impel us to make what we want to see out of whole cloth. Stendhal wrote a lovely and cynical book, *On Love,* telling in pitiless and yet happy detail how a lover forms a misguided idea of the person he loves and distills it into a perfect crystal. He worships the crystal, no matter what his lover might actually be like, until the moment comes when the insistent presence of the woman herself shatters the crystal and the love affair is ruined. The crystal is an entirely mistaken image of the beloved, something built out of things that have been mis-seen and misunderstood. According to Stendhal—and he was a bit of a sexist by our standards—a love affair is a triangle, made of the man and the woman, who actually exist, and the crystalline version of the woman created by the man.

What is this image of a mermaid (figure 2), if not a picture of someone's desire? If the need is pressing and the world is not forth-

■ FIGURE 2

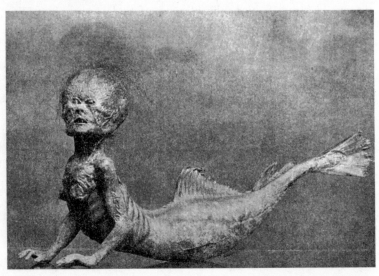

coming, then vision will dictate how the object of desire can be created. This wrinkled confection was someone's crystal. A visual hunger produced it, and it was kept as long as it mattered that such a thing could be seen. Pictures and seeing work in some of the same ways, and pictures have much to tell us about the ways we see. A picture is not only a view onto the world or onto someone's imagination: it is a peculiar kind of object that sets us thinking about desire. If I see a mermaid, a silk shirt, a snapshot, a gorgeous landscape, a picture of bread and butter, or photograph of a eunuch, those images are not just passively recorded in my mind. Looking immediately activates desire, possession, violence, displeasure, pain, force, ambition, power, obligation, gratitude, longing . . . there seems to be no end to what seeing is, to how it is tangled with living and acting. But there is no such thing as just looking.

I N thinking about these things, it is important not to become too enraptured with the idea that seeing is desire, because it tends to split seeing into the ordinary occurrences of life, when we behave as if seeing could be disinterested and passionless, and the reflective moments, when we become archaeologists of our desires. In my profession of art history, that is what people routinely do. We construct theories about how all seeing is fraught with gender constructions and power relations, but then we study works of art as if we were just trying to appreciate them—as if we had no desire to possess them by writing about them and reproducing them in our books, as if we had no urge to capture and domesticate the odd things of the world. When a historian reproduces a famous painting and writes about it, how is she different from the Parisian doctor with his exotic eunuch? We write books about art and leave ourselves out, as if we weren't involved. Just as it would never have occurred to the Parisian doctor to say anything about his own sexuality and his attraction to freakish things, so it seldom seems appropriate among the members of my profession to connect their own lives and loves to the pictures that they study. That may be prudent, since it is difficult to connect private thoughts with professional ones, and it is also appropriate in a deeper sense, because our reticence makes art history a good match for the dynamic of pictures. A picture presents itself as an unapproachable object forever detached from the nets of possessiveness and violence, and yet it urges on its viewers, impelling them to walk up to it, to touch it, to move into it or run away. In my profession we do the same by exhibiting artworks in an appreciative but disinterested way, and that only makes them that much more seductive. Art history and pictures mimic the world in this, since seeing itself works the same way: the world is simply there, and it can be described and appreciated from a distance, as if we were all operating lunar landers and training their glassy eyes on impossibly distant objects. But I suppose astronauts know better than most of us that the lure increases with the distance, and the most inaccessible object is the one that is the most desperately attractive.

There is a wonderful novel about this kind of drama, Alain Robbe-Grillet's *Jealousy*. In the opening pages it seems to be about a banana plantation and a woman who lives there. The writing is strangely finicky, and the narrator lavishes his attention on peculiar details, like the exact shape of the sun's shadow on a porch, the smudge of a squashed centipede, the wobbly outline of a car seen through a wavy windowpane. The descriptions seem to be objective, impartial, and a little inhuman, and they are impeccably precise. The days pass, and everything seems fairly normal—until the reader guesses that the narrator, who does not seem to be part of the story, is actually living at the plantation with the woman. The people in the story barely acknowledge that he exists: every once in a while the woman will sit at a table with a male friend of hers, and there will be three glasses instead of two. The third one belongs invisibly to the narrator. There is something weirdly wrong with the narrator's scientific, nearsighted precision. Slowly it becomes apparent that the narrator is invisible not because he is a naturalist who likes to describe what he sees, but because he is out of his mind with jealousy for this woman and does nothing with his life except observe her as closely as he possibly can. Every detail of the plantation that he sees is motivated by his obsessive jealousy.

Jealousy is an exact allegory of the way we usually think about seeing. We imagine that seeing is entirely objective: after all, the world gives us what there is to see, and we cannot do anything but open our eyes and see it. But like the observer in *Jealousy,* we are so deeply involved in the world, so desperately dependent on it, that we must pretend that we have some distance in order to go on at all. In the national parks there are signs reading, "Don't take anything but photographs." It is true that the landscape suffers only infinitesimal change when it loans me a few photons. But we mistake that for the nature of seeing. I may not change a pine tree by taking its picture, though I obviously *do* affect a bison or a bear by taking its picture. Some national parks have problems with tourists who lure bears with food in order to take their pictures. (And this is where there is truth in that phrase, "*taking* a picture.") Years ago in Yellowstone I saw a group of cars parked by the side of the road. People were standing at the roadside with their binoculars, looking out across a wide valley. When I got out my binoculars I could see what they were watching: in the far distance a man with a camera was running full-tilt after a bison. I doubt Yellowstone has any problem with people mobbing pine trees or patches of turf. What the tourists see is driven by their desire: on the one hand they want large animals, dangerous scenes, and close encounters with white fangs, and on the other they want bucolic, sublime, and picturesque landscapes. Wildness and wilderness are the two goals, and there is very little seeing of botany, geology, miscellaneous zoology, or unpicturesque landscape. Most of Yellowstone is invisible, even though it is there to be seen, just as in *Jealousy* the world has shrunk to a bit of shadow, a few glasses on a table, and a squashed centipede.

Our "objective" descriptions are permeated, soaked, with our unspoken, unthought desires. Seeing can be a strange experience, like reading *Jealousy.* First there is the eye, "just looking" at the objects, just taking some mental notes on their names and their places; but just beneath the surface there are other forces that can't quite be spoken, twisting their way through the viewer's thoughts, forcing the eye here and there, suddenly focusing it on a charging bison or a crushed bug.

• • •

WHAT is seeing, then? Even though I can't just look, can't I simply see? Isn't there such a thing as mere biological sensation, so that my eyes might be technically considered just as passive recipients of phenomena, like my tongue or my ears? In a scientific sense, aren't my eyes just tools, like a blind man's cane or a carpenter's tape measure? But as soon as I start asking questions this way, comparing one sense to another as an eighteenth-century philosopher would have, the answers get thrown back in my face. My ears are anything but passive recipients of noise. Out of the buzzing continuum of sounds I listen for certain things: I am acutely sensitive to voices, to rhythmic tappings that might be footsteps, to whistles, howls, shrieks, creaks, and whines. I am capable of entirely ignoring whole ranges of sound: in an airport I scarcely hear the jets, and when I'm cleaning house I don't even think of the deafening vacuum cleaner. The photoreceptors in my eyes have evolved so that they are acutely sensitive to single bursts of energy—twinkles of light from a department store display, or a momentary glimpse of a moving face—but the cells in my ears have evolved so that they can sift prolonged, faint signals from the world's constant random background noise. That's the scientific way of putting it, and it implies my ears are specialized: they don't just pick up everything, but they actively search. The same could be said about my tongue, or my fingertips, or the blind man's cane.

Once I wanted to write a book with the title *The Observer Looks at the Object*. It would have been an academic exercise, designed to destroy its own title, to tear it apart and show how little sense it makes. The idea was to begin with the least objectionable, most elementary sentence describing the rudimentary facts of vision: after all, there has to be an observer, something to be observed, and an action such as looking. From what I've been writing so far, it already seems that the sentence says too little, as if it meant, "The observer *just* looks at the object," or as if it were only half a sentence and would need to give its reason: "The observer looks at the object *in order to* do something or get something."

Originally what I liked about the idea of dismantling the sentence was that it would seem the work was finished as soon as the word "looks" no longer sounded right. But I think there's much more wrong here. The whole sentence is suspect: there is no such thing as just looking, and there is also no such thing as an object that is simply looked at by something else called an observer. Looking is much too complex to be reduced to a formula that has a looking subject and a seen object. If I observe attentively enough, I find that my observations are tangled with the object, that the object is part of the world and therefore part of me, that looking is something I do but also something that happens to me—so that the neat architecture of the sentence becomes a morass.

Paintings are an interesting example, since we often think of them as isolated objects: There is the *Mona Lisa,* protected by its glass shields, cordoned off from people and placed apart from the other paintings in its room in the Louvre. There is the "sofa painting" hanging by itself on the white wall. There is the picture that is up above my desk as I type this. (It's a ferocious battle scene of swimming centaurs and demure mermaids clubbing one another with bones and sticks.) Paintings seem to be exempt from the world, as if their frames were parentheses letting the text of the world flow on around them, or little fences keeping the picture from straying into the world.

But objects do not exist one by one in isolation, so that an observer could look at *just one* object. My picture of enraged centaurs looked quite different when it was in the bedroom, hanging over the bed—then it seemed to be more of a romantic fable and less of a story about hard work and fighting. I noticed that the centaurs seemed to protect the nereids and that it was really a love battle. Now, when it's over my desk, I tend to look at the clubs and sticks. The *Mona Lisa* would turn into a diva if she were hung in the Paris opera, and if she were hung in the Paris Métro she would look like a homeless person, wrapped in rags. The room in the Louvre that houses the *Mona Lisa* is transformed by her presence. The painting and its case are like a reliquary or an altar, and they make the room function like a little church. People line up to see it like worshipers waiting for the Eucharist. The other paintings look somehow less sacred—which is odd, considering that the *Mona Lisa* is not a religious work and the room contains several wonderful religious images.

For the same reasons a movie in a suburban theater is different from the same movie in an inner-city theater. I saw John Carpenter's *The Thing* in a huge old theater in downtown Chicago that has since been destroyed. It was a deep, cavernous space, decorated in faux-Baroque shields, twisting columns, parapets, and plaster statues. There was garbage under the seats, and people were talking and lobbing popcorn across the aisles. The sound was turned way up so that it could be heard over the noise. The people who were watching would yell at the screen, as if they were helping the hero:

"Look out!"

"Oh, my God, you idiot!"

"Don't look in there!"

Later I saw the same movie in an affluent suburban shopping mall. It was the kind of theater in which the cheapest available purple polyester curtains covered cinder-block walls painted in blue enamel. The audience was stony and silent, as if they were trying hard to scare themselves. Afterward they left grumbling and snickering. In effect, I have seen two movies: one that is mingled in my mind with a fusty ancient theater, with noises and smells and interruptions, and another that I remember along with a slightly cold, cryptlike space that smelled like a new car. There is no such thing as the movie *The Thing* in my mind apart from those two experiences.

This painting (figure 3), which has the traditional title *Icon with the Fiery Eye,* is in a church in Moscow; but it also exists in many different sizes and shapes on postcards and in books, including this one. Each one is a different face. Even the reproduction on page 37 will change, depending on where you are right now as you're reading this. It will look different if you're on a sofa, or eating, or reading in bed. (I was once told not to look at religious images in the bathtub. Presumably that was because I could see holy bodies and my own body at the same time—but I was never quite sure why that was bad.) Each time you glance at this picture it will mean something slightly different. At first it might be just a picture of Jesus, and then on second look it might seem oddly frowzy or troubled (at least that's the way it looked to me at one point, since it is not the symmetric face found in many icons). Then you might notice the cracks and flaws, and it may suddenly seem ancient. On

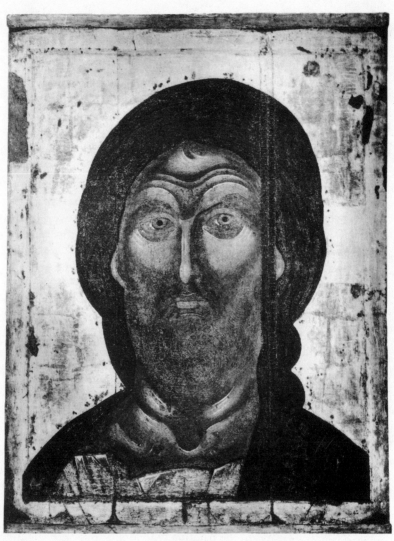

■ Figure 3

later inspections you might take note of the single curl on the fore-head, and the face might become a little more human. If you're reading these sentences in between glances at the picture, you're also mingling memories of the text with changing images of the *Icon with the Fiery Eye*. After a few moments, you might decide to give it a really thorough look and let its strange, surprised expression bear down on you in full force. After a long look at something, I usually shift my position a little or scratch my head. And each move I make moves the image in my mind. If you get a slight crick in your neck and press your hand over it, the icon might take on a subtle under-tone of discomfort. If you're lying in a bubble bath, that furrowed brow might look a little more relaxed and a bit less puzzled. In the end, when you've seen it enough and it's time to move on, the image will be quite complex—a kaleidoscope of thoughts and im-ages that coalesce from all the individual moments that you spent thinking and looking. Many people in my profession are attracted to a beautiful, bloody picture by the Renaissance painter Titian that hangs in a small town in Slovakia. I have never seen that painting, and I probably never will; but I have learned to love it by looking at reproductions in books. My idea of the picture is composed of all those reproductions, in black-and-white, in color, and in slides, to-gether with all the remembered and half-remembered things I've read and heard.

I am simplifying a little here, since I am pretending there are only two players in this drama: one object and one person looking at it. But seeing and being seen is more complicated than that. Say you're in a museum, looking at a painting that has a number of people in it. There may be up to ten different kinds of looking involved: (1) you, looking at the painting, (2) figures in the painting who look out at you, (3) figures in the painting who look at one another, and (4) figures in the painting who look at objects or stare off into space or have their eyes closed. In addition there is often (5) the museum guard, who may be looking at the back of your head, and (6) the other people in the gallery, who may be looking at you or at the painting. There are imaginary observers, too: (7) the artist, who was once looking at this painting, (8) the models for the figures in the painting, who may once have seen themselves there, and (9) all the other people who have seen the painting—the buyers, the museum officials, and so forth. And finally, there are also (10) people who have never seen the painting: they may know it only from reproductions like the ones in this book or from descriptions.

A complementary source of complexity comes from the fact that we never see only one image at a time. Even up to this point in the book, if you haven't looked ahead, you will still be mixing a eunuch and a mermaid into your ideas of the picture of Christ.

But I'd just as soon leave these sources of confusion aside: they all depend on the primary scene, where one observer encounters what appears to be one object.

H o w can the observer look at the object if it is multiplying and changing under his very eyes? The supposedly static object is a moving target, like the exit door in a hall of mirrors. In a good hall of mirrors, the exit cannot be seen at all, and it seems there is no way out—and then a moment later, with a slight change in position, there are nothing but exit doors wherever you look. Some of them are only half visible, and you can't get a clear look at them. Others send out curving streamers, copying themselves into infinity. The elusive exit door is the analogue to the fixed object. Any object dissolves and shatters itself if it's seen too long or sought for too carefully. Perhaps "the observer looks at the object" should be "the observer looks *for* the object" or "the observer looks *among the objects*."

And all this so far supposes there is an observer. We need to think this, even when we have given up the idea that looking is straightforward or that objects are stable. I need to think that *I* am the one doing the looking and sifting one version of an object from the next. But what if I were changing along with the objects? What if the sentence were "The *observers*"—the multiple moments of myself—"look among the objects"?

I am not a member of the Eastern Orthodox church—I'm not among the intended viewers of this icon—but since I'm an art historian I am used to looking at images like this. If I were Hindu or Parsee or Navajo, the face would lose the aura that any Westerner senses in Judaeo-Christian images. Even if you are Eastern Orthodox, born and raised in Russia (where this icon was made seven centuries ago), the icon will look quite different if you've just been to the Eucharist, or if you're about to stop reading and go to the Eucharist, or if you've just skipped the Eucharist and you're feeling guilty.

In European churches it happens that local worshipers walk right by "important" paintings and sculptures and kneel in front of "unimportant" images instead. In a church in Italy, I saw a crowd of townspeople gathered in front of an altar that had a cheap, Holiday Inn–style painting and a plastic baby-doll Jesus draped with Christmas lights. Less than twenty feet away was one of the masterpieces of Western art, supposedly full of noble and uplifting religious feeling. In both chapels the Christ Child glowed with the light of the new Sun: in the "important" painting, his body was mysteriously luminescent, and it cast a daunting cold light on Mary and Joseph. The plastic doll in the other chapel had a bulb inside it that made it look like a tacky novelty light. On the afternoon I was there, the worshipers ignored the painting as completely as the tourists ignored the plastic doll. How can I begin to understand the people who would rather worship a novelty light? What do they see? And for my part, could I ever worship the painting? And what do I fail to see when I lecture about the masterpiece as an example of the art of painting? These are the kinds of questions that art history professors have a great deal of difficulty in answering. In the art historical textbooks that discuss this church, there is no mention of the plastic Jesus, and I doubt there are any books on it except perhaps some tongue-in-cheek study of postmodern culture. People who worship the plastic Jesus do just that, and often only that—and they do not write books or give lectures. And we are no less guilty of failing to speak about our own ways of seeing: our own irreligion, our assumptions about what is of interest.

An art historian I know tells a story about his first trip to Italy. He was in a church, taking notes on a sculpture by Michelangelo, enjoying its subtleties and its elegance.

Then I noticed some commotion in the dark recess . . . under the sculpture, as an older woman, dressed totally in black, dragged forward a young girl by the hair and knocked her head, again and again, on the base of the sculpture, chanting all the while. Horrified, I dropped my notebook, realizing that the image I was describing as a work of art was something else for this woman, something she was using to drive evil spirits from her daughter's mind.

The worshipers who prefer the plastic Jesus and the woman who tries to purge her daughter's soul are seeing very different objects from the ones I see, because they are very different people than I could ever be.

No two people will see the same object: that's a truism that is proved each time two artists try to draw the same object and end up with two irreconcilable versions of it. What makes it more than a common truth is that it applies just as well *within* a single person. I am divided, and at times my modes of seeing are so distinct from one another that they could belong to different people. At other moments they coalesce, but I am normally aware that differing viewpoints collide in the ways I see. Within limits, I do not *want* to see things from a single point of view: I hope to be flexible, to think in as liquid a way as I can, and even to risk incoherence. And above all, I want to continue to change—I do not wish to remain the same jaded eye that I was a moment ago. Art is among the experiences I rely on to alter what I am.

I expect pictures to have an effect on me, and I hope that the effect will not wear off: I want to see something new and to have an experience I can remember years later. Some pictures affect me for a few minutes, and others make permanent alterations in what I am. If you spend time in front of a painted portrait, the figure's mood will begin to change the way you feel. That new mood might become a part of you, recurring months or years later in very different circumstances. Some people go to the art museum every day, and they go to the same room to look at the same painting. Some of them work nearby and visit during their lunch hour, and others are retired or out of work and stay for hours on end. These are people who have developed a need for particular images. I teach a course in an art museum, and the students in the course set up their easels in the galleries and copy paintings. Their experiences are very different from the experiences of the people who are used to visiting their favorite pictures. At first the students have a hard time looking at one image hour after hour, week after week. As the semester wears on and they spend five hours a day, two or three days a week, standing in one place and looking at one image, they tell me that they begin to have dreams about the paintings—and some of them also report nightmares. Many students rebel against the power of the images, and they complain that the paintings dog them, recurring like hallucinations when they are trying to eat or watch television. Eventually, though, most students end up feeling attached to their images: by a slow process the pictures find permanent places in their imaginations. Over the course of the semester the paintings have surprised and bored them, chastised them in their daydreams, scared them in nightmares, and eventually seduced them.

And this can also happen almost in the blink of an eye. There are pictures I love that I have seen only very briefly. The few moments I have spent in front of them are strong in my memory, and I can conjure them and continue to think of them whenever I want. Images like that take on a life of their own, like actual people, and they can appear suddenly to my mind's eye the way a friend might turn up unexpectedly. I might be riding on a train or on the point of falling asleep, and suddenly the image will appear to me. Each time that happens, the associations I already had mix together with whatever else I have been doing and seeing and feeling that day, and after a number of years my memory becomes rich and entangled, just as it does with people I have known my entire life.

These are important experiences, no more and no less central in their way than my friendships. They not only add to what I am but also *change* what I am. The *Icon with the Fiery Eye* is not one of my favorite images, but even so I would not say that when I saw it I simply added it to some mental file of Russian icons. An image is not a piece of data in an information system. It is a corrosive, something that has the potential to tunnel into me, to melt part of what I am and re-form it in another shape. Some things in me are different because of that image, and that means—if I am willing to let down my guard and be honest about how this works—that I am not the same person I was before. When people talk about experiences changing them, they usually mean that the change adds to them— the essential core of what they are remains the same. Philosophers are sometimes fond of speaking about the cloudy flux of the self, but it is not at all easy to acknowledge the absence of an architecturally solid foundation—the indestructible, immutable ''I.'' If pictures are corrosives, it is because light itself is an acid: it burns into me; it remakes me in its own image.

My sentence, ''The beholder looks at the object,'' is in serious trouble. There is no simple looking, there is no fixed object, and there is also no fixed observer. If I were a logician I would be tempted to write a syllogism something like this:

> The beholder looks at the object,
> but the object changes the beholder,
> and therefore the beholder does not look at the object.

But it's not as dry as that. *The* beholder is many beholders, and *the* object is many objects, and there is no scene in which a single beholder stands and absorbs facts and forms from an object while remaining impassive. The sentence is true only for a split second, before there is a chance to think about what is being seen or who is doing the seeing—which is to say it is never true. The sentence reminds me a little of a military action: ''The soldier kills the enemy.'' It sounds like a crisp action, a one-way gesture, with empty space between the protagonists. Like a bullet, the gaze shoots out toward the object; but the act of killing changes the killer, and like a bullet, light travels back from the object to the observer. When it comes to seeing, objects and observers alter one another, and meaning goes in both directions.

These are not things that happen sometimes, or under special conditions. They are not subtle nuances or refinements to the way we look at objects. Instead, they are the conditions of seeing itself. A picture *is* the ways and places it is viewed, and I *am* the result of those various encounters. In order to salvage the sentence, I would have to destroy it completely. I would need a new vocabulary of hybrid objects: "observer-objects" would be observers altered by objects or fused with them through the act of seeing; "object-observers" would be objects altered by observation. It would no longer be possible even to write the sentence, because its subject, verb, and object would have fused together.

Some philosophers proceed this way, coining compound words and trying to push the grammar to make room for them. If this were a philosophic treatise, I might go ahead and do that, and start writing about seen and unseen observer-objects and seeing and unseeing object-observers. The sentence would deliquesce into an exchange of emerging identities, with "looking" rewritten as the force that causes objects and observers to appear or disappear. This subject is both important and complicated, and if I veer away from those possibilities it is not because I want to simplify things. Instead, I think it's important to remember the superior force of the sentence itself. "The observer looks at the object": it is how we live; we live by that sentence, and we need it to keep looking. Luckily, it's one thing to know that something is a lie and another to try to live with the truth.

AND yet these are haunting ideas. I don't really exist apart from the objects I see—what a strange thought. I am neither independent observer nor object in someone else's eyes. Whatever calls itself "I" must always move, as Martin Heidegger said, "in the *between,* between man and thing." There is ultimately no such thing as an observer or an object, only a foggy ground between the two. It's as if I have abandoned the place in the sentence that was occupied by the words "the observer" and I've taken up residence in the verb "looks," literally between the words "object" and "observer." When I think of things Heidegger's way, what I have been calling the observer evaporates, and what really takes place is a "betweenness" (for lack of a better word): part of me is the object, and part of the object is me. There is no such thing as a pure self, or a pure object apart from that self. This sounds unlikely, and it goes against intuition; but it is only a consequence of an idea we recognize every day when we say a person or an image is "inside" us or that we are "lost" in a scene or a memory.

And so looking has force: it tears, it is sharp, it is an acid. In the end, it corrodes the object and observer until they are lost in the field of vision. I once was solid, and now I am dissolved: that is the voice of seeing.

Two

THE OBJECT
STARES BACK

I A M alone in my bedroom. It is night, and soft lights play on the walls and ceiling. The curtains shift in the breeze. They sway together like an aurora, merging and changing in pastel colors.

I undress in the green light of the cat's eyes. The bed is dim, but I know it by touch. The cat jumps up and pads around looking for a spot to rest. The mirror over the dresser is dark, like a tunnel into another room. If I turn my head, I can see a few stars above a black silhouette of trees.

For a moment I stare back into the cat's eyes. It seems she is not really looking at me—it is as if she's looking through me—but she probably knows she is attracting my attention. In a way her eyes are blind, like reflecting posts at the side of the highway—they seem like eyes but they are really only signals in the dark. Perhaps she doesn't see anything when her eyes are open like that.

After a few minutes, the cat begins to drift off to sleep (or perhaps she was asleep already, with her eyes open, and now she's woken again inside a dream). The green lamps close down and the cat becomes an object, a blurry cushion at the foot of the bed. I know that human eyes don't reflect light like a cat's eyes, and I wonder if the cat could even have seen me looking back at her. Perhaps my eyes are as dark as the mirror. With no eyes left to see and no one else around, I begin to feel sleepy. The room is dim and quiet, and I am about to leave it for the invisible lights of my dreams.

I know the cat is still awake, because I can see its ears pressed slightly back. It is listening, watching me in its own way, paying attention to where I am. I know that if I move, the cat will instantly open its eyes; but even with its eyes closed, it can watch me, as if its body can see. I know that it knows exactly where I am, and I guess that it even knows I am watching it—it does not need eyes to see me looking at it. I wonder if the same is true of me: do I need to be looking at the cat to know it is aware of me? I can feel a slight pressure of the blanket against my foot where the cat is resting. Could I sense from that small clue that the cat is in its sphinx pose, with its paws curled under in front, instead of sprawled out in unconscious sleep? Could I tell from that slight lean, that small insistent pressure, which way it is facing?

And for that matter, can I be sure nothing else is watching me? There is a dense woods behind the house, and tonight is especially dark. Even now, after ten or fifteen minutes in the dark, I can't see anything in it. I know where some trees are, and I think I can pick out their shapes, but I can't be certain. How many creatures might be able to see me in their different ways, with their various eyes, in their alien minds? A squirrel might be looking in at me, or a drowsy bird. Even a tree frog or a cricket or a gnat might sense me. I know that it's possible to hunt spiders at night by walking through the forest with a flashlight—the spiders' eyes glow red. There must be many spiders' eyes out there now (eight eyes to a spider), and some may be looking my way. A mosquito might see my outlined form under the sheets as it tries to get in the window. And as long as I am entertaining this fantasy, I wonder if I should restrict myself to creatures that are outside my window. My dog, who sleeps downstairs, is very smart about when I get up and when I go to sleep. He definitely knows just where I am, and he might know that I am still awake. Perhaps it's because I am half asleep, but I would almost say that the whole world could be connected by this kind of direct and indirect sight, so that everything is visible at all times, and nothing is hidden. Some neighbor's dog might sense that my dog is awake, and that dog might be watched by my neighbor . . . and so on to the most distant part of the world. Even a worm, cramped in a narrow passageway under the lawn, would be sensed by other worms, who would be seen by beetles and ants, by mice and birds . . . some of whom would also see me.

In this frame of mind, it occurs to me that I am still thinking along narrow lines. Why confine vision to things with eyes? Why shouldn't vision be universal? And with that the room begins to seem full of eyes, full of vision. The veils of light from the curtains play on the walls. Before, I hadn't noticed it, but they dance as if they could see one another. One faint ocher light moves toward another, slowly turning in mimicry of the curtain shifting in the window. It comes near another light, a sharper band cast by the window frame. The two lights regard each other, they get closer, they move away, and then suddenly merge into a bright yellow band. A dim greenish strip of light waits off to one side. It never approaches. Surely these lights have eyes.

Mirrors are like empty eyes, blind until I step in front of them—then they produce copies of my eyes, staring back at me. At night the hollow socket of the mirror looks on quietly, waiting for morning. I can feel, as I see it in my sleepy eye—or in my sleepy mind's eye, since my eyes are closed now—that it is somehow like an eye with nothing to see. Its emptiness is not just a vacuum but the absence of an eye, the absence of sight. All eyes are like this in a way. If I look into someone's eyes and think of the fact that the eye is nothing but a rotating sack of fluid, then an eye becomes an unsettling thing: I see the eye but it does not see me. What *sees* is the mind, the person connected to the eye, but the eye itself is just tissue—it would be like looking at someone's palm or at a nipple. That thought, which is so useless for practical purposes (I never *need* to notice that the eyes I see can't see me), has a deep resonance when it comes to thinking about looking at things that are not eyes. An open palm *can* see me, in a way: it is opened toward me, responding to my presence. A nipple *does* behave like an eye when it attracts my attention, and I may look at it the way I look into someone's eye. Everyone is an Argus, covered with eyes, and the same is true of objects. The mirror has a special kind of empty eye. It waits to see, but it cannot see without me to see it. At night, that absence is even more ominous, since it is entirely dark and hollow.

The bathroom door is ajar, and if I were younger I would probably start to wonder what eyes were hidden inside; but now I think I can go beyond that kind of hallucination toward a more evocative one. I can imagine the entire bathroom as an eye: it is a place where I look at myself and see myself seeing myself. It is a place that makes me think of appearances and looks. A bathroom is an eye because it is about seeing, and also about not being seen. When I want absolute privacy, the bathroom is the place to go: the only room perfectly sealed against seeing. But I go there also when I want to see how I look, since it is the room best designed for seeing. The whole idea of seeing is concentrated in that room, and I think of it now as I try to look into its dark doorway.

The night has reduced a picture hanging on one wall to a gray smudge, and as I look, its outline undulates in the half-light. It moves in response to what I try to see: I think I can make out the hilly landscape that I know is there, but suddenly it assembles itself into a staring face, and then into a little mannequin chopping wood. The mannequin has a little stick-figure head. It performs in response to what I imagine: it knows I am here, it sees me. For a while we look at one another: he smiles at me as best he can with his stick-figure face, and then he turns back to his work and splits a log. When the light streaks on the wall join in, pick up axes, and start splitting logs, and when the cat reveals itself as a picnic basket, then I have passed beyond vision and I am truly asleep.

All this has been a waking dream, this benevolent hallucination of eyes, but like many delusions it has its truth. Even when I am wide awake and working in my office, objects have a certain presence. The world is full of vision, full of eyes, as in this nineteenth-century picture of a sentient universe crowded with seeing stars (figure 4). As the poet Yeats knew, the presence of objects can grow into a terrifying, smothering claustrophobia when everything seems to be watching us:

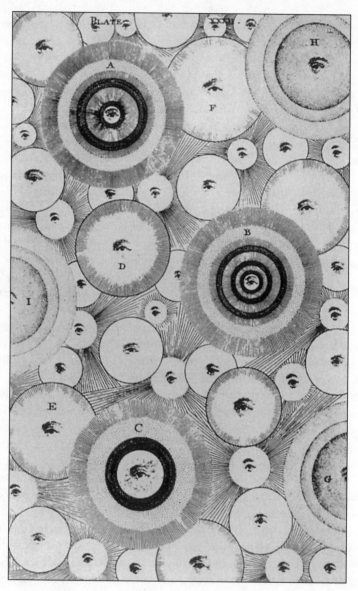

■ FIGURE 4

> When a man grows old his joy
> Grows more deep day after day,
> His empty heart is full at length,
> But he has need of all that strength
> Because of the increasing Night
> That opens her mystery and fright.
> *Fifteen apparitions I have seen:*
> *The worst a coat upon a coat-hanger.*

The simplest objects can be the most unsettling because they remind us that the world is full of apparitions. Every object sees us; there are eyes growing on everything. In daily commerce we don't think about objects, but a half dream or a childish fear or an old man's lonely mind can bring back their power. To see is to be seen, and everything I see is like an eye, collecting my gaze, blinking, staring, focusing and reflecting, sending my look back to me.

THIS is a beautiful subject, and I want to work my way around to it by thinking of two related phenomena that may be easier to accept. First, I want to spend some time thinking about all the myriad things in the world that surround us without our noticing, and then about the things we cannot notice unless scientific techniques make them visible. Out of the whole world, we see almost nothing, and all the things that are out there show how unexpected and finally how uncontrollably frightening the world can be—how much like an apparition it is, and how its objects surround us and stare back at us with thousands of eyes.

In the first chapter I mentioned objects that do not correspond to desire—blank stretches of walls, objects so useless and familiar we no longer see them. There are also spectacular, astonishing things we routinely overlook. I remember one late afternoon, walking home from the university library. There had been a cloudburst. Large drops of rain were pelting down, and most of us were running across a field that leads from the library into the city streets. People kept their eyes down and covered their books with their coats. When they reached the buildings across the way, most of them walked close in to the walls, brushing against them with their shoulders. For some reason I stopped after I had run across the field. I leaned back against a building, perhaps to catch my breath, but perhaps also because I sensed something, and I looked up and saw a most amazing sight. The street led straight away to the east, and it was lit by the brightening sky at the end of the storm. There on the horizon, perfectly centered over the street, was the most magnificent rainbow I have ever seen. Only readers who have seen truly amazing rainbows will know what I mean by that. This bow had supernaturally strong colors, and they were echoed several times inside the bow, forming a concentric series of rainbows (I later found out they are called supernumerary bows). The primary bow had all the colors of the spectrum, and the ones inside it were blurred into red and green, and finally into a luminous gray-brown. Inside the bow, the sky was brilliant white, and, just outside, it was deep azure (that effect has also been named; it is called Alexander's dark band). It was as if the entire sky had been pierced by a hole punch or as if curtains were being raised on a bright stage. And off to either side was a second rainbow, echoing the first. I remember I stared at it for minutes on end and that I even tried to point it out to a few people who passed by, probably because I was a little embarrassed at standing out in the rain gaping at the sky. The rainbow was especially wonderful because it was so utterly obvious and yet so easy to overlook. I could easily have turned down that street, walked all the way home, gone inside, turned on the television, and missed that rainbow forever.

The experience rekindled a childhood interest, and I began researching sky phenomena. I read about rainbows and white fog bows and about aureoles and the mysterious Brocken specter, and I discovered how mirages work. Along the way I found out some fundamental things about the sky that I had never known. Whenever there is a reasonably clear sunset, without too many clouds, if you look toward the east just as the sun sets you will see a dark purple band just on the horizon. If you keep watching for about five minutes, you will see the band rise up into the sky and then dissolve in the darkness. That band is nothing less than the earth's shadow: the shadow cast by the earth itself onto the sky. It's an amazing thing, watching the shadow of the entire earth and feeling the globe of the earth turn underneath your feet. And it's very common; I saw it the same evening I first read about it. Another common sight, uncommonly seen, is crepuscular rays, the beams that radiate from the setting sun. Those rays continue very faintly far up into the sky, and on some evenings you can trace them up overhead and even completely across the sky and over onto the side opposite the sunset. When that happens, they do not keep diverging but come together again at a point in the east directly opposite the sun. The sun and the "antisun" are balanced, tied together by curving orange-violet bands. One evening I watched a sunset with four crepuscular rays, and I followed them up overhead and down again, and I saw the faint antisun where they come together. They seem to bend like a photograph made with a fish-eye lens, so that the whole sky is striped. The effect is an illusion, since the sun's rays are effectively parallel to one another. It is exactly as if you were to stand in the middle of some railroad tracks and note how they seem to come up from one side, bend around you, and converge again on the other side—but crepuscular rays are much more dramatic.

Many people have noticed sun dogs—they look like fragments of rainbows, and they appear on either side of the sun. On a cold winter day, in the later afternoon when the sunlight shines through a veil of cirrus clouds, the sun dogs can be exceptionally brilliant, like colored cellophane or iridescent Mylar shimmering in the sky. (They have an especially ugly name, and they should be called "sun peacocks" or something of the sort.) Now that I know to look for them, I see sun dogs five or six times a year, and they can appear in the summer as well. Even though they are bright and colorful, they can be completely invisible unless you expect to see them. Once I saw a pair of sun dogs out the window of a restaurant, and I had ten people craning their necks to see them.

And there's more, since it turns out that sun dogs are only the most common in a whole encyclopedia of ice halos. When the conditions are right, the sun dogs are revealed as two fragments of an entire circular halo around the sun, and there can even be another halo around it. Those halos take up most of the sky, and they can produce a startling effect. That is as much as I have ever seen, but they are only the beginning of what can happen in the sky. There is also a circular halo that goes around the entire sky like a horizontal ring, passing through the sun, and there are arcs and bands that branch from it. The full panoply of arcs, pillars, sun dogs, antisuns, and halos can make the sky look like an ice skating rink scraped with intersecting circles. Most of the more exotic phenomena are visible only in the Arctic and Antarctic, where the sky is likely to be filled with tiny ice crystals, and even then they are very difficult to photograph well (figure 5). Once or twice a century they appear in the skies over Europe and America, where they used to cause sensations and were interpreted as miracles. The few halos I have seen are nearly impressive enough to make me want to go to Alaska or Antarctica and wait out a winter watching for them—*nearly* enough, but not quite.

The world is filled with things we do not see, even though they are right in front of us. When I was younger I kept a collection of insects, and for several years I was especially entranced by moths. With several friends, I used to go out each evening and make the rounds of the neighborhood, looking at everyone's garage light to see if any moths had been attracted to it. Later we bought an ultravi-

■ FIGURE 5

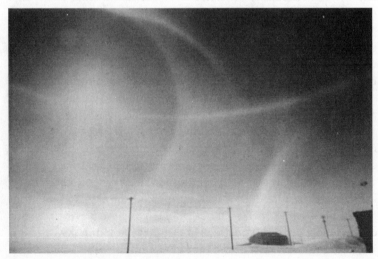

olet light in order to attract even more moths. We used to drape a
bedsheet over some bushes and put the light in front of it. The idea
was to stay up as late as possible and then go out into the yard and
see what had accumulated. But the most interesting experience—
the one that altered the ways I see the world—was sugaring for
moths. Some kinds of moths don't care about light at all, and they
stay in the woods and fly only at night. For that reason they are
particularly rare. To catch them you mix a pail of beer, mashed
rotten bananas, and molasses and walk through the woods painting
it on tree trunks with a house-painting brush. Then late at night, if
you go out again with a flashlight, you'll see all the moths, and other
insects that spurn the light but cannot resist something sugary and
alcoholic. The moths we were after also have excellent camouflage,
and their wings are perfect facsimiles of bark. Even with a flashlight,
it was easy to miss them when they sat still off to one side of the beer
slurry or when they rested down in the leaf litter after they had
gotten drunk. After several summers sugaring trees, I developed a
special eye for the subtle outlines of those moths: I learned to see the
little rounded triangle of their bodies, the very slight shadow they
cast when they pressed against the wood, and the minute differences
between their patterned wings and the texture of bark. Sometimes I
would be walking through the woods in the daytime and be able to
see them against the trees, still alseep after their night of partying.

And now, over twenty years later, I still have the ability to spot
those moths. It seems to be built into my neurons, because it kicks
in at the strangest times. I might be walking down the street, thinking of the business of the day, when I find myself suddenly looking
with piercing attention at some patch of peeling paint on a wall, or
the torn corner left when someone has pulled a stapled notice off an
electric pole. Something in my subconscious must still be scanning
for that particular shape, and it breaks into my conscious thoughts to
warn me when it thinks it has discovered a moth. Every once in a
while I do find moths that way, but now I don't want to find them,
and so I take note and move on.

There is something in this that is akin to ancient hunting instincts:
I can imagine prehistoric hunter-gatherers following trails along the
forest or watching for broken twigs where bear or moose might have

passed by. Those hunters would have been alert to minute differences between twigs that had fallen naturally and those that had been
broken by squirrels or by larger animals. They would have been able
to distinguish leaves matted by rain from those stepped on by moose
or disturbed by smaller animals. There is a cultural historian, Carlo
Ginzburg, who connects those primordial activities with the mod-
ern-day profession of detectives. When Sherlock Holmes enters a
room, he sees much more in it than anyone else, and when he is
given an object—a hat, a cane—he can peer and sniff at it and
deduce its owner's age and occupation, where he lives, and whether
he has murdered anyone lately. In the Edgar Allen Poe story "The
Purloined Letter," the inspector solves a case by finding the missing
letter in plain sight. After the suspect's apartment has been searched
from top to bottom, the inspector walks through the rooms and
points directly at the letter: it had always been right there in plain
sight, turned inside out and tacked up on a board with other letters.

I T is difficult to break through the wall of usual seeing and begin
to discover how many other things there are to see. It requires
practice and special information—you have to know what you're
looking for—and it also requires energy, since it involves special
concentration. If a person who has grown up in the city takes a walk
in the forest, she will not see very much. I have been told that
inner-city children who are taken on trips to the rain forest tend to
huddle together: they know that the jungle is full of things, but they
can't tell any of them apart. For all they know, a stinging plant might
be right in front of them, or a snake just underfoot. An average city
person can certainly enjoy the outdoors; the national parks are
jammed with people from large cities. But what do they see? If they
can't tell the plants apart and if they don't know the animals and
don't recognize geological formations, then they can see only general
categories: bird, mountain, stream. Vast amounts will pass them by.
Two rocks, one reddish and one reddish brown, will look the same,
even though they come from different strata millions of years apart
and even though those strata are laid out like a diagram in the
mountains across the valley. A bird will fly past nearly unseen, even

though it is calling out in an attempt to lure the person away from its nest, which is just on the other side of the path.

We are all guilty of not seeing, and I think most of us don't see most of the time. In the building where I work, there is a back stairway that I walk up and down each day. Pipes run along the walls, and some especially large pipes run down the center well of the stairway, just on the other side of the banister. Sometimes I absentmindedly tap those pipes as I climb the stairs, and they make different musical tones. But only recently did it occur to me that I have no idea what they are. I can't tell hot water pipes from cold water pipes, or heating pipes from sewer pipes, and I can't tell which pipes have wires inside and which have water, which have phone cables and which electricity. I pass junction boxes on each landing without even glancing at them. To someone else, that same stairway would be a key to the building's construction, and she would be able to tell how many bathrooms there were on that side of the building, and how many offices, and how the building is heated and ventilated. To me it is all a blank. I didn't notice the pipes, and I didn't notice that I didn't notice. I was trapped in a double blindness; now at least I realize that there are things I have not seen.

Superhighways are another example. I know someone who was hired to watch the construction of a new highway. He is an ecologist, and his job was to make sure that the construction of drains went according to environmental law. He inspected things that every American has seen thousands of times but virtually none of us have noticed: the little sluices that lead down on either side of the grassy slopes that are cut for the superhighways, and the design of the conduits that pass underneath the highway when it crosses a stream. The sluices are supposed to end in gravel pits or drains, and there are regulations about their slope and their length. As we drove along the highway he pointed out those things, and I began wondering if the regulations had changed over the years and if the little curbs and low bridges and shoulders and median strips might be datable—if it would be possible to tell an embankment made in 1950 from one made in 1970. When a superhighway goes over a stream, the engineers build a little concrete wall or steel railing on the side, just enough to help prevent cars from going over the edge. Since they are so simple, they have practically no forms at all: no columns or decorations, nothing much to look at. As we saw one in the distance, we would try to see if we could guess when it was made. Many have little cornerstones with the dates on them, and we began reading them as we went by. After a few hours, I could discern tiny differences between them—the color of the concrete, the exact slope of the top surface—that allowed me to begin to see the highway as something that had a style and belonged to a certain period in history. It wasn't the most exciting afternoon I have ever spent in my life, but it demonstrated how even something that seems absolutely devoid of detail and interest can hide visual forms. Anything in the world, it seems, can be seen if we know how to find it. Wittgenstein liked to say that the most difficult problems are the ones right in front of our eyes, the ones we don't see *as* problems. Those are the ones we have to struggle just to perceive. Problems that are at a more comfortable distance, like the conventional questions of philosophy, are in a way much easier because we know what to do when we meet them.

I think Carlo Ginzburg is onto something when he connects prehistoric habits of close observation with modern ones, but that kind of seeing is unusual and exhausting. Ginzburg's primary examples, the experiences of tracking and hunting, are like a crash course in intensive seeing. In hunting, all of a sudden it *matters* that the forest is a blank, and it becomes necessary to try to see as much as possible as quickly and carefully as possible. I have spent time crouching in trees long before dawn on freezing cold mornings with a bow and arrow held ready in case a deer walked by. As the light began to fill the woods, I would peer as intently as possible in the direction of the slightest sound. No one who has not hunted can imagine how noisy the forest really is. A single leaf dropping would catch my attention, and I began to be able to tell the difference between a bird landing on the forest floor, a twig falling, and a cautious deer stepping slowly on a fallen branch. A squirrel jumping through a thicket is deafening, as if a tray of plates had fallen to the floor. I was acutely conscious of my own body and its every movement: each minute rustle of clothing, each careful slow breath. Those intense moments must be the remnants of an ancient way of getting along in the world—a way that makes us all seem very dull and blocklike in comparison.

Science has helped a little to stir us out of our complacence, alerting us to things we haven't been seeing. First there was high-speed photography, which proved that horses don't gallop gracefully with their legs outstretched like rabbits (that is the way that painters had imagined them, and if you look at old pictures you'll see horses bounding that way, in graceful U-shapes). A gallop is an intricate gait, and most of the time the horse's legs are tangled together as if they were tied in wire. About the same time came the first photographs of lightning, reminding painters that lightning does not fall in a schematic zigzag but in a very organic-looking, branching pattern. (Painters had learned that several centuries before, but it was a lesson they kept forgetting.) Lightning and galloping horses are things that people might have noticed if they had looked closely (and if they had *wanted* to notice them, which is another matter). Other images showed us things we can never see.

Beyond Vision is the name of a book by John Darius that illustrates the things science has shown us that will never be available to our unaided eyes. There are pictures of subatomic particles, of the insides of the body painlessly cut by magnetic resonance imaging, and of the earth from space. Though I try to keep up with what happens in scientific imaging, there are some images I cannot understand at all. Everyone interested in images should take out a subscription to the journal *Ultramicroscopy,* because it publishes the most unusual images in any field. What happens at the very limits of microscopical vision, when scientists are looking at individual atoms, results in pictures far more interesting and more original than anything that is being done in the visual arts. Practically any other kind of image will look somehow familiar: I can recognize an electron micrograph of a cell, and I know a computer-generated image when I see one or a medical image of the human body. I probably won't know the detailed science involved, and I may not know exactly what the object is— whether it's a mitochondrion, a distant galaxy, or an electron trail— but I will usually recognize the kind of image. A picture made through a telescope has a certain look to it, and one made by George Lucas's Industrial Light and Magic has another look, and one made by a biologist looking at DNA has another. Contemporary painters work in certain ways, and so do scientists. A radar screen is different from a sonar chart, and they are both different from a stock market graph. After a while, images sort themselves out fairly neatly, and I find I am rarely surprised by the format or the look of a picture. But *Ultramicroscopy* is different. The scientists working at that frontier between the merely microscopic and the theoretically unvisualizable produce kinds of images that have never been seen before. Here are three beautiful images of that sort (figure 6). The top one looks as if it might be a picture of three stars, or three tiny tears in a black sheet. The lower photograph on the left reminds me of pictures of the refraction of light waves, and the one on the lower right looks like a satellite picture of a coastline. But they are far from anything so obviously visible. The top photograph is a Fourier transform of a hologram, and the lower images are described as the modulus and the phase of the image wave. I am entranced by images I do not understand, and doubly so by images of objects I do not understand, and I am almost disappointed when I begin to see what they are. Photographs like this are at the outer bounds of the concept of image itself, not because they record phenomena invisible to the unaided eye—many scientific photographs fulfill that criterion—but because they fall outside of anything I can intuitively grasp as objects of any sort.

Scientists now have the ability to move single atoms and photograph the results (figure 7). Here some sulfur atoms have been removed from a crystal surface to spell "nanospace," the infinitesimal spaces occupied by atoms. The sulfur atoms are each about two nanometers high, and so the word "nanospace" occupies about fifty nanometers on this crystal—fifty billionths of a meter. That is too small a scale for a human to appreciate, and the very idea of seeing an atom is something we have to accept in a pragmatic spirit and not try to relate to our relatively gargantuan existence. So the photograph is conceptually challenging, but it is also extremely conventional. The surface of atoms is very like the surface of a table or a landscape, and the writing is only slightly strange (the two *A*'s are tilted in order to conform with the array of sulfur atoms). The atoms seem to be lit as if by ordinary light, instead of modeled by electrical

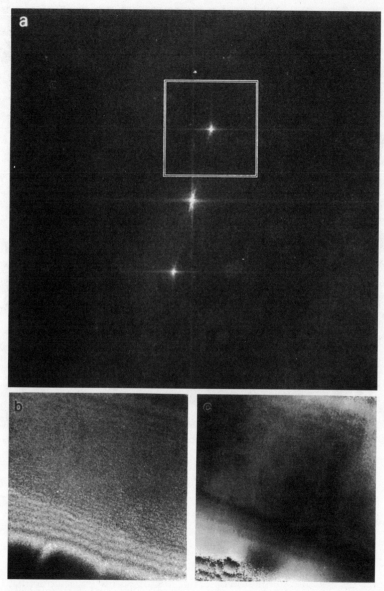

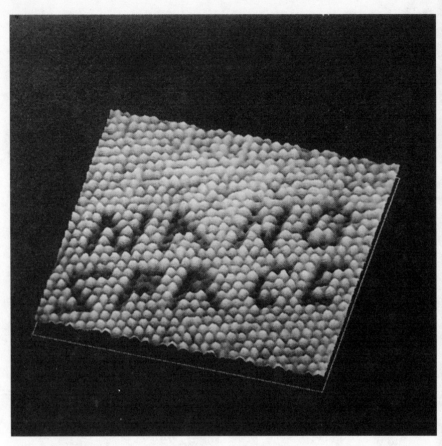

■ FIGURE 7

potentials as they actually are, and the whole sample is cropped into a rectangle and set inside another rectangle. So it is easy to understand *as a picture,* even if it is forever incomprehensible as an object. The Fourier transform from the journal *Ultramicroscopy* is a different matter. It is also submicroscopic, but it disobeys my expectation that an image should be a picture of an object.

Naturally this is only an impression, and as I learn more about the science involved I can see how the Fourier transform is indeed a picture of an object and how it uses the same photographic conventions as many other images. But that's where I lose interest. It's the inexplicable and counterintuitive aspect of scientific imaging that is most intriguing. Scientific images show us parts of the world we haven't seen (like horses galloping) and parts we can never see (such as atoms), but what is ultimately engaging is the possibility that science can confound my expectations about the visual world, showing me things I cannot comprehend either as objects or as images of any sort.

THE world is full of things that we do not see, and when we begin to notice them, we also notice how little we can ever see. Scientific images show that best, and a few more examples of scientific seeing will help bring me back to the idea that the world is full of eyes and apparitions.

It is almost as if seeing is too full, too powerful to indulge in without careful rules and limitations. Books of art history tend to review the same kinds of images over and over, making visual art seem to be only a matter of paintings, sculpture, and architecture. Even with new kinds of art such as installation and video, the mix is not that challenging. I would love to open an art history textbook, turn to a chapter on Renaissance wall paintings, and see this image (figure 8). It's a picture of a hidden defect in what the author calls "an ancient fresco": we are looking straight *through* the cement wall into an air pocket behind, where the fresco has begun to separate from the building itself (the fresco itself is shown in the inset). The picture was made with a "digital speckle pattern interferometer" and it entirely bypasses the painted surface of the fresco in favor of an invisible defect. It shows a fringe pattern indicating the dimensions of the gap, and it erases the painting, the wall, and the rest of the building. What a difference it would make if art historians tried to come to terms with this kind of seeing. The image reminds us that a fresco is also an object with a peculiar relation to a building, partly on it and partly off it—here literally falling off. Now that I have seen this image, I will never be able to see frescoes in quite the same way. I will always imagine the invisible ringed form hiding in the wall.

There are many ways of seeing aside from those that can be

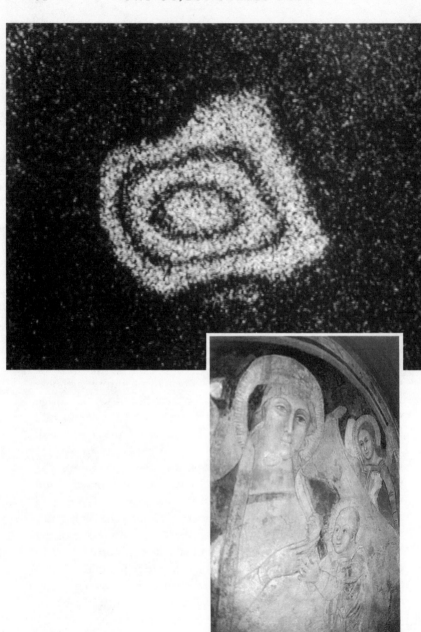

■ FIGURE 8

captured by pointing photofloods at an object and documenting it
in Kodachrome. A few years ago there was a special slide film called
color infrared, which mixed visible light with near infrared to produce unexpected colors. Pictures of autumn leaves would come out
partly the way they naturally look and partly glowing pink-and-
turquoise. A picture of a hand would look a little waxy, with the
surface veins showing through as if the skin had become transparent.
The color infrared film was also a way to think about the vision of
other animals. Some animals see different wavelengths than we do;
this raises curious questions about how they perceive the world.
Apparently frogs can see color but tadpoles can't: is the metamorphosis from tadpole to frog like the change from black-and-white
Kansas to colorful Oz? Bees can see some ultraviolet, so that they
can look at flowers that appear perfectly white to us and discern
patterns in them. At the same time bees cannot see the other end of
the spectrum—they can't perceive red, and so their vision begins in
the ultraviolet, continues up through the spectrum of purple, blue,
green, yellow, and stops at orange. To us, the two extreme ends of
the spectrum look very similar: red on one end seems to blend well
with violet on the other. In terms of wavelengths they are opposites,
but in our perception they seem like a good match. That is the
reason why artists have been able to bend diagrams of the spectrum
into color circles, connecting the red to the violet to make a continuous (and unscientific) cycle of color. If you think of what happens
when you mix the deepest red with the deepest violet, you can only
imagine a color very much like red or violet. Most colors mix to
produce new colors, so that, for example, blue and yellow make
green; but red and violet seem to only produce more red and violet.
That's odd if you think of the spectrum as a number line. Violet at
one end of the spectrum has a wavelength of around 420, and red is
about 660. You might think that if they were mixed, the result
would be in between—say, about 540, which is the wavelength of
green. But red and violet do not mix to produce green. Bees are
different, and they see mixtures of *their* two extreme colors (ultraviolet and orange) as a third color, which we cannot even begin to
imagine. It is called bees' purple, though there is no reason to assume
it looks anything like purple. Perhaps to bees it is more like our

yellow or our indigo . . . or perhaps it's something entirely new. We have no capacity to imagine new colors. No matter how hard you try, each color you imagine is going to be a color that exists and probably one you've seen before. You can make up a new color—the philosopher Nelson Goodman made up "grue" and "bleen"—but you cannot imagine how a genuinely new color looks. We are stuck with the spectrum and its mixtures, but we know that other animals may not be.

And what about other ways of seeing form? Animals that can change their color, like flounders, octopi, and chameleons, provide a way to think about that. A flounder will not only change its color to try to blend in with its surroundings; it will also change its pattern (figure 9). The flounder in these pictures has a fairly good idea of what a dot pattern looks like, even though it ends up making dots that are several sizes too large. But it messes up the large and small checkerboards. Faced with a small checkerboard, it produces some small white patches, but there are too few of them and they are unevenly spaced. For the large checkerboard it manages larger spots, but it cannot get the evenness of the pattern, and its silhouette remains clearly visible. In describing things this way I am of course seeing as a human, and what these pictures may show is the way that the flounder sees those patterns. It could be that, for the flounder, those are perfect matches, and a large checkerboard really *is* a mottled black surface with some blotches of white. The flounder might be communicating its vision with its body, letting us glimpse the world through its eyes.

From my point of view there is no reason not to think of instruments in the same terms. If there is flounder vision, frog vision, and bee vision, then there is also microscope vision and digital speckle pattern interferometer vision. Currently radar systems are being improved so that they can show more than just a blip when they encounter a ship or an airplane (figure 10). By its nature radar is sensitive to distances in a way that our eyes are not. In order to perceive how far away an object is, I need to use both my eyes, so that my head turns into what the military calls a binocular range finder, capable of comparing the view of an object from two slightly different positions. I also guess at the distances of objects from expe-

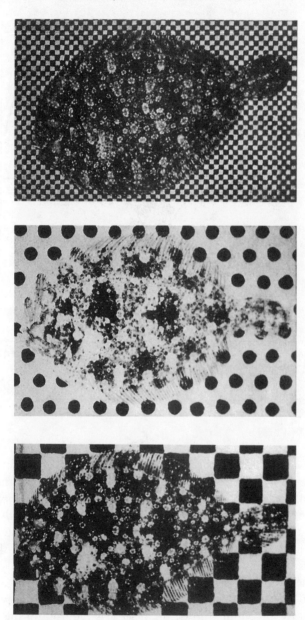

■ FIGURE 9

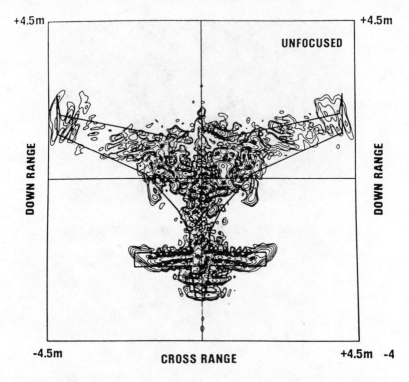

rience and by sensing the muscles in my eyes as they focus in and out. Radar is different, since a single beam carries with it information about the exact distance of an object. It is as if I were to look at a point of light in the dark with one eye closed and tell exactly how far away it is. Unfortunately it is not easy to get radar systems to make images in the normal sense. They are insensitive to shapes, since radar has a very long wavelength. (The smaller the wavelength, the smaller the object that can be seen.) In this experiment, a radar system has managed to see a plane as a disconnected set of wobbly shapes. As the outline shows, the radar gets the front of the plane very well but sees the wings as watery blobs. The radar also sees parts of the plane in back, where there is no plane, as if it cannot stop seeing when the object ends. This is the way this system sees: hard, smooth metallic objects come out as moldy lumps. It would be nice to see an entire radar cityscape made the same way, with streets reduced to pools and buildings to swarms of gnats.

The author of the article where this picture appears cites a standard definition of "image" in order to place the concept of a radar image among other kinds of images. The definition casts a very broad net. An image is said to be "a spatial distribution of a physical property such as radiation, electric charge, conductivity, or reflectivity, mapped from another distribution of either the same or another physical property." An oil painting, for example, would be a spatial distribution of visible light mapped from another spatial distribution of visible light. Artists would have difficulty with that word "map," since there is no systematic correlation between the original and the image in visual art, and often enough there is no original at all. But I like the definition because it reminds me how broad the range of vision has become. Radar seeing, speckle interferometer seeing, and bees' seeing all influence the way I see the world.

I N most of these images from science and technology, the "eye" —that is, the machine that helps out the eye—needs to send out something in order to make the object visible. Like a studio photographer using a flash, the scientist has to illuminate the object instead of just taking in light the way the eyes do. To make the electron micrographs, the crystal has to be bombarded with electrons; to see the sulfur atoms, the surface must be electrically charged; and to make the image of the plane, it had to be bathed in radar beams. In modern thinking this idea of *sending out* something in order to receive it back, and thereby see an object, is not a common notion. There was a period when philosophers thought that the eye saw objects by extromission, sending out streams of light and collecting their reflections, or catching beams of light and hauling them in. But opinion turned against those theories, and in recent centuries we have learned to think of our eyes as passive recipients of ambient light. Psychologically, the older theory is stronger. After all, it is not

easy to imagine how the air can be so filled with crisscrossing photons that the tiny fraction that make it into my eyes are enough to
see every object I look at. For me, at least, it is impossible to understand how a star at the far end of the galaxy could be sending out so
many photons that they spread through the entire universe, even
spilling into the infinitesimally small openings that are my two eyes.
For those reasons, the extromission theories still have some power
over our concepts of seeing. Sometimes, even though I know better,
I choose to imagine my eye emitting visual rays or fiery ether.

Since these speculations have long been disproven, it is philosophers and psychologists who think along these lines, rather than
scientists. The psychoanalyst Jacques Lacan has an attractive theory
about vision that borrows from these ancient possibilities. He thinks
of seeing as a reciprocal process: as I look at someone or something,
it looks back, and our gazes cross each other. My gaze finds its
answer in the person I see, so that I can see its effect in her eyes. If I
am looking at an inanimate object, it has a certain presence—it looks
back, and again I can understand that as the echo of my gaze. I see
and I can see that I am seen, so each time I see I also see myself
being seen. Vision becomes a kind of cat's cradle of crossing lines of
sight, and Lacan thinks of the whole scene as a kind of trap: we are
"caught," he says, "manipulated, captured, in the field of vision."
As I lie awake in my bedroom, feeling the force of vision everywhere
in the room, I am entering into a complicated game. Objects (and
also my cat, if she isn't only an object) are no longer just things out
there to be seen but also places where I can think about seeing and
being seen. Each object has a certain force, a certain way of resisting
or accepting my look and returning that look to me.

This is a very peculiar state of mind, one that I started this chapter
trying to describe. There is something fundamental about it, something that goes into being human. I *need* to be seen by objects and
by people; I need to be caught in that intersection of gazes. Certainly
I have a deep desire to see people I care for and to have them see
me, and Lacan has emphasized that I have an equally important need
to see myself in a mirror. By looking into the mirror each morning
I check to make sure that I am the same person who went to bed
last night—the person who dissolved into darkness and dreams. Of

course I know that, but I also need to see it. It could be that the first few times I glimpsed myself in a mirror, when I was still too young to speak, I realized in some infantile way that I had a certain shape and a certain look and that I was not just a few flailing limbs or a crying sound—that I was like my mother a little, and different from her as well. Being a psychoanalyst and believing in the importance of early experiences, Lacan put great stress on those forgotten encounters with the mirror. I have seen infants find their first mirrors with absolute disinterest, and I do not see any reason to insist that such a drama need ever take place. But I love the concept behind the theory: that we all put together an idea of what we are by looking at ourselves and that without mirrors our sense of ourselves would be very different.

It seems to me that something of this kind happens every time I see a person, and in a different way each time I stare at an object. If I am just meeting someone for the first time, I will probably be acutely aware of how I look, and I will watch the person carefully for signs of my appearance reflected in her face. It's not so much approval I'm after, but a more nuanced response—I want an updated sense of myself; I want to know how I appear to the world, what kind of person I am. In short, I am in the process of continuing to define myself, adjusting my sense of who I am by watching for the way the person responds to me. At times I'm aware of this process —for example, if I'm meeting someone important. But it happens when I talk to anyone. I see myself in the other person's gaze, and so I see myself being seen. It is like the old theories of vision: I send out a version of myself, and I watch as its echoes come back to me. And there is no reason to stop at people, because objects also send back our sight. The radar image of the plane contains information about the plane, as the radar sees it, but it also contains information about the radar array itself. When I see a book I understand something about the book and also something about myself.

The only problem with this way of thinking about things is that it's easy to overstate it. It is more fluid and subtle than Lacan makes it sound, and everything interesting about it is unconscious. As a theory about vision, it is rather harsh and static, with its rebounding gazes and surrealist objects. When I do think about what happens with mirrors, I am usually preoccupied with something trivial: I worry about how neat my clothing is or if my hair is in place. Sometimes I try to project charm or confidence (that's a telling phrase, as if I had charm rays to send out). And when I look at objects, it would not normally occur to me that they might some-how be returning my gaze. But what does it mean to say that people need human contact, unless it is this? And why would I need to keep looking around my apartment, thinking about the arrangement of furniture, buying and cleaning and tending to objects, unless I needed to see them?

And objects do have eyes. The knife sees me: it gleams from the tabletop and says, "Pick me up." As in *Alice in Wonderland,* food seems to speak. A cookie looks at me with its single eye and whis-pers, "Eat me." And ultimately, objects all say one thing: "Look at me." Objects look incomplete or inviting; they seem to be waiting for us to notice them. In a painting, the bright gleam on a teacup is an artist's trick to make it look real, but it is also a hypnotist's device to keep our eyes on it. Is it too wild to say that at times objects that are off by themselves can begin to seem lonely or rejected? As I look around my desk, I see a box that I have shunted into a corner. Ordinarily if someone asked me why it was over there, I would say I hadn't used it in a while, and so it got pushed aside. But there is more to it than that. The box reminds me, very, very gently and unconsciously, but also quite firmly, of certain things about myself. I was given it as a present several years ago, and I associate it with memories from that time. For various reasons, all of which are too subtle for me to put into words, I don't want to be reminded of that part of myself when I work. It's not a bad memory or even a strong memory of any kind. Most objects don't have that kind of emotional meaning. It's more like a gentle feeling just at the edge of thought. At any rate, whenever I see the box, it works like a little mirror, returning to me a small part of my image of myself. I see myself being seen—again, without the thought ever crossing my mind—and I turn away, or I put some other object between my eyes and the box.

It's already too much to describe things this neatly. What I should have said is that these cat's cradles of seeing and being seen are like single spider's threads. Like the wispy lines that snare shoppers, they are invisibly fine, and when I am caught in one I may not even notice it. At the same time, there are hundreds of thousands of them, filling the rooms I inhabit, streaming between my eyes and the eyes of the person I see. The air is thick with this weightless skein of vision, just as a physicist would say it is thick with photons, dashing silently here and there.

S T I L L , there is something creepy about this idea of objects staring back. Normally we are comforted by the exactly opposite impression. I am happy sitting in my living room because I know that the clutter of furniture around me is not a crowd of people staring at me and that the easy chair I'm sitting in is not assessing my body to see if it approves. Hopefully there is no Big Brother in the television looking back (though people with black boxes might know what it feels like to have the television watch *you*). Every gleam from a teacup is not an eye, and I am happy about that. I can live with the idea that I glance at my furniture in order, at some ill-defined low level of mental activity, to revise and affirm my conception of myself. But to raise the possibility that all these things are eyes and that they look back at me is to go against the grain of common experience. It happens that I think this way only when I am aware of myself and paying attention to the ways I see. In ordinary life, all this is beneath the surface. In a grocery store, I do not think for a moment that the rows of vegetables and the cans of soup might be looking at me as I speed down the aisle.

Or do I? I think that in the most evanescent way possible—a way so ineffable that the word "ineffable" is too coarse to describe it—I am aware of every single object in the store, which is to say I react differently to the presence of every object. Sometimes I return their gaze and even decide to buy them, as in my example at the opening of the book. More often I am scarcely aware of them—the entire aisle of health foods goes by in a flash and doesn't even enter my consciousness—but my actions are ways of defining myself, and I have a particular relation to each one. In my living room there are two large bookcases, each one eight feet tall, and they have about five hundred books between them. If I step up to a shelf and look at the books one by one, I can remember something about each. As a historian once said, some stare at me reproachfully, grumbling that I have never read them. One may remind me vaguely of a time when I was interested in romantic novels. An old college text will elicit a pang of unhappiness about studying. Each book has its character, and even books I know very well also have this kind of wordless flavor. Now if I step back from the shelf and look quickly across both bookcases, I speed up that same process a hundredfold. Impressions wash across my awareness. But *each book still looks back* in its own way, answering the rude brevity of my gaze, calling faintly to me out of the corner of my eye. At that speed many books remain wrapped in the shadows of my awareness—I know I have looked past them and I know they are there, but I refuse to call them to mind.

A psychoanalyst might say that we need to believe that vision is a one-way street and that objects are just the passive recipients of our gaze in order to maintain the conviction that we are in control of our vision and ourselves. If I think of the world in the ordinary way, I am much reassured. Everything is mine to command: if I want to see a movie, I go see it. If I want to look at my cat, I look at her. But this implies something darker: that if I resist the idea that objects look back at me and that I am tangled in a web of seeing, then I am also resisting the possibility that I may not be the autonomous, independent, stable self I claim I am. I may not be coming to terms with the thought that I need these reciprocal gazes in order to go on being myself. Lacan was extreme about this, and he sometimes said that the very idea that we are unified selves is entirely fictional, a lie that we tell ourselves in order to keep going. In reality (that is, in the world we can never face), my sense of myself is a desperate fiction, a "symptom" of being human.

This is the kind of idea that is popular in academia because it is so exhilaratingly radical—but at the same time it is almost entirely unbelievable, which is to say we *cannot* believe it if we want to keep going. To the extent that it is true, it means more than just being aware that nets of seeing and being seen are necessary to sustain my sense of self. Here the object not only looks back at the observer; it *makes* the observer by looking, and the other way around. What is really happening, what I can never really see or else I will go mad, is that I am not the spider who weaves the web, and I am not even a fly caught in the web: I am the web itself, streaming off in all directions with no center and no self that I can call my own.

THE world is full of eyes, and sight is everywhere. But there is a special category, another kind of eye that is neither real (like my eyes) nor metaphorical (like the "eyes" of rainbows and halos). It sees, and yet it is blind. I mean the fake eyes that some insects grow on their bodies in order to frighten away predators. Butterflies and moths tend to have these eyes on their lower wings, so that they can keep them hidden under the upper wings until they need to flash them in some animal's face. The effect startles practically any animal that can see: it keeps away birds, lizards, frogs, and small mammals, and it also scares many people. So many animals are frightened of eyes that biologists have a word for it—cyclophobism. The odd thing about this is how nonsensical many insects are about their protective strategy. It seems reasonable to have an extra pair of eyes hidden on your body to scare off a predator, and some insects throw in a half dozen more eyes for good measure. The beautifully named pearly eye has a half dozen small eyespots scattered over its wings and rows of tiny eyespots along the margins (figure 11). How scary can those little eyes be? To me they look like decoration, and that's what most of them must be. To say they are decoration is to say they are used to attract mates, and so perhaps the pearly eye has two real eyes on its head for seeing, two false ones on its wings for scaring, and several dozen others for attracting. (By comparison, humans have a poverty of eyes, and we have to use the same pair for seeing, scaring, and attracting.) But the problem with that neat classification is that the pearly eye's smaller eyes are also a little unsettling, and the larger ones are also attractive. A huge eyespot is frightening, and a wingful of eyes is unsettling, and a pattern of little circles is just a little interesting. Somewhere along the line the fright drains out. When is an eye just a spot, and when is a dot an eye? The microscopic protozoan euglena has an eyespot, a little red mark in its green

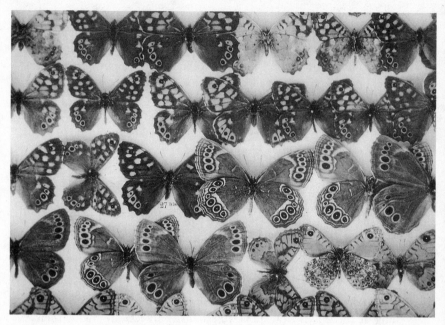

■ FIGURE 11

body. As it swims around under the microscope it seems to look this way and that, even though the most the eye can sense is change in the light level. As soon as I know that the red dot is an eye, I pay attention, and even though I know that the little eye-shaped markings on the butterfly are not eyes, they have a certain claim on my interest. In biology real eyes are distinguished from protozoan eyespots, and both eyes and eyespots are distinguished from these lepidopteran ocelli. But are they really that different? Isn't this ©️ also an eye? And this • also? What round shape is not a magnet for my gaze?

The Amazonian lantern fly has a large false front built over its real head, and it seems to mimic a crocodile (figure 12). It's a weird attempt to make a crocodile, if that's really what it is supposed to be. The lantern fly is much smaller than even a newborn crocodile, and the "head" is puffy and bloated, more like a helium balloon than a

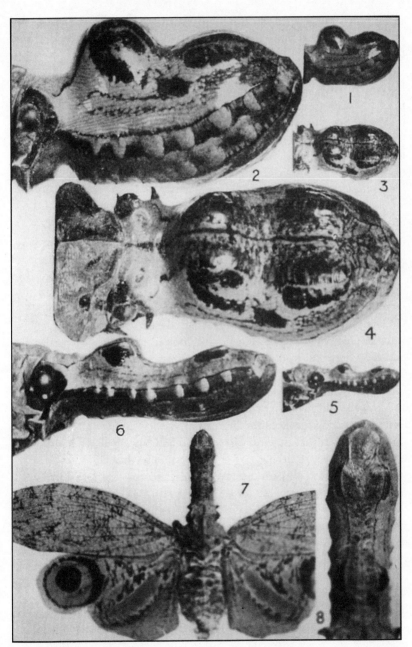

FIGURE 12

real reptile. Still, it's an admirable job. It has a double row of teeth modeled in three dimensions and big globular eyes that even look wet.

Scientists who have tried to explain the lantern fly's evolution have had to say why a bird or a monkey—which are what would normally want to eat a lantern fly—might be scared by a tiny alligator's head that they encountered high up in the trees instead of down in the water. One biologist tried to argue that size was unimportant to the "animal mind," and he gave the example of his own pet dachshund, who rushed up to a four-inch-long porcelain dachsund "with the utmost interest and excitement." A monkey, he thought, would be scared by any size crocodile head. Another biologist, Roger Caillois, was unsatisfied with that kind of explanation. To him the hollow crocodile head is an archetypal form: a scary, bulging-eyed, toothy face that would be horrifying to *any* animal under any circumstances. So the lantern fly did not evolve in imitation of the crocodiles, but both the crocodiles and the lantern flies evolved in imitation of an archetypal horrifying mask. Caillois recalls the Greek myth of the Gorgons, who had flat noses, hair made of snakes, and a double row of teeth. They didn't look like anything on earth, but they were still frightening. Both Gorgons and alligators would then approximate some fundamental, inbuilt criterion for petrifying fright. An accurate version of that primordial terror would be too awful to see and live. The hero Perseus cut off one of the Gorgons' heads by looking into a mirror instead of staring directly at her, and Caillois suspects that he didn't have to do any cutting at all: he just turned the mirror to her face, so that she could see herself.

I don't know if this makes any scientific sense—the lantern fly does look an awful lot like an alligator, and it couldn't be chance that it lives near alligators. But Caillois might say that doesn't matter, since it can still be that they are both wearing the masks of something worse. The idea of ultimate horror is very appealing, and it helps account for many frightening things that are not eyes. Why do I recoil from a yellow-and-black wasp? Why do I feel creepy around a furry brown moth? Why do I flinch whenever I notice a spider dangling just in front of my face? Are those just human prejudices, something I feel because I was brought up in the twentieth century and in America? Or are they more universal than that? Some people believe that there is no inbuilt fear of insects, and my parents brought me up to be unafraid by showing me insects whenever they could. After I was safely grown, my mother admitted that she had always been a little uncomfortable about insects and that she had stifled that feeling in order not to pass it on to me. And it worked, since I don't usually mind insects. Even on a hot summer night when I go upstairs and find that I have left the window open and the light on, I can fall asleep in a room that is buzzing and fluttering with insects. But that doesn't mean I don't appreciate the creepiness of some insects, and I am left to wonder where that residual feeling comes from. Is it an inevitable slip in my mother's strategy? Or is it an innate sense reasserting itself? Many things can be frightening that are not full masks and have no eyespots or false teeth. A little piece of something that doesn't seem to belong can be the most terrifying imaginable experience. A "coat upon a coat-hanger" can be worse than a multi-million-dollar horror film.

And here, I think, is the key to these enigmas. What really counts is whether or not an object fits in with its surroundings. A tiny balloon alligator high up in a tree is definitely frightening (I think I would probably fall out of the tree if I encountered a lantern fly). So is a real alligator, because it appears where there was only murky water and algae. I have some snapshots taken in the Okefenokee swamp in Georgia, showing mangrove trees, vines, and leaves in the water (figure 13). I took them during a boat ride in the swamp, and each picture is really a picture of an alligator or a poisonous snake. But by the time the film was developed, I had forgotten where the animals were. This is a typical tourist photo, taken with the wrong lens, and the animal that seemed so threatening at the time has entirely disappeared. In the boat, each sighting gave me a little shiver, since I realized the swamp was thick with animals I could barely see. The photograph has a residual echo of that sensation, since I know it is not just a picture of undergrowth. In other photos from the same series I can just discern the smooth curve of a snake or an alligator's snout. Here I cannot see anything, and the more I look at the picture the more alarming it becomes.

The startling appearance and mysterious disappearance of Okefe-

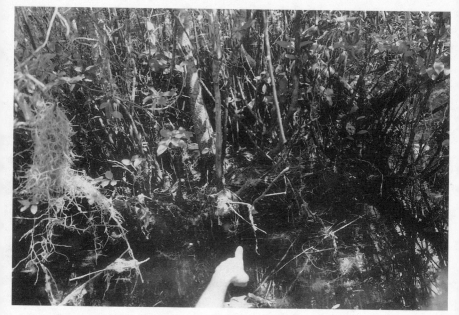

■ FIGURE 13

nokee animals finds its parallel in natural strategies of coloration. Brown moths try to creep away and hide by blending with dead leaves, twigs, mold, moss, or bark. A yellow jacket's stripes, on the other hand, draw attention to it and serve as a warning. Eyespots and fake alligator heads have the same function: it's not the mask that matters; it's the difference between the creature and its setting. (If all the trees in the Amazon sprouted alligator heads, the lantern fly would be in trouble.) Some butterflies have flash coloration: they are camouflaged when they are at rest, but when they fly they look like strips of brightly colored paper. In the language of biology, they are aposomatic: their patterns distract us from the idea of their body.

If the world is a setting, then all creatures have two choices: either to be a part of it, to fit in somehow like a piece of a jigsaw puzzle, or to stand out against it. I especially like to think of the world as a picture or a picture-puzzle. There is a picture of some vines in a swamp, and there are animals hidden in the picture. There is a picture of a tree trunk, and there is a little brown moth somewhere in the corrugated bark. The moth wants to fade into the picture of tree trunks, to be like a little stain in a mottled patch of the world or like brush stroke in a painting, meshed and blurred with every other brush stroke. Nudibranchs—unshelled snails that live in the ocean —are a wonderful example of this. They make magical apparitions in the coral reef, floating by with their edges undulating gently like dazzling little Persian carpets (figure 14). Many of them have gaudy iridescent colors (outrageous purples and oranges, pinks and yellows), and others try instead to disappear into the dingy ocean floor. One species has a wobbly grid pattern, and it is supposed to look something like a mold or stain growing on a sea fan (figure 15). Above it to the right and left are spiral deposits of its eggs, and they too are meant to be invisible. (Perhaps they look like molds on the other side of the sea fan.) This is an especially entrancing photograph

■ FIGURE 14

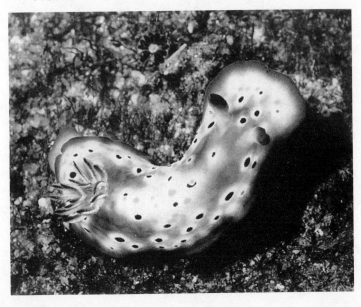

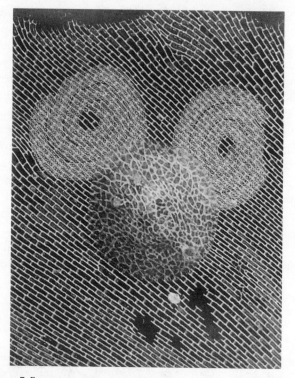

■ FIGURE 15

because the entire arrangement happens to resemble a startled human face, and that might just be an effect that the nudibranch wants: that way it could be moldy and frightening at the same time.

This is a versatile theory, and it applies just as well to people. Sometimes I dress to fit in, so that I can blend with the crowd and not attract attention. When I do that I am imagining the world as a picture, and I want to find a place in the picture where I can disappear. As I walk down the sidewalk or enter the conference room, I want to be nothing more than a blotch among other blotches. But on many other occasions I have exactly the opposite effect in mind. I dress in my best clothes and I make sure I look just right, because I want to make an impression: I need to stand out; I want to be noticed. Makeup does both those things. Some people wear it in order not to look out of place, and others wear it to attract attention. A woman who is made up in this way is exactly the same as that nudibranch. She wants to be striking and also invisible; she wants to be arresting and yet uninteresting—depending on who may be looking at her. Of course the nudibranch hopes that it will be striking and *frightening,* so it won't be eaten, and the woman hopes that she will be striking and fascinating, so that she will be devoured in another way—but that's a different subject.

Like some people, some insects have outlandish decorations. Where fashion is concerned, anything is possible—though, in the insect world, fashion is much more overtly a matter of sexual attraction. Some insects carry heavy weights on their backs that look like abstract sculptures or television antennae (figure 16). Creatures like this show that there is more to being interesting than growing an eyespot or a fake head. It is possible to stand out from the crowd by not resembling anything—not an alligator or an alligator's eye or even an archetypal mask. This body sculpture has the same purpose as any outrageous outfit: it attracts mates and challenges rivals. Sexual adaptation in insects is as senseless and quick changing as fashion in the human world. In this way these insects are just spectacular versions of everyday desires. Some humans are every bit as unusual—I am thinking of the strange hats popular in the nineteenth century (some with stuffed birds) or the fetishistic dresses worn by some street people. A person who walks around near where I work has a three-foot-tall hat adorned with pinwheels that looks very much like the abstract sculptures on these insects.

So part of what it means to live in a world full of gazes, where objects, animals, and people all define one another by the ways they see and are seen, has to do with this underlying difference between the shy and the overt. Objects might stare at me invisibly, like the spiders I imagined in the woods outside my window. To see them, I would have to look hard or do something unnatural—I'd have to go out spider hunting with a flashlight and catch their eyes in the act of seeing. Other objects stare at me insistently with obvious eyes or frightening eyes. But in the end, seeing and vision do not depend on

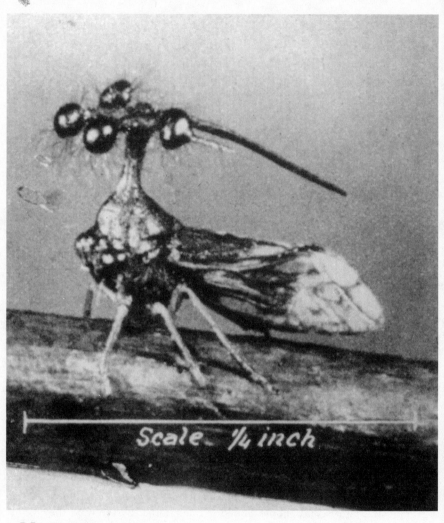

Scale 1/4 inch

■ FIGURE 16

eyes at all. A bright stripe, a shining color, a fragment of a face, "a coat upon a coat-hanger"—they are all things that see.

ALL this puts me in a strange mood and makes me think again about paintings. If we all want to be pictures to some degree, then it may be that when we look at visual art we are seeing examples of that desire. Every landscape painting gives me clues to the way I might hide in a landscape. I don't mean that I usually look at a landscape and think, "I could creep into that corner and never be noticed"; I mean that the landscape shows me how objects can blend and harmonize, and I dimly sense my own desire to fade into forms. A portrait shows me how a face might look, so that I can think how I could resemble it, and even an abstract painting makes me think of patterns and harmonies in the world and how I find my place among them. When we say that pictures can be escapist or that we can be transported into them, we are talking about a literal version of this desire. Some pictures do invite us this way (science fiction book covers and some romantic landscapes do that), but what I am describing here is a deeper motion of our minds. We want to *be* pictures, not just to be in them, and so when I look at a picture I am also looking at myself, at a way that I might be. I want the relationship between my self and my world to be like the relationship between the parts of a picture, and so I look to pictures for advice on the ways that might happen. It may be that one of the reasons visual art is so highly valued and so important to so many cultures is that it provides examples and models for how we might fit into the world.

Three

LOOKING AWAY, AND SEEING TOO MUCH

So far I have painted a picture of seeing that looks like a web or a cat's cradle. Vision runs back and forth from objects to eyes, and whatever is seen also sees. If I see a shoe or my cat with its eyes closed, they see me in return. And seeing is self-definition. Objects look back, and their incoming gaze tells me what I am. Our sense of ourselves is like a television station always going out of focus, and we tune and clarify ourselves by seeing. Everything from our wives and husbands to our shoes and the grass in the park looks back and tells us who we are.

All this happens unnoticed, even though it is the common thread of vision. And now I want to move into more turbulent waters and start to think what happens when vision goes wrong. In the end of the book, that will lead to thoughts of blindness and death, but I want to begin with seeing that is merely difficult or unpleasant. First there is the fact that seeing is never complete—especially when the subject is charged with sexuality or with danger, it is impossible to see all of it or to see it in a relaxed and measured way. Instead, our eyes jump from one place to the next, trying not to apprehend the whole. This skittish seeing also has its echoes in everyday life, when we cast irregular glances over rooms and landscapes. Following a French surrealist writer, I will consider three things that throw the eyes into so much confusion that they may not be able to see at all: the sun, genitals, and death. Confronted with objects like those, vision goes out of control, and we see where we do not want to, or we fail to see where we should, and our eyes no longer obey our conscious wishes. Death, in particular, may be the hardest thing to see, and I want to take a close look at the most powerfully affecting pictures I know: photographs of executions and beheadings, taken in China in the 1920s and 1930s, that come very near to representing the moment of death itself.

CONSIDER, to begin, the problem of looking at naked people. What practices and institutions involve people with clothes on, standing around and looking at naked people? Hospitals, for one: in a hospital, a patient may be visited by a roomful of doctors and medical students, and in those situations anything can happen, depending on the illness—patients may be asked to expose themselves, or to sit up while the doctor demonstrates how a lung is drained or a catheter is inserted. Since the Renaissance, patients have been paraded onstage in theaters full of students. Nineteenth-century hysterics are the most famous examples of that—they were brought out onstage naked, and the doctors tried to induce hysterical episodes by speaking to them and touching them in certain ways. Bedridden patients could be examined by lifting them up (figure 17).

So hospitals are one place where naked people are displayed to curious observers. Another is the pornography industry. I have had the pleasure (and the displeasure) to see a fair amount of pornography in connection with a course I teach on the subject of the human body. The first year I taught it, students complained that I wasn't showing slides of real porno but only pictures that I had found in books with titles like *Erotic Art Through the Ages*. Pornography is an important subject in contemporary art, and I had to admit they were

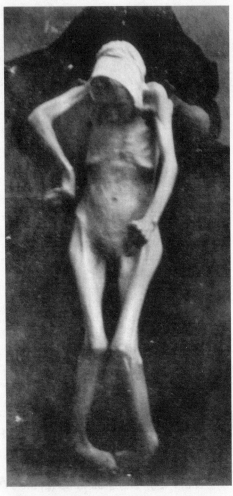

■ FIGURE 17

right. So the next year I brought in some fairly timid slides I had shot from mass-market pornographic magazines. Several students that year criticized me for being too narrow in my choices, and they brought in alternate images. In that way I have seen a wide range of pornographic materials, from nineteenth-century photographs to "sophisticated" videotapes. There is a remarkable diversity in the kinds of images that go under the general name of pornography, and they tend to be lumped together by the press, and by feminists such as Catherine MacKinnon, when it becomes necessary to characterize their nature or effects. But virtually every image I have seen conforms to this one theatrical criterion: it involves people with clothes on observing people who are naked. If a pornographic image is imagined as a scene, instead of as someone's projected fantasy, then it is necessary also to imagine the room in which the actions take place. In many cases there is more than one person behind the camera, and there are commonly lights and props offscreen as well. People who are not involved in the sexual act are bystanders, professionals who have ambiguous—and sometimes unhealthy—relations to what the camera records.

Naked people must often have been observed in jails, too. Strip searches are common enough, and there are many stories about contemporary jails where prisoners are kept naked as humiliation or punishment. Amnesty International publicizes cases of that kind, and during wars the incidents become too numerous to record. There are accounts of concentration camps that describe inhuman variations on this theme (a line of women paraded naked in front of a line of naked men) and scenes that are too strong to clearly imagine (a woman raped and killed in front of her husband). These examples may seem to differ from what happens in the pornography industry or in hospitals, because they are forms of torture. At the least they involve embarrassment, and at the worst they are murders. It is true that what happens in prisons, in wartime, and prisoner-of-war camps has many times been worse than what normally takes place in hospitals and in pornographic films, but the distinction between them is one of degree rather than kind. There is humiliation in all three settings, and people are coerced in each of them.

A fuller answer to the question (about the practices in which people who are clothed observe people who are naked) brings us to very different examples—to nude bathing, for example. There are nude beaches in many countries, and nudist camps in America and in Europe. I grew up in Ithaca, in upstate New York, a college town with a strong contingent of ex-flower children and radicals. One of the perennial customs in Ithaca is to bathe naked in one of the city reservoirs, and since the landscape is scored with deep rocky gorges, many of the streams serve the same purpose. At the largest reservoir a crowd of naked people sunbathing and swimming is always watched by a crowd of clothed voyeurs, some of them lurking in the woods and others just walking around among the naked bodies. The police used to raid the large reservoir several times each summer in an attempt to drive the swimmers out. For their part, the swimmers protested that their bodies did not make the drinking water poisonous, at least no more than the dead fish and raccoons that also floated in it. There was also outdoor sex, and I remember once being a little embarrassed when I was out walking along a stream bed with my sister and a friend and we turned a corner and saw a couple in the distance making love. As we waited patiently for them to finish (I remember my sister's friend saying irreverently, "He's almost done now; I can tell"), we chatted about various things, and the couple said hello when we passed them. There are places where naked people do not mind being watched by crowds of clothed people, and I suppose I would have to include borderline examples such as strip joints and topless bars. They can be benign, and there can be a relative absence of pressure, discomfort, and pain.

And I can think of one last answer to the question: live models in art schools. The practice of drawing and painting from live models seems consensual and harmless, and it has been around since the middle of the fifteenth century. The models are not coerced, except of course by the need for money, and there is rarely any problem. But I have participated in enough life drawing classes, both as a student and a teacher, to know that they are not always free of the problems that mark the other examples on the list. It is a simple, inescapable fact that looking at a live model is a charged experience. No matter how used to it we get—and studio instructors can persuade themselves, over the course of years, that models really are nothing but interesting furniture—it still possesses sexual and social overtones. It involves a person whose body is openly displayed being silently watched by a crowd of people whose sexuality is more concealed. It entails that the person who is being seen remain perfectly motionless, and as live models report, that can be very uncomfortable and difficult. It normally means that the model keeps quiet, though conversations are not uncommon. In each of these ways the model is turned from an individual into an object. As in pornography, the model's personality is erased or drastically simplified, so that he or she expresses only a single mood. There is an unequal power relation, as there is in hospitals, between the naked unmoving model and the actively creative students (and also between the model, the students, and the teacher, who supposedly orchestrates the entire activity). Life drawing classes can be unpleasant when it becomes apparent that the models are unhappy or suffering because they are unable to find any other work. Just as nude bathing is normally done without sexual excitation, so life drawing classes are usually not overtly sexual. But there are exceptions, and life drawing classes can sometimes be more like pornographic photo sessions. Anyone who has been around life drawing classes long enough will recall some examples of male and female models becoming aroused and of the range of responses that elicits in the students, and I am sure the opposite happens as well.

Hospitals, prisons, pornography, and nudism all echo in the life drawing classes. There are also racial and class issues at stake in life drawing, depending on the configuration of models and students. There can be elements of sexual inequality, humiliation, coercion, racism, class difference, sexual desire, sadism, masochism, voyeurism, discomfort, and even pain. But these things are seldom mentioned: no one talks about prisons or pornography, and instructors do not mention sexual issues. I remember a class in which a black man and a white woman were posed on a table that was draped to look like a bed. Certainly there's nothing wrong with that, but the instructor was behaving as if it were a random arrangement, as if he had put a pear next to an apple. No one mentioned the fact that this particular configuration was sexually and racially loaded. Instead, the students were critiqued for their use of form and color. It is dishonest and a little silly to look at a naked person for three hours and then talk about lines and planes; but in general, art instructors treat models as if they were nothing more than objects that are difficult to draw. But if that were all that is at stake, instructors would use toasters or spoons instead, since they are just as challenging.

Students and teachers negotiate these problems by an elaborate process of *not seeing* them and *not thinking* about how they are suppressed, in order to get on with the business of producing academic nude studies. Still, the silence is not effective. At some level each student knows as much, and it comes out in the drawings even if it is smothered in the class conversation or buried in the students' unconscious thoughts. If art students' life drawings are interesting at all, it is because they have controlled these issues in a complicated and not entirely successful way. A life drawing of a male model might have an intricately detailed penis, or it might have only a gap where the penis should be. Some students depict penises and testicles as cylinders and spheres, or else they group them together as a triangle, while others lavish attention on them as if they were the most interesting part of the body. Those kinds of choices are the most obvious effects of the suppressed sexual and social dialogue that accompanies life drawing. Usually the results are more subtle. A drawing might highlight a shoulder or a wrist at the expense of other body parts. A student might choose to concentrate on the face and make a kind of nude portrait, or else create a drawing that abstracts the whole body into geometric planes even more general than the drapery that surrounds the figure. Some life drawings feature strong staring eyes, and others omit the eyes altogether or do not come to terms with the face. All these results are the effects of a particular kind of seeing. In the end, each drawing expresses important decisions about the relation between model and student: Is this person potentially attractive to me? Is this situation embarrassing? Do I wish that the model were facing away from me? Do I want to think of the model as a person like me? Can I really imagine the model as a pattern of light and shade? No matter how silent a student or a teacher may be, those questions are asked and answered at the level of the drawing.

This is inconstant seeing, a way of looking that skips over some parts and emphasizes others in the service of some unrecognized anxiety or desire. Those readers who are artists might try this experiment: next time you visit a life class, think of your eye movements as you study the model. I find it is nearly impossible to look from head to toe at a constant speed. If you're not an artist, you might try the same experiment wherever you see naked bodies. I have not tried this in the bedroom, because it could be a little cruel and strange—but cruelty and strangeness are exactly what typify life drawing and the other examples.

Yet people have not always seen bodies this way. There is little evidence that Albrecht Dürer flinched from any part of his own body, improper or not, when he drew this *Self-Portrait* (figure 18). The face is just as wrinkled as the testicles, and even blank swatches of skin are endowed with textured marks. This is powerful seeing: it despises decorum and succeeds, at least for a few moments, in not flinching. Most of our pictures are different—they follow our habits of seeing and they harbor blind spots. We see a little more constantly if we are looking at things other than naked bodies. But only a little. If I look at a bird, I see mostly the head, and then my eye might travel down the back or the wing, with a glimpse perhaps at the tail or the claws. But I don't linger on the place where the bird's crotch should be, partly because I know I won't see anything there and partly out of an entirely displaced sense of decorum. If it occurs to me that birds don't seem to have ears, I may spend a moment looking for the ear, but otherwise I would skip that area entirely. Dogs may be the creatures we look at with the most constancy. Their penises are well known for being embarrassing and obvious, and dog owners will look over every inch of their dogs' bodies in search of shedding hair, fleas, or injuries. The same kind of seeing is lavished on infants by their mothers.

These are possible exceptions, and I think most seeing is fairly even in comparison to the way we see sexual bodies. I look up and down a tree without fear, and I think I look equally at every single word on each page of a book I am reading. As experimental psychologists have discovered, those are illusions on my part, and no human gaze proceeds evenly from left to right and top to bottom. By monitoring the direction of the pupils it is possible to make a map of the points where the eyes fixate as they move over an object, and that map is never a grid. Still, there is more involved here than the sum total of momentary fixations of my eyes: I am thinking of the emotional investment and the thought that are directed along with the gaze. A student may spend quite a while looking at a model's penis, but the resulting drawing may not show that attention at all. I find it

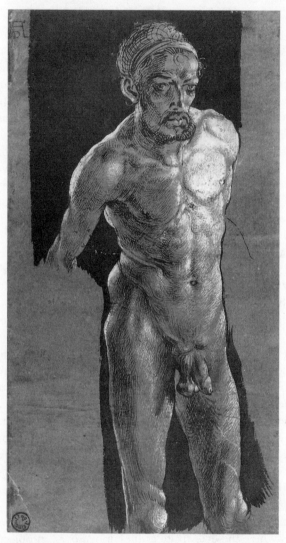

• FIGURE 18

easier to look at objects that are not naked bodies—easier in the sense that I do not feel my vision is constrained. No force impels me; no impropriety restrains me. Although I see everything with an inconstant eye, I see naked bodies most inconstantly of all.

THESE are charged examples, but they touch on something universal in vision. No matter how hard I try, there will be things I do not see. No seeing sees everything, and no skill or practice can alter that. Every field of vision is clotted with sexuality, desire, convention, anxiety, and boredom, and nothing is available for full, leisurely inspection. Seeing is also inconstant seeing, partial seeing, poor seeing, and not seeing, or to put it as strongly as possible—as I will in the last chapter—seeing involves and entails blindness; seeing is also blindness.

Here's another simple experiment. Next time you come upon a beautiful view, make a mental note of what seems interesting about it. Say it's a wooded valley with a red farmhouse in the distance. There is a pasture with a faded wooden fence and a herd of cows, and a shallow rocky stream on the near side of the pasture. Then turn away from the scene and take note of the blank spots in your mental picture. What was over to the left of the pasture? Were there trees separating the pasture from the stream? Were the hills entirely covered with trees, or were there other houses? When you turn back, the view will be suddenly more complete as you add those areas to your image of the scene. The same thing can be done again and again. Each time the mental picture will have gaps in it—often large ones—and in my experience it can be difficult to assemble a reasonably complete scene.

This is not a matter of seeing details, the way it was in the last chapter when I was thinking about hunting and about detective stories. Instead it's a question of trying to see *more* than details, more than a fraction of the world. If I were a plumber, I would see those pipes in the stairway, but I might see *only* the pipes and nothing else. The inspector in Poe's story sees the one detail that no one else can; but what else does he see? Sometimes I rehearse this game in a quicker way, by trying to force my eye to fix on the one object I would be least likely to ever notice. My gaze skips from place to place, searching out the one spot that is so entirely uninteresting that I might not ever see it, even if I lived here and saw the same landscape each morning. Perhaps the least interesting part of this landscape is the pasture: first I might look at the cows, and then, moving away from them, I might see a patch of thistle, or the cows' shadows, or a bit of dry ground . . . until finally my gaze would come to rest in a place utterly without features—and only then would I begin to understand how much I had not been seeing. The view that looked so complete at first was really just a poor sketch. In my mind it may have resembled a picture postcard, but it was more like a diagram with big labels for "pasture," "farmhouse," and "stream." A great deal of the world around us is blank without our noticing.

ARTISTS know this phenomenon very well, and they have to watch the world in a particular way in order to remember even a small fraction of it. That was made clear to me after I had seen a stuffed aardvark in a natural history museum. It's a strange animal: this one was huge and intensely muscular, like a monstrous rat with rabbit's ears. It had long, sparse white hair, deep wrinkles, and gigantic yellow nails, as if it were constructed out of close-ups of an old man's body. I was captivated by it, but when I went home and tried to draw it, I found I couldn't start. I couldn't remember how the legs went—did they come forward or back? What shape were its eyes? Was its nose black or gray? I had forgotten—or to say it more accurately, I had never seen. As artists know, in order to draw something new you have to study it with the express purpose of seeing the necessary parts and remembering them. As you look, you have to also be thinking of drawing, so that in a way you are recording what you see on a mental sketch pad. This is a specialized kind of seeing, which entails the thought of drawing and the thought of seeing together. Without it, drawing from memory is hopeless. It does not have to do with skill or even practice, though they influence the outcome: but it requires some idea of what a drawing is and how it might work, and that idea has to be brought into play while seeing is taking place.

An aardvark was something I had never seen, and in this important sense I still haven't seen one. There are many animals that I can't draw at all, not even a little, because I have never tried to see them with anything more than the kind of glazed attention I give animals who gallop by on television nature shows. The same is true for many other objects, all except the ones that are so simple that their names or their concepts practically *are* the objects themselves. I can draw plates, books, needles, and even shoes for that reason, but I cannot draw the building I work in, or the storefronts on the street, or my office phone, or the chair I am sitting in. And what's most unsettling, I couldn't draw my mother or my father either—but that's a problem I want to save for a later chapter. My world is full of holes, and there are probably more holes than there are objects. The way I see is a little like the way a blind man taps along the street: he knows just that one spot where his cane touches down, and he hopes he can pretty much guess the rest.

I N part it is a relief to think that we don't have to see everything. Certainly we couldn't *notice* every detail around us—if we did, the world would turn into a fluttering, buzzing confusion. But we would also be overwhelmed by just becoming aware that we see everything, without even looking closely. Merely registering that such and such a form is a tree, a segment of sidewalk, a blade of grass, or a pebble would be enough to overwhelm us and divert us from what we want or need to see. Out in the countryside, you might become preoccupied with the species of grass in the pasture and entirely miss the fact that there are cows as well. On the street in the city, you might be hit by a car while you were checking to make sure each brick in each building really *is* a brick. In order to be able to see at all, we need to peform these intuitive reductions and omissions. If I see the texture of grass in one place, I assume the rest of the pasture is not barbed wire, and if I see the outline of one skyscraper, I assume there aren't important gaps in it or other buildings inexplicably entwined with it. All these operations are the concern of experimental psychologists and neurobiologists; they are the ones who are trying to explain how we can get away with seeing so little.

So I'm happy with this, but I am also a little uneasy. The whole scenario assumes that if I wanted to, I could look at an entire landscape, see the barn and the cows and the pasture and the stream, and finally see everything down to the smallest specks my eye could resolve. When I first thought of doing this, I imagined sitting under a tree and patiently looking at every leaf and blade of grass, until I would eventually fall asleep like Rip Van Winkle. But I have tried it, and what really happens is that I am baffled from the very beginning. If you look at a tree on a distant hillside, you can see it has branches, and you may think you see its leaves, or at least some of them. But are those spots leaves? Or are they bunches of leaves, blended by the distance and by the limits of your eyesight? The strange fact is that you can *never* inventory a landscape, not even in a lifetime, because most of the objects you think you see are only rough guesses. Those of us who don't have serious eye problems do not pay much attention to the limits of our eyesight, and even people who wear strong glasses or contacts imagine that good vision is crystal clear and capable of resolving everything. But most objects are only blurred colors, and we guess the rest.

Our daily obliviousness to the limits of our eyes was brought home to me when I bought a telescope for my apartment. I thought the telescope would let me explore the view better, see the names on the passing ships, or resolve the houses across the bay. But the telescope did not improve anything: it gave me a wobbly, fuzzy view of things I could already see, and as I shifted my position, trying for the best views, I realized the telescope was revealing the limitations of the glass in my windows. (With a window open things were different, and the telescope did reveal many details that had been invisible.) I began looking at the glass in my windows. Thanks to what the telescope had shown me, I could see the way the glass made the world just a little distorted. It was an unhappy discovery: a moment before, I hadn't given a second thought to the window-pane, and I would have said it was perfectly transparent; now it was like looking through eyeglasses smeared with Vaseline. The distortions of the glass were just barely below what I might have noticed with my naked eye, but when I knew what to look for, they were obtrusive and annoying. I felt a little trapped, as if the window had become an obstacle or a wall, or as if it were a permanent defect in my own eyes. Even now I dislike seeing through those windows, and I always open them to have a good look.

Trying to see a whole landscape produces a similar result. In quick succession you realize that you have not been looking at leaves or grass but bleary patches you assumed were leaves or grass. You can never see an entire landscape, because views of the world are built from the ground up out of reasonable assumptions. The texture on a far hill will show itself to your eye as if it were trees, but that is only an unconscious assumption, and those "trees" are never composed of leaves and branches. They are phantoms, forms without structure.

All this happens in front of our eyes. Things are even more dubious when it comes to objects we sense out of the corner of our eyes. What do we really see out there beyond the sharp focus of our gaze? In the nineteenth century the master experimentalist Hermann von Helmholtz spent time trying to see, and also to calculate, what takes place at the blurriest margins of the field of vision. It turns out we are acutely sensitive to peripheral motion (in modern terms, the retina has motion detectors at the edges of the retina), so that if I stare straight ahead and hold my arm out to the right, I cannot see my hand until I wiggle my fingers. The hand out there is not a proper hand: with some effort, I can see it as a flesh-colored pad with five loose appendages, like a salamander's paw. (Incidentally, some animals prefer to see motion all across their visual field. If you have a dog, try this game: walk into the woods and press yourself against a tree trunk. Stay within sight of the path, but keep close to the tree. Then whistle for the dog and it may run right by you, even within a foot or two, and it may not stop until it loses your scent and realizes its mistake. Dogs are very good with motion and smell and comically bad with static visual patterns. Maybe that's why they are not interested in pictures.)

Everything at the margins of vision looks higher and skinnier than when it's seen head-on. Helmholtz demonstrated that mathematically with a clever proof, and you can verify it by standing in a dark hallway with a bright open door exactly to your right or left. If you look straight ahead, the doorway will seem too high and a little too narrow. These phenomena tell me that things I see peripherally are not just blurry but also differently proportioned. They are distorted and hallucinatory, and they need motion in order to exist. The fifteenth-century painter Piero della Francesca said it best when he supposed that everything out there is nothing but a mess of spots. I don't know much about my peripheral vision, because it is a real strain trying to learn about it. It is not easy to look straight ahead and think about what you see in the margins: and I say "think" because that's what it is: a kind of seeing that is really thinking. Even though you see whatever is out there, in a way you can't see it at all until you think hard about it. And that unusual partnership of thinking and seeing feels as if something is wrong, like twisting a foot around until it faces backwards. Helmholtz was a kind of hero in this respect, and just reading his book makes my eyes turn red in sympathy: there was a person who really *used* his eyes.

EVEN though these experiments can be entertaining, they are really all unhappy thoughts. Your eyes don't give you the world like a photograph, crisp from one corner to the other. First off, your field of vision has an irregular margin. If you look around, you can see your eye socket: your nose, eyebrows, and even the lower outside corner of your cheek (though that may be a little painful to bring into focus). But that's not the real issue. What matters is that when you are looking more or less straight ahead, everything at the edges is radically undependable. It's spotty and evanescent. It's not just out of focus; it's dilapidated. And then there's the problem of resolution: you may think you can see grains of sand on a beach or threads in someone's coat, but when you look closely you may be thrown into confusion. It's hard to realize you have not been seeing familiar objects like distant trees but drawing conclusions based on tiny samples and guesses. And worst of all, you actually see very little. Out of a panoramic scene, we tend to pick one or two convenient picturesque details or essential objects, and we can scarcely force ourselves to see the remainder.

Still, unless we think of these things, we can be perfectly content. I know that if I want to, I can use my eyes up to their natural limits. If I have the patience, I can see everything I need to see. The fact that I am hardly ever aware of these issues does not disturb me, because I've been using my eyes to good effect my entire life. As long as I command my vision there is no serious problem: that is, I can live with corrupted vision if I know that I am capable of seeing everything my eyes can resolve, if I need to. But is that really true? Is it possible to look really hard at that distant tree and say what it looks like? If I hold my hand to one side and look straight ahead, can I concentrate long enough to accurately describe what I see? What are those shifting blurry lights I was calling leaves? Can I throw off the impression that they're leaves long enough to see them for what they are? Can I force my eyes *not* to draw conclusions, and see the visual mess for what it is? Perhaps Helmholtz could, but I can't. It is very hard to see something that has no shape or name: if I try to force myself to suspend judgment about those leaves, I see them as clothes tumbling in a dryer, as a child's kaleidoscope, as a dirty rug . . . as anything at all, but not as the nothing that they are.

In this way I come to understand that I see nothing—the objects I see are constructed out of nothingness; confusion is the porous stone from which I build visible things. This is a fundamental discovery for me, but it is safely pushed just outside the limits of ordinary seeing. I can choose to notice it and become perplexed at how I make vision out of nothing; or I can ignore it and go about my business without doubting my eyes.

F E W people spend time thinking about things they cannot see. Visionaries imagine worlds that cannot exist, stocked with unicorns, mermaids, and other ravishing creatures. But those are all things that can be seen, both in imagination and in real life, when they are painted or built out of wood and wire (or, like the mermaid, out of a fish tail and monkey skin and glue). It's alluring, this idea of visualizing the invisible. Photographs of UFOs are always curious because they are attempts to give form to fantasies and at the same time to make the vision conform with whatever will seem real. Part of a UFO picture is the embodied imagination—the invisible thing appearing before our eyes—and part is the effort of trying to marry that to the requirement that it look real: hence the compelling look of the best UFO photographs. They mimic grainy news photographs, overexposed snapshots, and blurry video frames, and they also obey the orders of the imagination. Over the centuries standards have changed, but whatever seems unreal must still be accommodated to whatever is taken to be real. It would be lovely to believe that we might see an electrical flying machine like the one in this eighteenth-century engraving (figure 19), but I just cannot think how I could fly using a heavy wood box, big clumsy gears, and two objects that look like breasts. And the style is all wrong: I wouldn't

■ FIGURE 19

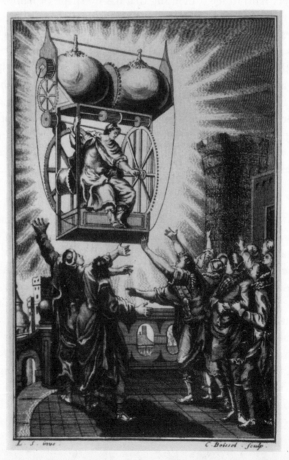

trust a scientific journal that used copper engravings or scientists who dressed in togas. It is easy to make the invisible visible, but difficult to make it believable.

And I am not really interested in fantasy. The machine doesn't make sense, either as a way to fly or as a machine (some gears aren't connected to anything, and it's not clear how the whole thing hangs together), even though I have no trouble seeing what it is meant to be. Each part of it is clearly delineated, and nothing is hidden from my gaze or my imagination except the possibility that such a machine could fly. So even though it is impossible, it is too easy. I'm much more interested to know if there are things that actually do exist but that I can't see. Is it possible to think of something we want to see but that we cannot visualize? Can we have an idea of something and fail to form an image of it? And most interesting of all, can we have an image of something—an actual image or an imagined one—and fail to see it?

There's a provocative theory about these questions, proposed by the surrealist Georges Bataille. He said that there are three things that cannot be seen, even though they may be right in front of our eyes: the sun, genitals, and death. Bataille tended to be portentously serious: he said he loved overwhelming laughter and sobbing, "the excess of raptures that shatter me," horror, voluptuousness, pain, and "unbearable joy." It can be difficult to take him as seriously as he took himself. Still, the list is interesting, and I wonder if there is sense in it.

What about seeing the sun? It is not true in any absolute sense, because I *can* see the sun for a moment or two. It is painful, I think (I'm not really sure if the sensation I feel is pain—it's more like the anticipation or memory of pain), and my vision is temporarily scarred with sunspots. It might be better to say that we know that the sun is a place where we should not look, and so we habitually look around it. The same happens when we pass by a construction site and catch a glimpse of a welding torch. One afternoon years ago I was wandering around some artists' studios, and I came into a room with a huge pottery furnace. The room was hot and dark, and there was no one around. There were several tiny holes in the sides of the furnace, and I could see orange light inside. I walked toward the furnace, intending to put my eye up to one of the holes and see what was inside. At the last moment I noticed a fine, nearly invisible jet of flame coming out of the hole: one or two more steps and I might have blinded myself. From that experience I learned to add the holes in pottery kilns to the list of things that I must not see. Together they form a small class of objects I believe are not visible because they are too strong. (Their opposites would be the things I know I can never see because they are too weak: for example, stars above the sixth magnitude, which are not visible with the unaided eye, or the stray light in a darkroom when the safety lamp is off.)

Mothers always say, "Look at the sun and you'll go blind." But do children really stare at the sun? Has any child of normal intelligence and functioning senses ever gone blind staring at the sun? Did I need to be *told* not to stare at the sun? I don't think so. Infants wince at the sun, and as they grow older they may become curious about the world's most obvious object and why they cannot see it clearly and steadily. That moment, according to the mothers of the world, is a dangerous one. But is it? Even if I set out with absolute perverse determination to see the sun and not to stop looking until I have really seen it, I can't do it. This may be different from other minor adolescent perversities, like holding a finger over a candle flame or opening a golf ball to see if it will explode. Gordon Liddy held his wrist over a candle until it burned, but could he have blinded himself looking at the sun? If it were possible, history would be full of cases of prisoners protesting by blinding themselves and ascetic philosophers choosing blindness over sight—and so I conclude it must not be possible to blind yourself looking at the sun. In this opinion I have at least the testimony of one student, who reported to me that he had often stared at the sun "for minutes at a time" when he was younger, and he had perfect eyesight. Still, the sun is impossible for me to see in at least two different senses: because it overwhelms me and because I simply know it is something I can't see, without knowing why or how that should be true. Perhaps it is the myth told by thousands of mothers that makes the sun into one of the things I cannot see and ensures that I do not see it. I would give this much to Bataille: the sun is the best example of an object that I know I cannot see without pain.

Bataille's other two suggestions may belong on another list, apart from the sun, acetylene torches, ventilation holes in furnaces, candle flames, and exploding golf balls. Genitals are hard to see in any normal way, but they do not cause physical pain, and I *can* see them if I want. They provoke discomfort of another order. Couldn't I force myself to look at the model's penis? Well, yes, I could. And I could produce a microscopically detailed rendering of it if I had to. But there would be consequences: my life drawing would be lopsided, betraying pools of attention and inattention, lines of force and resistance.

Perhaps Bataille need not have been so spectacular about genitals either. I have a peculiar inability to remember the colors of people's eyes. I seem to be the only one with this defect, and virtually everyone else in the world puts great stock in the colors of eyes. But even now I can't be absolutely sure that my father's eyes are blue. Even if I try to take note of a person's irises, I forget after a few minutes or a day. It doesn't seem to be worth expending energy in this direction, because I still can't see what I'm trying to look at. When I told someone about this, she suggested I was a little color-blind, and I was offended. After all, I said, it's not that I can't distinguish colors; it's that I cannot recall colors in that particular setting. The same colors in carpet samples or test strips would be easy to remember. But with irises there's a problem. Couldn't I just put aside my habits and start taking notice of people's irises? I could, but I would be seeing strangely, giving up my normal ways in favor of a single trait, and that goes against the grain.

A painting by Gustave Courbet called *The Origin of the World* is a brightly lit scene of a woman's crotch with her legs spread and one breast visible (figure 20). There is a tangle of black hair and a small stripe of red labia. I find that picture induces two kinds of seeing: either I reflexively look away or I stare at it too much. Because Courbet is a well-studied artist, I have seen photographs of the painting many times, and I have read essays about it, so the effect on my eyes is minimal. Yet each time I see it there's a little tug on my attention. I am aware of a force, as if something were pulling on my eye sockets, turning them away or else pressing them into place so that they are compelled to see. It's as if I am no longer entirely master of my own eyes, as if some mechanism that normally lies

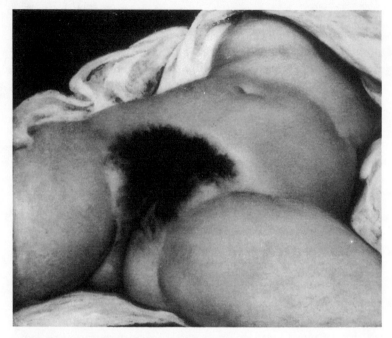

■ FIGURE 20

dormant had been turned on, putting my eyes in someone else's control.

If I looked at *The Origin of the World* for several minutes, would I be burned in some way analogous to the actual blindness I might suffer if I looked at the sun? Or would something instinctual shut down my eyes, so that I would stare without seeing? And would that instinct be somehow parallel to the instinct that makes me shut my eyes to the sun? There are similarities here, but they are not easy to draw out. An important difference is that the sight of genitals often impels us to *act*, not just to see. If I see someone's genitals in a bedroom (it's a strange subject, isn't it, that raises questions like this?), then I receive a message along with the image, urging me on or motioning me away. A penis or a vagina is not just a pattern of light and shade: it is a force. Somehow I am aware that it belongs in a sequence of sights and feelings that lead toward or away from sex, and I sense—at a level much less conscious and far less determinate than the awful step-by-step descriptions of sex that biologists have given us—that it means something has to be done. The sun is not this way, though it might borrow some of its attraction from the dynamics of sexual images. When I am attracted to the idea of looking at the sun, it's because of a faint perversity. I want to see something I know I shouldn't see. I think it might burn me, so I toy with it because it's dangerous. All these are sexual thoughts—a little coyness, some outrageous behavior, and the lure of the forbidden.

There probably isn't any way to think very clearly about these issues. Seeing the sun does have to do more with sheer inexplicable impossibility, but it also makes sense to talk about genitals that way: it can be impossible to see them, literally and figuratively. The sun can entail physical pain, but there is also pleasure involved in daring to see it—and isn't that exactly the way it is with sex? I probably cannot force myself to look at the sun, but some people enjoy looking at it and do so with equanimity—and isn't that also true for sexual preferences?

Perhaps the most interesting of Bataille's terms is the last one, death. First off, I wonder what it could possibly mean to *see* death. I can see someone's crotch and I can see the sun, but isn't the idea of seeing death only a metaphor? Aspects of death are terrifying, and so I do not see them, in the sense that I avoid thinking about them. It is frightening how death becomes more and more obvious as we get older, until people who are dying can be unbearable to see, because they are deeply immersed in death—death hovers over them and waits, as they used to say. The worst encounters with the idea of death are those moments when we talk to someone we haven't seen for a while and he looks much worse than he used to—even if he is young and healthy, we can clearly see that death is beginning to write on his face.

Those moments are terrifying, and we normally do not want to see them. Like most people, I usually try to think *around* death. Sometimes I prefer death as an abstraction, as if it were a proposition in mathematics, and other times I imagine it as impersonal, as if it only happened to people in the obituary columns. Painters think around it by showering it with symbols. What are hourglasses, young women looking into mirrors, skulls, candles, decaying fruit, withered flowers, and old books, if not ways of making death visible without discomfort? In art history, we say an hourglass is a memento mori, a reminder of death—but it 'isn't; it's a way of *not* thinking about death, not looking at it and not thinking about it. Only a very few images have to do directly with death instead of its costume jewelry of signs and symbols.

In a grisly book called *Violence in Our Times* there are two photographs of Chinese executions (figures 21, 22). In the first one the man's severed head lies on the pavement while his neck squirts three streams of blood into the air. The photograph was taken a half second after the decapitation; I know that because the blood is still on its way up into the air and the hair on the man's head is still blown back by the fall. The head looks static, as if it were kissing the ground, but it has just made impact and it will probably roll forward. The executioner's sword is poised, probably on the upswing. Perhaps he is about to push the corpse onto the ground. Is this a picture of death? Where is death in this picture? The body, it seems, is still living, hanging in the position it had before the executioner struck. The rest is symbols: decollated trunks spurting blood can be found in medieval illuminated manuscripts, and so can rolling heads and bestial executioners seen from behind. Those are all signs of death, akin to the hourglasses and skulls of later painting.

The other photograph is from a moment nearer to the beheading. The sword is still on its downward arc, and it moves only an inch below the falling head. Death is much closer here. The head itself is a black smudge, giving me an uncanny feeling: death must be right here, within seconds or inches of this place. Even the shadows have not had time to record the death: in his shadow, the man's head is still on his shoulders.

This makes me think that Bataille may be right and death can never be seen. It is most horrifying when it seems inescapably close, closer than a man to his shadow. Several years ago, browsing at random through a large library, I came a across a series of four photographs of a Chinese execution known as the death by division

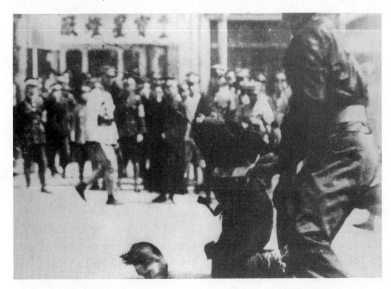

■ FIGURE 21

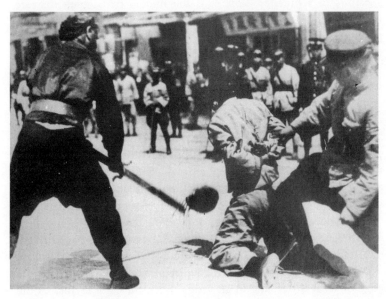

■ FIGURE 22

into a thousand parts (figure 23 A–D). The name conjures an utter carnage of body scraps or a floor strewn with pieces. According to the original Chinese law, the nose, ears, toes, and fingers are to be cut first, and the pain is to be prolonged as much as possible, but the few photographs that exist show that the division was done in a few dozen parts. A strange thing happens in looking at these images, something like what prisoners and soldiers describe who have seen such things. The eye begins, at the first frame, with a woman: she is whole, though she looks as though she may be drugged with opium to lessen the pain. The eye ends, at the last frame, with a piece of meat: it is blurred by the photography, but certainly no longer living or human. In between comes pain and then death. And yet these are not four equal photographs in a sequence. What changes as I look from the first scene to the last is my ability to see, to take in what I am looking at: The first frame is comprehensible, though when I first saw it I tensed in anticipation of what would happen next. (In the original publication, the four photographs are on four successive pages.) The last frame is gruesome, but it too can be seen: it is meat, a carcass in a butcher shop. It is the middle two scenes that are hardest to look at. The pain in those scenes is enough to cause physical changes in my body, and when I have shown these images in lectures, I have seen viewers wince, rub their arms, and blanch. Afterward I have had students complain of the continuing shock of thinking of those images. Bataille discovered some other photographs of the same ritual, and even to his jaded eyes they were the most "insane," "shocking" thing he could imagine. And there is also a nearly unbearable immorality to these images. The crowd of complacent executioners moves aside each time the photographer wants another shot, and the photographer did not protest or run away or intervene. The pictures are also difficult to come to terms with because the victim is a woman, even though the German sociologist who wrote the article accompanying the pictures was a man, and so were all the executioners and bystanders. The horror there is that adulteresses were among those most often punished in this way.

All of these are reasons why the sequence can be right at the edge of what is bearable in an image. Even the poor quality of the photographs conspires to make them hard to stand, because there are

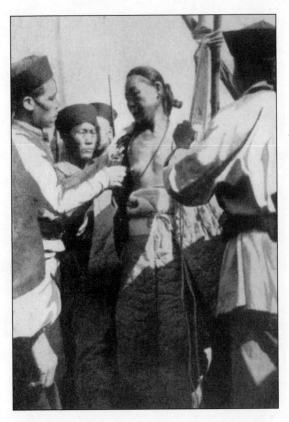

■ FIGURE 23A

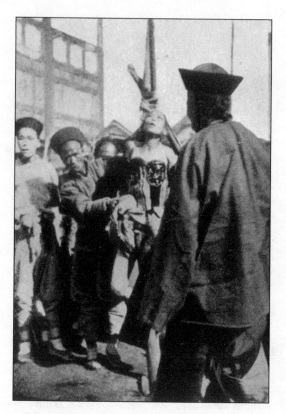

■ FIGURE 23B

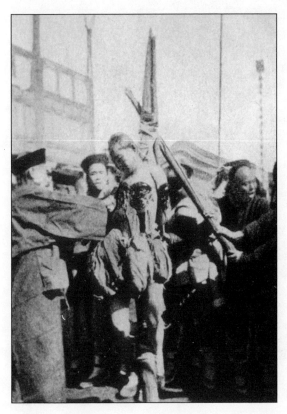

■ FIGURE 23C

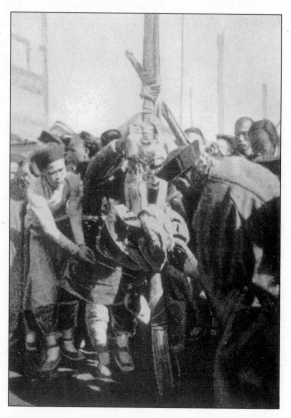

■ FIGURE 23D

no distracting details and because, despite everything that is shown, there is a great deal that is not shown. Like the black smudged head in the older photograph, the blurriness of these scenes makes them effective carriers of our own fantasies and projections. These are not dry symbols but living nameless forms.

Still, despite all this, I think that something more is needed to account for the singular power of this one sequence of photographs. They are not merely expressive of pain, immorality, sexism, or uncontrollable fantasies. This is one of the most powerful sequences of images I know in any genre and from any period, and the reason, I think, comes from the way they hold the idea of death. In virtually every other instance, death is something that happens just after or moments before the image. In real life, if I watch someone die, I see them before, and then I know afterward that they have died. In pictures of warfare, the dead lie in ditches and in heaps, and in front-line footage, a person may be alive in one frame and then instantly dead the next. But here I know that death must be in the sequence, trapped between the frames. I may not know exactly where it is (it could be between the second picture and the third, or the third and the fourth), but I know it happens before my eyes and that it happens over and over again as I look at the sequence.

Ultimately, this is what I think of these images, which have gotten me in many heated discussions since I first discovered them: I think we can finally get used to the pain (doctors become entirely anesthetized to pain; it comes easily with practice), and we must finally accept the sexism and immorality as historical facts (just as we must come to terms with newspaper reports of atrocities and injustices). But the *way* that death is trapped here, both in the sequence and somehow between its frames, is permanently unsettling. As long as I look at these images, they cause me some pain; in Bataille's terms, they are painfully close to something I know I cannot or must not see.

T H I S may be a good moment to make some general remarks about the images I have chosen for this book. There are some caustic pictures here, some of the hardest to look at and think about that I could find. In this chapter, I have used them to try to say something about things that we cannot see, that we must look away from. In the next chapter I will be exploring the idea of the inside of the body, and in Chapter 5 I will be talking about the definition of a face: what makes faces, what the minimal requirements are for faces, and what happens when faces are damaged. It seems to me that the only way to speak fully about the act of seeing is to think about all seeing—the happy and inconsequential (seeing birds, cows, and pretty landscapes), the boring (observing bridges on superhighways, staring at bricks or grass), and the intense (both intensely pleasureful and intensely painful).

Those are my principal justifications for these images, but there is another reason as well. Images that are extremely powerful are also rare. Especially in the art world, where artists continuously struggle to be noticed and there are few boundaries to what is possible, it is odd that most images are not this powerful. The reason is not that artists are conservative or that they are afraid of censorship, and I don't think that artists tend to shy away from images like these because they are about specific subjects such as execution or birth defects. (Any image can be put in the service of a wide range of purposes.) The answer is in the nature of the power itself. It is too strong for most image making, and if an artist attempts to put one of these images in a larger composition, it will poison whatever is around it. The sheer visceral power of images like these is too much for any modulated, well-considered composition, no matter what its subject might be. So I like to think of this as a problem of relative energy rather than as a question of revulsion against some specific subject matter. In order for us to be able to stand in front of an image and experience the kind of richness of feelings that we associate with art, the image must be able to speak in several registers. These images shout all other images down: they are harsh and importunate, so that they are not only hard to see; they also make everything else hard to see.

PERHAPS death can be seen after all, but these pictures express only the warning pressure that makes us turn away when we might be in danger of seeing it. Who knows what other experiences are possible in the face of death? I am not sure what can be seen and what can't, but I know that seeing is sometimes extremely difficult. I don't want to see, I wish I hadn't seen, I saw too much, I don't know what I saw, I don't remember what I saw, I didn't see anything —those are the phrases that policemen hear from traumatized victims. They are not the voice of reason, but of shock. And in everyday life, even when we think we have seen, we may not have. We have looked directly at the thing and have not seen it, or we have looked away and seen too much.

As a reader, you choose to open the book, and you choose which images to look at and how long to look at them. You may be surprised by an image, but that's a common feature of the world we live in, and after the surprise you are again in control. You can rip the offending page out of the book if you like, or keep it to see again and again. These images are like a gust: they buffet me; they make it hard to walk in a straight line. Ultimately, however, they are all images that can be seen—briefly and with consequences, but we *can* see them.

But there is good reason to think there are also images we cannot see, even when they are in front our eyes. If they exist, they would be like the censored images we are not allowed to see, except that the censor would be ourselves—our own unconscious. The United States government forbids us to see child pornography or snuff films (films depicting an actual murder), and the great majority of us have never seen them. They are forbidden images, and in other countries nonsexual images are also forbidden. There are also images we forbid ourselves to see, even though the government doesn't care. In the United States, mass-market pornography is a good example, and even people who buy pornography will normally forbid themselves to see certain kinds of pornography. Then there are images we forbid other people to see, even though we may not forbid them to ourselves: we may keep children from seeing violent cartoons, even though we may sometimes watch them ourselves.

"Forbidden images" is a phrase coined by the art critic Thomas McEvilley, and it's apt. It shows how government censorship is deeply related to self-censorship, and it helps me think about the connections between pornography and a much wider class of images that I do not see. Those images may be political, or childish, or pornographic, or violent, but they all share a common trait: I haven't seen them and I do not intend to. Sometimes I may bridle against the government or some other authority for denying me things I want to see. But censorship is like a snake with its tail in its mouth, and it turns on me when I realize how much I deny to myself. I do not need the government to forbid me from seeing some kinds of pornography, since I would freely deny them to myself; on the other hand, the government doesn't care if I watch Saturday morning cartoons, but I happily avoid them.

There have been times in history when images were censored both by governing powers and by the people who lived under them. Pornography is an example for the later twentieth century. The art historian Leo Steinberg has provided over a thousand examples of another sort in a book called *The Sexuality of Christ*. He collected images of Christ's penis in Renaissance paintings, and he argues that the sexuality of Christ was represented in order to demonstrate that Jesus was fully incarnated, so that the miracle of his appearance on earth could be complete. He was not a half god who had sent his image to earth while remaining in heaven, but God himself, who could achieve perfect fusion of human and divine forms. Renaissance paintings demonstrate Christ's sexuality in many ways: by having the infant Jesus wear a translucent loincloth, by letting the Magi peer up his diapers as he sat on his mother's lap, and by exaggerating the loincloth into wildly suggestive shapes (figure 24). After the Renaissance, all this was forgotten. Steinberg shows over and over that Christ's penis is an object that we have not let ourselves see. After the Renaissance, viewers became prudish and started ignoring the fact that the paintings are full of penises being inspected and shown off. For centuries, until Steinberg's essay, art historians and observant Christians alike had ignored a central fact about the images they studied and esteemed.

It takes a historical example like this one to prove that there are things right in front of us that we do not see. In everyday language we speak about a person blocking or screening an unpleasant memory. For psychoanalysis, this is repression, and it could be called

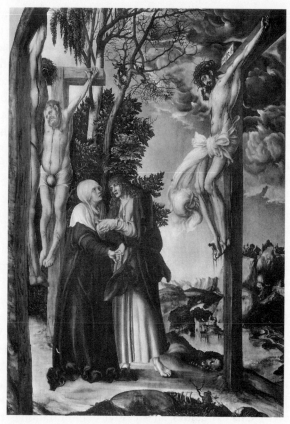

■ Figure 24

visual repression—the involuntary disappearance of an image from
the visual field and from the imagination. Or it could be called,
following Steinberg, "deflected seeing." It makes me think of my
vision streaming toward the image, heading right at it, about to strike
its surface head-on, and then suddenly veering away like a bug
sweeping past the windshield as I drive. Or else it's like magnetic
lines of force, bending and curving around an object and utterly
incapable of contacting it. No matter how hard people looked, they

could not see what was literally the most obvious part of the image that was in front of them. There is no good reason to think that the sexuality of Christ was the only delusion in the history of vision, and I assume my vision is deflected continuously without my noticing it.

When I look at a live model and find myself paying more attention to a hand than a penis, my vision is being deflected: not as strongly as in Steinberg's example, but just as insistently. I can easily become aware of that fact, and I can work to minimize its effects on my drawing and my habits of seeing. But I cannot get rid of it and make my eyes see straight. Vision is curved, and nothing can be done about that. The phenomenon of forbidden images has its reverse side as well: deflected seeing is half the story, since there is also seeing that zeroes in on its target with insistence and even with violence. I might also experience that when I look at the model and end up seeing nothing except the penis. The attractive object—penis, aardvark, whatever—creates a vortex, pulling us in, monopolizing our attention. Before I read Steinberg's book, I was interested in this painting of the crucifixion for many reasons: I loved the volutes and whorls of the storm clouds (they recall ripped napkins), the kinky curlicue twigs, the winding rivulets of blood, the way the Virgin's robe is like a wrinkled old tree. The textures and materials are all wrong: the ground is soft and fleshy, the leaves are crinkly, the distant mountains are like the inside of a shell, the landscape like melted Jell-O. Even the robes are rubbery and moist. The painting is an encyclopedia of oddities, an excessive demonstration of tendencies common to German art of the time. But after I read Steinberg's book and saw the apparition of the helium-balloon erection, those forms faded a little. Before, my seeing was deflected so that I saw everything *but* that one central fact; now, my seeing zeroes in on that fact and the rest goes out of focus. Both kinds of seeing are pathological, and both disturb the painting. Though I have no way of knowing, there may be things that I still miss, parts of the picture that my vision still bends away from, things that repel my vision so effectively that I do not know they are present.

I F we look at looking too long, it falls apart. Underneath the benign surface of the orderly world is the "optical unconscious," a deceptive, fragmentary domain that has to be forcibly reconstituted in order to make daily sense. Some writers like Bataille tend to go at this idea so strongly that they topple the complexity that makes vision so interesting. The most compelling objects are not always genitals, suns, and death. Someday a physicist and a psychoanalyst might write a book on the laws that curve vision: What bends my vision away and how tightly do the visual rays curve? What rules govern the curves of attention as they speed toward an object and then turn aside—or become trapped in whirlpools of interest? Such a book would be unimaginably beautiful, and it would have pictures of the ways my vision is trapped in pockets of detail or flung away from impossible objects that I can never see (figure 25). Sexuality would have to play a large role in those equations, and so would fear and pain—but I would be disappointed if desire and instinct were the only forces at work in the field of vision. I would like to think that the equations for curved vision are spectacular effects that play themselves out across a field that is already unstable. I want to think about all the things that go wrong with seeing, about each brief moment when seeing fails.

The historian Daniel Arasse has written a book just on the details of paintings, about the way that little pieces of pictures slowly press forward and tear into the fabric of what we see. In the background of one of Botticelli's paintings there is a small tree just behind a figure who is probably Botticelli himself looking out at us (figure 26). It is some kind of conifer, but it's also an impudent little detail, perching on his shoulder or sprouting from it. It does not look much like a tree, and it fails to resemble the other plants in the painting, which are more realistic. Furthermore it's not necessary. The picture is a nativity scene, and the only indispensable figures are the Virgin and Child and the three Magi. This tree is especially gratuitous and distracting. As Arasse says, it is "nothing," a blotch of color. Even so, after I've spotted it I'm hooked. It's a little vortex pulling in my eye, ruining the experience I might have had and reminding me how uneven seeing can be. Arasse says it's a bit like a signature, as if Botticelli had painted a little self-portrait in his picture and signed it; whatever it is, it certainly fails as a gesture that would make me think only of trees.

And that can't be the end of it, since the tree is not the only

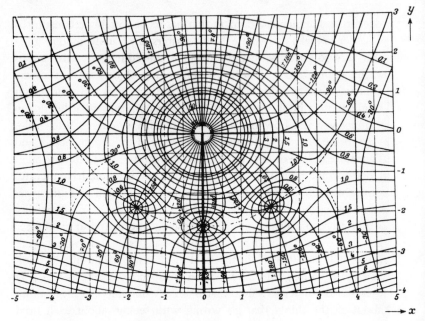

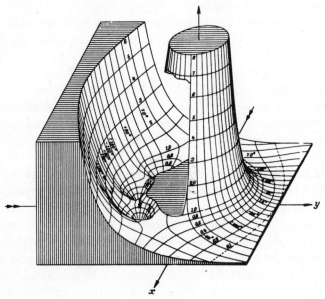

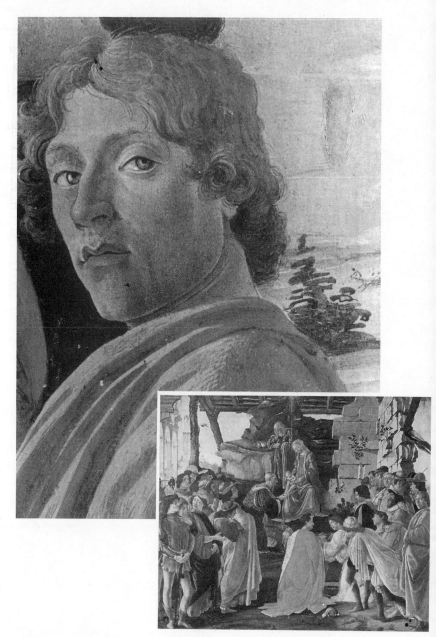

quirky mark in the picture. Arasse might have gone on and noted the way the sloppy tree makes me doubt the funny landscape just above it (is that a cartoony cow just to the right of the tree?—if so, it's much more outrageous than the tree itself) and the wavy hair on Botticelli's head (it looks like spaghetti, which reminds me that Italians use one word both for "hair" and for a kind of pasta). And I wonder about the slightly tilted right eye and flattened nose, and gradually I doubt the other figures in the painting, the manger and the ox and the ass, until the whole scene begins to swirl with odd attractions. Thinking this way I can quickly reach a state in which I am puzzled and entranced by almost everything in the picture and unwilling to say I can accept anything for what it claims to be. Is Botticelli's left eye any more convincing, any less abnormal, than the tree? What am I really seeing here? Every detail is lopsided, a senseless smear. My eye wavers and undulates trying to understand what it sees. And the greatest puzzle is how I can negotiate all those little traps and pull the scene together, make my vision work, and see it once again as a representation of a holy drama.

Vision is not a simple act of volition. We want to see, but we cannot; we try not to see, and we see in spite of ourselves; we try to see everything, and we see next to nothing. Seeing is not easy: it is not easy to do, it is not easy to control, and it is certainly not easy to understand.

Four

SEEING BODIES

OUR eyes are built to seek out complete figures. If I am shown a triangle missing the midsections of its sides, I will complete it in my mind. We instinctively repair fragments into wholes and search for continuous contours and closed curves. Shards present our eyes with a problem, and unwittingly we cast around for patterns, assembling pieces into shapes. Our eyes prefer practically any object to a borderless scatter of points.

Those, at least, are the facts of vision. If a building is half hidden by the branches of a tree, we literally see it in fragments: subtract the tree and you would have a floating collection of irregular building pieces. But the eye completes the puzzle and sees the building whole. Psychoneurologists call the phenomenon subjective contour completion, and it helps explain how we can routinely see a single building instead of disjunct pieces. On a deeper level, subjective contour completion answers to a desire for wholeness over dissection and form over shapelessness.

The night sky is such a shapeless thing. It is a chaos: it has no pictures; it does not represent any earthly forms. It has no border, no picture frame, no outlines, no up or down, no beginning or end. For those reasons it is beautiful but intolerable to our eyes, and we make it into a tapestry of patterns and pictures, of mythical creatures, asterisms, and geometric regions. I still find a sense of pleasure and wonderment when I look straight up on an August night and see Cygnus, the Swan, silently flying across the Milky Way. Having learned how to pick out its vast wings and its long thin neck, I can never again see those stars as random points. It is not surprising that Cygnus has been a bird since before the Greeks, though it has not always been a swan. In early texts it is a hen, a big goose, a pigeon, a horned owl, an ibis, a mottled desert partridge, and a roc (the bird that carried off Sinbad the Sailor). Yet from the moment it was first seen as a bird, it was destined to always be a bird, and that is the way it usually is with constellations. With force of will, people have been able to see other things in the night sky; at one time the pagan heavens were Christianized so that the believer would see nothing but saints in the night sky. In one atlas Saint Helen sits on the cloudy Milky Way, holding up the true cross she had unearthed on Calvary. The arms of the cross occupy the same place as the outstretched wings of the flying swan, so that the swan's body becomes a sign for the cross. I find Saint Helen hard to see and instinctively revert to the swan. That may be evidence of my own bias, but it also shows that the images we first form are likely to be the ones that recur.

In the Southern Hemisphere there are some even more tenuous fictions. Because the Southern Hemisphere was first mapped during the fervor of Enlightenment rationalism, it has constellations named after scientific instruments. There is the Telescope, the Air Pump, and the Microscope—very unlikely objects to imagine floating in the sky, and decidedly unromantic. The obscurer instruments have traditionally given mapmakers problems. Each generation of atlas makers has redrawn the constellation of the Microscope to suit its own idea of a microscope (figure 27). One astronomer thought of the first microscope, designed by the Dutch physician Leeuwenhoek, and another imagined a modern binocular model. Few of them fit the stars very well, but the point of constellations is to make

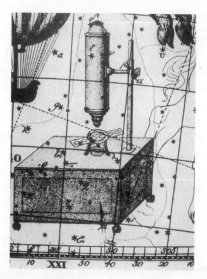

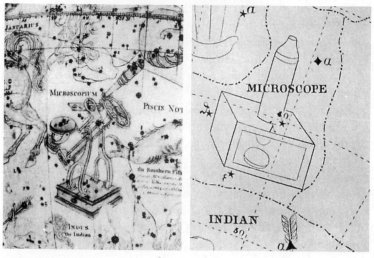

a comprehensible unity out of an underlying chaos, and it takes only one or two stars to anchor a fantasy as odd as a microscope to the heavenly vault. The one star at the top of the microscope and the other below are like quilting points, the buttons in upholstery: they force the fabric into contact with the frame beneath just enough so the two remain connected. The rest is stuffing. The other stars and the other parts of the microscope don't need to be anywhere in particular. As long as the quilting points hold, we will see the microscope. Bird or saint, desert partridge or mythical roc, Leeuwenhoek-ian or binocular microscope, it doesn't matter. All that counts is that we are not thrown back on the incomprehensible field of nameless stars.

The urge to make a continuous shape out of the pieces of our visual world runs very deep. Aside from the psychoneurological research, there are also comparative studies in animal behavior that suggest the impetus to wholeness is an instinct. When a chimpanzee is shown a chessboard with a black square missing, it will attempt to color in that square. If the animal is shown a page with two black squares, it will provide a link between them. The same motions can be detected in human artists. Obsessive draftsmen like Edvard Munch draw round and round their figures, weaving them into sealed cocoons of lines, as if to protect them from falling apart—or perhaps to smooth them into infantile forms. The ragged outlines of old age become the swirling curves of a young woman, and finally the rounded egg of an embryo or the teardrop of a sperm. His gentle, insistent curvilinear lines are like a mother's caresses, testing and proving the bulk of the child, making sure it is whole and round. These were Munch's particular obsessions, but he is not the only one who has dreamed of a simple body, a round droplet without organs or orifices. It is a subject of great fascination to psychoanalysis and philosophy, since it seems to be entangled not with a primordial desire for human wholeness but with a deep-seated dissatisfaction with the body and with ordinary life. In the psychoanalytic account, what we want with wholeness is to reject the imperfect machinery of the body in favor of the prehuman egg, or zoocyte. The urge to see whole bodies would become the urge to *be* such a body: to seal the body, to purge it of its messy organs, and finally to cancel human life in a protozoic implosion. Aside from that wild possibility, and apart from the scientific findings, the desire for complete bodies also makes reproductive sense, because it means our eyes are designed to search for smooth continuous contours like those that would be found around a young human body.

What we want is not just complete figures (microscopes, swans) and not just smoothed outlines (eggs, infants) but complete *bodies*. We need to see figures that are like bodies, and ultimately, we need the bodies themselves. When I see a form—any form, any shape at all—I am also seeing a body. I may be looking at only a smudge on a piece of paper, but I see it as a single form, a unit unto itself, a thing, a body. A lover is very different from a smudge, but ultimately I take an interest in every isolated smooth continuous object because I am interested in bodies.

When we are confronted with an unfamiliar object—a blot, a funny smear, a strange configuration of paint, a mirage, a frightening apparition, a wild landscape, a brass microscope, a building made of brick and rock—we seek a body in it; we try to see something like ourselves, a reflection or an other, a doppelgänger or a twin, or even just a part of us—a face, a hand or a foot, an eye, even a hair or a scrap of tissue. In other words, we try to understand strange forms by thinking back to bodies. Even odd bodies, things that are manifestly not human, get referred back to human bodies when we try to understand them (figure 28). I know that a sea dragon is not a human body, but I cannot help myself when I look at it: I see the arched back, the lanky neck, the pert upturned buttocks, and mincing feet. It's weird, this little aquatic body, but only because I make it so by referring it to human bodies. I see a clownish hallucination where I should be seeing fish parts.

As we go farther afield, away from human forms, the instinct to see bodies continues in full force. The Mandelbrot set is a mathematical graph made on the same principles as a high school drawing of a parabola, yet it is irresistibly also a body formed of faintly unpleasant parts: round cheeks, a head and stumps for limbs, smaller warts, and filament hairs. This Lyapunov space graph, derived from the Mandelbrot set, is just as insistently a body (figure 29). Even though it had never been sighted before the latter part of this century, there

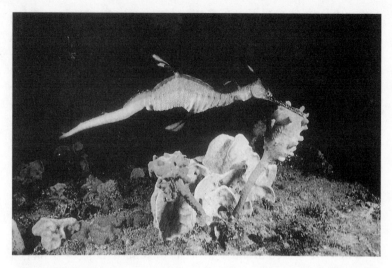

■ FIGURE 28

is no way to see it as something *other* than a body, and I even have to give it a stubby head and snaking arms. It's like a squashed louse, gooey and spiny at the same time.

Before any conscious intuition about what we're doing, we scan the visual field to see if it might harbor a body. Preferably, I suppose, we must be searching for a human body, but it seems that any body we can find will present itself as a solution to the search. I've somehow *seen* the Lyapunov graph when I've seen it as a body, and I'm happy to be impaled on my ridiculous reading of the sea dragon as an aquatic dancer. This quality of sight is a little pathetic. If it's my instincts that are impelling me to look for suitable human bodies, then that's the ordinary squalid business of evolution; but if I keep going until I find *any* body at all, and then *stop* there, I'm forfeiting the chance to see the world in some other way—to realize that the sea dragon is not a human body and the Lyapunov graph is not a body of any sort. The instinctual search for bodies might go too far, and satisfy me too easily.

And if the search for bodies fails entirely—if what we are seeing

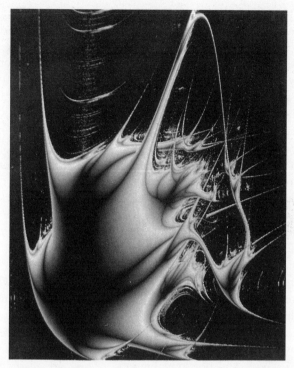

■ FIGURE 29

is positively not bodylike in any sensible way—even then we remain in thrall of the idea of a body. If we look at something genuinely confusing—an abstract painting, for example—we will see body metaphors and body echoes: uprightness, the breadth and height of a body, the symmetries of a face, the texture of skin, the warmth of an embrace, the position of one person near another. This happens even if we know there are other things going on in the picture, and it happens with decidedly uncorporeal forms such as graphs and charts. It is our inescapable, habitual way of coming to terms with things that are not bodies. A building can be strongly like a body when it stands off by itself and is clearly different from the ground.

Buildings are often, perhaps in the end always, made of body meta-phors. Eaves are like the hair that shades the forehead; windows are like eyes, and the door is like a mouth. Very few things are not like bodies or parts of bodies. Pages in a book have headers, footers, and a body of text, and some of them even have shoulder notes. This very page you are looking at might be comprehensible because you see it in analogy with the body.

There is a desire at work here, perhaps the most primal desire of all: we prefer to have bodies in front of us or in our hands, and if we cannot have them, we continue to see them, as afterimages or ghosts. It is an exquisite and complicated subject, the way our eyes continue to look out at the most diverse kinds of things and bring back echoes of bodies. First there is the question of motion and how we want to see bodies move: motion is life, but it can also accelerate into pain and still itself into death. We limit the experience of pain, I think, by dividing bodies that evoke feeling from those that leave us cold: some bodies make us sympathetic, so that we start to feel what they seem to feel, and others remain detached, as if they were machines, or unliving things. Then there are the even deeper questions of understanding bodies—how they have insides and outsides and a thin layer of skin separating the two; and how we know when a body *is* a body and not something else. These are all rudimentary questions, half buried in our instincts, and thinking about them is a way of seeing how we see the world *as* bodies and how things that are not bodies are not parts of the world.

ONCE we have seen a body, or imagined one, or found a body metaphor to rest content with, then another desire becomes visible: we also want bodies to move, to be alive. Lyapunov graphs don't actually grow, but every change in a parameter will produce organic-looking variations, as if the Lyapunov thing were moving around in its abstract Lyapunov space. A body must be able to twist and heave against itself, propel itself, huddle and crouch and stretch itself. Mi-chelangelo gave us our sense of this by inventing tortured figures absorbed in psychic battle with themselves. As the limbs wring them-selves into tighter spirals they express what we would call psychic unease. Too much motion has long been identified with death. The most horribly twisted are bodies that have perished from their suffering. The dead, decapitated Medusa at the feet of Cellini's famous *Perseus* in Florence is such a figure (figure 30). Tourists seldom realize just how awfully twisted it is: it grasps its right ankle in its left hand and bends backwards even more severely than its modern echo, Regan in *The Exorcist*.

Acceptable bodies have to possess the potential for movement, no

■ FIGURE 30

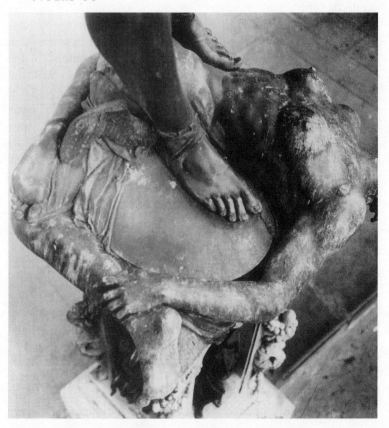

doubt because our own bodies are constantly in motion. We laugh and double up; we collapse into shivers of fever; our eyes bug out; our jaws drop open. We wave, we flinch, we tense. In saying this I am only naming the common lot of all humankind. We are pressed through the birth canal, swell to adult proportions, and shrink into old age. Our jaws grow thick; they sprout teeth; and then they collapse back into the skull. Our noses grow away from our jaws and then back toward them in old age. Our skin is elastic. If I pull up the skin on the back of my hand, it snaps back into place, but I know that will happen more slowly as I grow older. Eventually the pinched skin may take over fifteen seconds to smooth down.

A body is a thing that is in perpetual motion until the moment of its death. There are a thousand positions of tension and action, but there is no position of rest, no pose that represents perfect relaxation. In medicine there is a standard anatomical position (arms at the sides, palms forward), there is a standard position "at attention" in the military (the same, but with the stomach in, the shoulders back, the chin up, and the palms turned in). In dance, the second position is with the legs apart and the arms curved into an oval, with the fingers pointing toward one another. "At ease" is the same, with the arms behind the back. None of them are very comfortable. The fetal position is fairly relaxing, but it stretches the back. If I lie on my back in bed and try to relax, my feet splay out to either side, stretching the muscles on the inside of my legs. And as dentists and hypnotists know, even the most relaxed person will normally not relax his tongue. If I make a concerted effort to relax every muscle in my body, I always fail when it comes to my tongue. Even the slightest thought tenses the tongue—the tongue is very sensitive to being thought about. In preparation for a hypnotic trance, the subject sits in a chair and tries to relax; but it is important not to relax too much. Some patients are not appropriate subjects, because when the hypnotist says, "Now relax," the subject melts completely out of the chair. The total relaxation of hypnosis is really a slight tension, just enough to keep the body in place without drawing attention to any part of it.

Thinking of these things, I realize I have never been completely relaxed. There is no perfect position for the body, in which every

movement is equally quelled. The body is in constant motion with
no point of reference: the body, therefore, *is* motion. Every movement distorts some part of my body, putting strain on it, distending
or twisting it. No matter what position I choose, my body is already
distorted: there is no escape from distortion. The situation is similar
to the elementary problem of mapmakers. There is no way to produce an undistorted image of the round earth on a flat sheet of paper.
It is mathematically impossible, and so cartographers design maps
that will be good for some purposes and not for others—that is, they
will preserve some part of the earth without distorting it and pay for
that by having to distort another portion so strongly that it may be
useless. A map might preserve the angles between cities and pay for
that by distorting the distances, or it might try to keep the actual
proportions of Europe and pay by squeezing Antarctica into a narrow strip. Mapmaking has this advantage over the body, that its rules
have been worked out once and for all. It is possible to say, with a
map, that such and such a form is absolutely correct and that another
is off to an exactly determined extent. But if I shift my body ever so
slightly—say, I just turn my wrist a little to one side—then I am
moving between two distortions, and neither one is closer to my
undistorted shape. A picture or a sculpture of the body is a distortion
because it freezes the body, and if it's a picture, it also flattens the
body. Artists and art critics like to draw attention to the fact that any
representation of the body is a distortion, but that is not what is
distinctive about visual art. The difference is that the distortion becomes evident, that the art makes us think about it. The body already
is essentially distorted, and the artist chooses *another* distortion to
emphasize or minimize that fact.

''DISTORTION'' is a handy word, but it is probably not the
right one for what happens to the body. "Distortion" comes from
the Latin word *torquere,* "to twist," and so it means "a twisting
out of shape." Perhaps it would be better to call bodily motions
"deformation," which comes f om *forma,* meaning "form" or
"beauty." To deform is to misshape, or to destroy beauty. But there
is also "distension" (from *distendere,* "to stretch"), "dissolution"

(from *solvere,* "to loosen"), "dissection" (from *secare,* "to cut"), "disruption" (from *rumpere,* "to break"), and "disjoin" (from *jungere,* "to join"). It is a bloody list, conjuring violence and injury. But it is also a dry list, and like any etymological exercise it is more of an intellectual pastime than a way of getting at the truth. That distinction between violent words and intellectual exercises is built into the subject of bodies. The choice has to be made every time a body is represented: Will the pictured body express discomfort or pain, even if that pain is only spiritual? Or will it be something clever, something *thought out* rather than felt? Will it be a picture of violent death, or an abstract mathematical body? The same choice between feeling and thinking appears in everyday life. A headache or a broken bone exists in two states: in one, we feel it, and often we cannot think of anything else; and in another, we think of it, and feel nothing.

It's not entirely easy to name these two options. On the one side is physical deformation and on the other is intellectual deformation. The first evokes violence, pain, aching, discomfort, or just unpleasantness, but it would be too narrow to insist on that sadistic or masochistic aspect of it. Really it has to do with bodily sensation of any sort, including pleasure. When I am aware that the body is in continuous deformation, I am thinking of a general condition of being alive, a sensual monitoring of the body, a care or anxiety about its health and its status.

Proprioception is a neurological concept that is close to what I mean. It names the body's internal sense of itself, and it can be thought of as an extra sense in addition to the common ones. When I count up the senses, I like to number eight of them: sight, hearing, smell, taste, and touch are the usual five, but there are at least three others. It is not reasonable to combine the sense of temperature with the sense of touch, because touch involves pressure, and nothing needs to make contact with my finger in order for me to judge how hot or cold something is. I can feel cold without touching an icicle, and the sensation of the hardness of the ice is different from the sensation of its temperature. So heat is a sixth sense, and a seventh is gravity. I do not need to see where I am to know if I'm upside down or not. The labyrinth in the ear does that for me, independently of touch or sight. If I'm reading in a plane, I know when the plane has started to bank, because of my innate sense of gravity, not because I look out the window or feel myself pressing against the person in the next seat. Proprioception would then be the eighth sense: it is the body's innate sense of its own position. I get my knowledge of how my limbs are disposed without looking at them or touching them, because I have an inner sense of where they are. As I am sitting here typing this, I know where my left leg is without needing to bend over and look at it. I can sense how it is bent at the knee and how it is just a little tense. There are medical cases in which proprioception disappears, and those patients report a faint sensation on the skin (they can feel the wind blowing against it, or the light touch of objects) but a general helplessness about their bodies. They have to learn to look at their limbs to remain seated or to walk. Grasping objects is difficult, since it is not easy to monitor the strength of the grip by eye. A glass may shatter painfully when it is picked up, or it may slip and fall to the floor. Proprioception is minute-by-minute unthought monitoring of the body, and it's a good name for the general awareness of the body that I have in mind. If I let my leg fall asleep, proprioception becomes unpleasant tingling, and if I injure myself badly, proprioception might become pain. It is the inaudible muttering of a body in good health, as well as the high pain of illness. But usually proprioception is low-level awareness of sensation *inside* the body. Most of the time visual art that represents the body has to do with simple things like the feeling of a turn of the head or of an eye that rotates and focuses. Those motions have virtually no sensation attached to them, and yet they *are* sensations. If I think carefully about how my eye feels when I turn it, I can sense the pull of the muscles and the shifting of tissues around the eye. Even the most automatic and subtle motions create some sensation.

Another word for this bodily sense is "empathy." These days empathy has been corrupted by science fiction writers who imagine the wholesale transferral of pain or emotions from one person to another, like the transfer of files from one computer to another. Empathy is more realistic than that: it has to do with an involuntary sharing of sensation between our bodies and something or someone we see. Robert Vischer, who is credited with inventing the idea, said the body swells when it enters a wide hall. It sways, even in imagination, when it sees wind blowing in a tree. I am happier if I have just listened to a good comic, I'm irritated if I have to be around irritable people, and I am influenced in unsavory ways if I spend my time in a mental asylum. Vischer wrote about paintings because he was interested in the way that they can communicate feelings without needing language to do so. Pictures of the body elicit thoughts about the body, and they can also provoke physical reactions *in* my body. If I look at Medusa's body for too long, I may get a twinge of discomfort. Paintings of spindly figures might give me a crick in my neck, and Michelangelo can exhaust me as if I've been to the health club.

The Renaissance painter Matthias Grünewald had an uncanny feeling for skin that demonstrates the kind of sensitivity I have in mind: he loved the way it stretches tight over the arm, how it forms into fine wrinkles on the back of the hand, how the nearly microscopic fissures on the wrist grow deeper and become troughs and furrows (figure 31). When he drew skin, he *felt* it with an uncommon, neurotic intensity. Looking at this drawing is like putting on a magnifying glass and peering at your own wrinkles, slowly flexing and unflexing your fingers to see how smaller folds disappear into larger folds, discovering where the dry skin at the back of the wrist gives way to the moist skin in front, watching the loose flesh under your arm, imagining the fat hanging down in the bag of skin. After studying Grünewald I feel as if I have felt my arm for the first time and understood how the smooth muscles slide around the bone, or the glistening fat slips back and forth in its fascial sheets, or the skin pulls the whole thing together. It is an intensive course in proprioception.

Normally there is nothing obvious about empathy or proprioception, and most viewers seldom even notice them; but they are universal. If you go to a museum with these thoughts in mind, and if you spend more than a few moments in front of each picture, you will feel something of the bodily existence of each painted figure. The same happens, as Vischer would point out, with all sorts of pictures. I smell something, or think I do, when I see a picture of maggots, and I feel small and weak when I stand in front of a picture

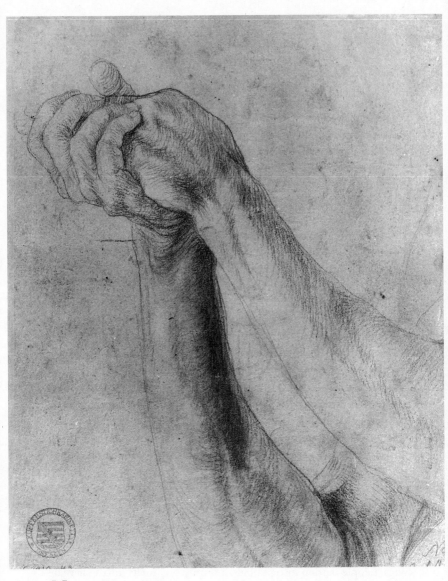

■ FIGURE 31

of Mount Etna. But the reaction is at its strongest when I am looking at bodies, probably because the origin of empathy is in the body.

T H E opposite of all this empathy, proprioception, sensation, violence, and even pain is not pleasure but *thought*. Even Grünewald can be discussed in sober philosophic terms as a person interested in the theological meaning of human suffering. The hypersensitive hands belong to Saint Sebastian, who enjoins us to meditate on our mortal fate. Medusa's coiled body is also a symbol of her evil nature and her ugliness. Michelangelo's figures are in torment, but their suffering is not caused by somatic complaints. Their problems are spiritual, and historians have described them as allegories and examples of philosophic doctrine. In the late 1920s Picasso went through an especially misogynistic period, painting women's bodies so deformed that they seem like abstract sculptures. In some images, the women's faces are grimacing succubi with three hairs, blind proboscises, and nostrils. The teeth are in a tightly clenched ring, like the circular mouth of a remora. The breasts fall and the legs rise, so that the body becomes a study in lumps and projections. In one painting Picasso mixed that wild misogyny with a bizarre little smile, making the effect even worse (figure 32). These images are about as violently antifemale as anything I have seen, but seeing them will not produce any effect on my *body:* instead they will engage my mind, making me think of the force of hatred, the stampeding violence that is necessary to flatten a woman into a harpy.

Even the grossest suffering can be rationalized. The torturer may be involved in a sadomasochistic relation to the person he torments, but he must also be removed—that is, he must also refuse to experience the body in pain. A masterpiece of this mentality is Ovid's *Metamorphoses,* a long poem about people that were turned into various creatures at the whim of the Greek gods. Ovid describes the most extreme transformations—a woman's fingers tighten into twigs, people harden into pebbles, a skinny boy melts into a salamander—all without a trace of pain. As we read, we are compelled to make mental pictures of these scenes, since Ovid is supremely skilled at description. A raped woman's tongue, freshly cut out of her

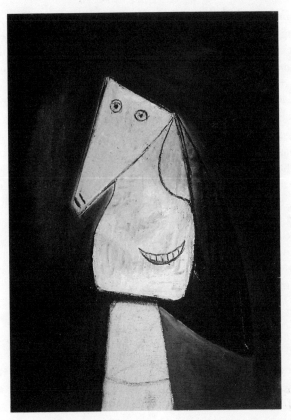

■ FIGURE 32

mouth, creeps toward the rapist like a caterpillar. It is a repulsive scene, filled with pain: but I don't think a reader *feels* anything, at least not viscerally. None of the metamorphoses are painful, and most of the victims feel no discomfort as their limbs are reworked into new shapes. That is what makes the book so strange: it is a joyous, even frivolous, romp through the most ghastly acts of cruelty, deformation, and violence, and somehow it remains in the realm of the thought rather than the felt. Perhaps that is the idea of metamorphosis itself: it is a way of coming to terms with extreme suffering by fantasizing a world in which everyone, to put it in current terms, is a metamorph. In computer graphics, morphing (as in *Terminator II* and other films) is entirely painless, and it's even used in advertisements, where pain would be a bad idea.

This is one of the few gifts that we are given when we are put in our bodies for the duration of a lifetime: that we can sometimes entirely forget that all bodies suffer continuous deformation and that deformation must involve sensation and probably also pain. I can enjoy the most outlandish pictures, like this one of an anthropomorphic landscape (figure 33), without once thinking of what it would be like to have little people walking over my face or to have the back of my head permanently soaked. I don't blink even when I notice that an eye being is used for target practice. Instead I think about the painter's wit and resourcefulness and about what it means to turn a grizzly face into a landscape or fantasize a hill as a half-buried man.

MEDICAL illustration is one of the places where these dual possibilities come together in especially interesting ways. The inside of the body is extremely difficult to *understand:* even after studying anatomy in textbooks, it can be hard to know what you're looking at in an actual body. First-year medical students are routinely baffled by the sight of cadavers. I've had this experience in a class on dissection. To prepare to dissect the abdomen, we studied its anatomy in a text, but the preparation was nearly useless when we were confronted with the real cadavers. I looked into the abdominal cavity expecting to see a labeled diagram or a large version of the plastic Visible Man. Instead I saw nothing: the belly looked like a bowl of curdled milk. My confusion was caused by the fat that ordinarily adheres to the intestines and to the fascia that bind them together. After a few hours' work, things began to be a little clearer, but those moments of confusion were repeated again when it came to different parts of the body. The palms of the hands, for example, are tough pads of connective tissue like the rough side of kitchen sponges. The pads are threaded with tendons, nerves, and blood vessels, and it is

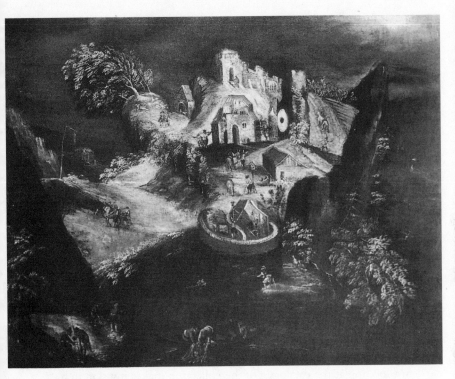

■ FIGURE 33

difficult to see them or tease them out. Dissection is an art that takes years to learn, and most medical students go on to other things. The masterpieces of dissection are kept in medical museums, and some are reproduced in textbooks. There are abdominal cavities cleaned of every blemish and perfectly dissected hands in which the most frail nerves and vessels stand out as if the surrounding tissue had just melted away. Those dissections are no less an accomplishment than oil paintings or bronze sculptures—they require a lifetime of practice.

That initial moment of confusion about the body's insides is a perpetual challenge for medical illustrators, because they need to reproduce enough of it so their illustrations are of some use to beginning medical students, and at the same time they must idealize the body into comprehensible structures. They have to turn the organic into the geometric without making the body into a machine. That choice is the choice between empathy and intellection, between giving a sense of the body's mass and texture and metamorphosing it into a painless diagram. Occasionally medical artists have tried to avoid the challenge by trying to reproduce what they saw, and the results are not always useful—and they sometimes incite so much empathic suffering that they can be hard to see.

The Museo della Specola in Florence houses life-size painted wax models of bodies and body parts. Women with their bodies opened recline gracefully on fresh linen sheets, and in the storage rooms are models of penises and individual organs, all done in perfect facsimile of the body's hardness and wetness. Some of that material has pedagogic use, but it is preserved mostly as a technical accomplishment and a historic curiosity. Elsewhere in the world there are private collections of actual cadavers that have been varnished to keep them from decaying; they can be nauseating as well as medically useless. A hospital in Paris features a monumental collection of painted wax tablets reproducing skin diseases. It has a powerful empathic effect— just looking at the catalogue of the collection makes my skin itch.

Relatively few works in the history of anatomic depiction have this kind of uncanny accuracy, and in most pictures of the body's insides it is a matter of trying *not* to see what is there. The physician Govard Bidloo tried to solve that by applying the expertise of the seventeenth-century Dutch still life painters to the problems of the human body. He employed a group of artists to draw and engrave his dissected corpses as if they were pieces of meat in Dutch market scenes, with knives, chopping blocks, ropes, and drop cloths all around. Some of his artists observed too well, with a precision that proved to be largely useless to medical students of the day. The artists would record each strand of muscle and stray blob of fat, giving the corpses too much detail and obscuring the medically important forms. Several plates in Bidloo's book are masterpieces of three-dimensional visualization (figure 34). This one captures exquisite textures—the gloss of the tendons, the matte sheen of red muscle,

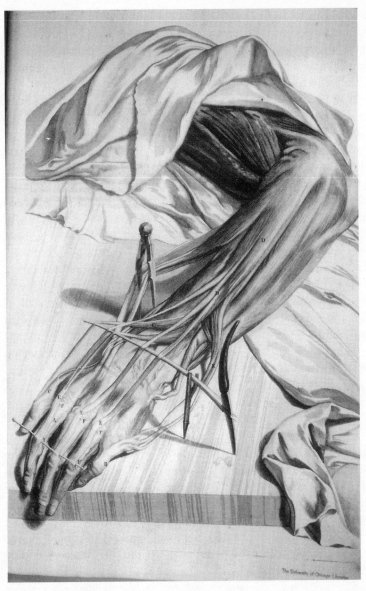

■ FIGURE 34

the hard metal of the improvised supports—and a circus of beautifully envisaged crossing forms. It is a human arm and also profoundly
alien, spidery and intricate. And it is useless for learning, since it
cannot make sense unless the observer already knows the muscles it
is supposed to teach.

Also poised between painful detail and painless schema is a book
by Charles Jenty that records a woman who died just before she
came to term (figure 35). Jenty's plates are mezzotints, a kind of
print ideal for the smoky darkness of the inside of the body. These
pictures do not reproduce well. In the original they are large, almost
overwhelmingly so, and the forms shine softly against their matte
background. The first plate shows the woman before she has been
cut open, and it is a little clumsy, as if the artist could not cope with
an expanse of unmolested flesh. To this artist, as to many who have
been seduced by the inside of the body, the uncut skin is a problem.
But with organs he is in his element, and the tissues are seen almost
lovingly. What clarity there is comes from his superlative ability to
see differences between each membrane and tissue. But for all its
skill and the deep absorption of the artist in his work, it is cold. I do
not feel discomfort when I look at this image, only an intense detached care for surfaces and light. This is as close to accurate seeing
of viscera as we get in the West before photography, and also perhaps
the closest to necrophilia.

T H E S E are interesting cases, in the psychoanalytic sense of that
word. When pain and intellection are firmly separated, as in the
Metamorphoses, the reader might sense a certain pathological denial
of the body, and when they commingle, as in Jenty's book, a viewer
might feel another kind of illness—a queasy sensation that metamorphosis must always be tied to pain. Yet none of this has stopped artists
from Leonardo to Picasso from joyfully making the most drastic
rearrangements in the body and not stopping to think what they
might be feeling at all.

The body has the capacity to give us the wildest images that
we can conceive and images wilder than any we can understand.
Something about the body has this power, as if it has weirdness and

unnamable force in reserve. In the entire field of vision there is nothing more affecting than images of the body, nothing more puzzling, nothing that is potentially more purely incomprehensible.

Figure 36 is a photograph of a rare deformation of the superficial muscle of the tongue. The doctor who wrote the article accompanying it tries to describe it in words. This is a working tongue, he asserts, perfectly functional but unaccountably deformed. Any normal body part can become distorted, and this particular condition affects only one organ. But what causes it? The doctor is clearly puzzled. At last he hits on the answer: the tongue, he asserts proudly, "gives the impression of the surface of a brain, with its folds and convolutions, or even a map where the countries and provinces are strongly outlined. It seems best to name the condition Cerebriform Tongue or Cartographic Tongue." He labels the tongue to show how it corresponds to the brain, and with that, the problem is solved and the article is concluded. But what has he shown? If the tongue is indeed turning into a brain, then is the brain also becoming a tongue? (What would it be like to think with a tongue?) All such questions come after the first, essential moment in which he finds a way to understand what he is seeing. When deformation is so strong that an object becomes incomprehensible, it is necessary to describe it by renaming it: the doctor finds an analogy—actually two analogies, since he thinks of brains and maps—and that renders the incomprehensible object *visible,* and the unthinkable is open for analysis. This is seeing with the help of analogies, a fundamental strategy for making sense of the world.

The history of the body is replete with examples of successful analogies. At one time or another the body has been a geometric diagram, a set of metal castings, a stack of bricks, a heap of T squares and charts, a remora, a vacuum cleaner, and a collection of levers and pulleys—to name just examples of twentieth-century artworks by Duchamp, de Chirico, Ernst, Picabia, and Picasso. We have already seen bodies that are maps, still lifes, circus tightrope acts (in Bidloo's dissection), mountain villages, and knots (as in Cellini's Medusa). Certainly the body is a fount of analogies, allowing us to understand things that are not bodies, but it is at least as important that the body receives analogies so well, helping us to understand it.

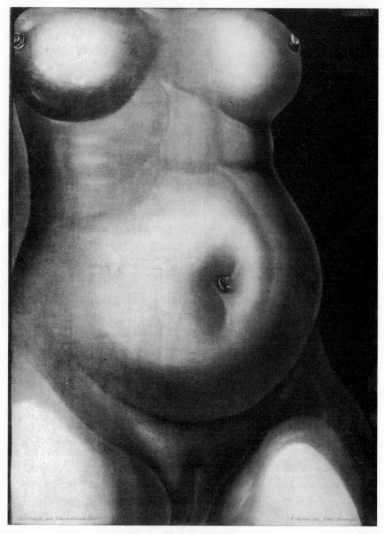

■ FIGURE 35A

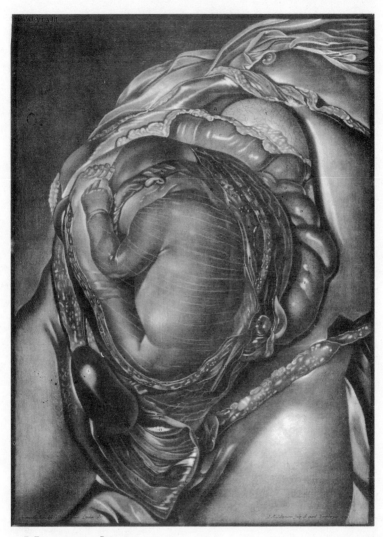

■ FIGURE 35B

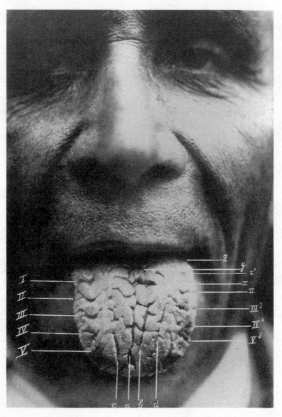

■ FIGURE 36

Normally it is easy to locate an apt analogy. The man's tongue is clearly like a brain. People can be stiltlike, barrel-like, potatoish, or blocky. Still, there are sometimes problems with analogy. In rare cases it can be hard to locate a convincing analogy. Then the object remains incomprehensible, waiting for some key to unlock its obscurity. Eventually, I think, we become visually desperate and cast about for any analogy at all. If an odd body is seen indistinctly, at a distance, or in a memory, we might say it looks like another thing, even if we don't really believe what we're saying. If I spot a recalcitrant object in a dream—say, a person's face on a pumpkin, with half a man's trunk and sawhorse legs, as in the Wizard of Oz books—then I might conceive it as a human who looks like a table. It's a tabular human, I might think, knowing full well that there must be more to it than that. Even in dreams there are reasons for things, and I can't rest content with a weak analogy. But the phrase "tabular human" allows me to keep looking, to keep seeing something while I think. Otherwise I would be disoriented and struck mute, the way Dorothy first was when she encountered the sawhorse man. The linguistic turn lets me get on with the business of figuring out what is happening.

There have been times in history when this kind of visual desperation was common. One is the discovery of fossil Cambrian organisms in British Columbia. The fossils date from a period just before the large extinction that gave us the forms and phyla we know today. Before that extinction, as Stephen Jay Gould and others have shown, life was far more diverse and did not follow the rules we imagine it has always obeyed. Initially the Burgess shale fossils were seen analogically, as examples of existing phyla: a wormlike creature, for example, was designated as an ancestor of some modern phylum of worms. The analogic explanations helped the paleontologists come to terms with what they saw. The incompleteness of that approach became clear in the 1970s, when the fossils were reexamined and it was discovered that some of them do not correspond with any known types. The analogies became useless, and the fossils had to be rethought in terms of new categories. That secondary process involved the creation of new terms and descriptions to replace the easy analogies.

Hallucigenia (figure 37) was named for its "bizarre and dream-like appearance." It was originally thought to be a kind of marine worm. It has a bulbous "head," which is not well preserved in the British Columbia specimens and was probably gelatinous. But it may not be a head, and it may not even be in the front of the animal. In one reconstruction, seven pairs of unjointed spines serve as "legs," and above are seven tentacles with two-pronged tips and six "tentacles." A tubelike "tail" bends upward. Almost every part of this animal has to be put in quotation marks because its function and orientation are

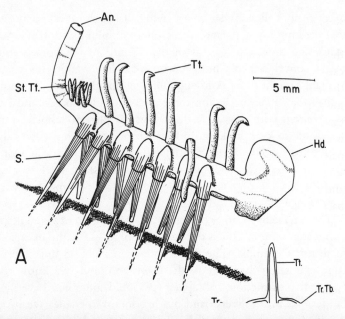

A

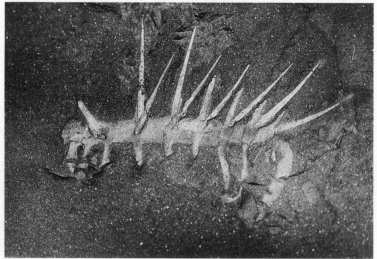

so unclear. *Hallucigenia* could have stood on the sea floor. But since the spines are attached to the body wall, paleontologists originally thought it couldn't have walked very well. The tentacles could have captured food, but how would they get it to the "mouth," assuming the "mouth" is in the "head"? It is possible that *Hallucigenia* had no mouth or head at all, and food passed down the tentacles, or even that it is a broken appendage of some larger animal—that the "head" is a stump ripped from something even less conceivable. Recently paleontologists have found another set of "tentacles" to go with the single row on back, and they have turned the animal upside down and decided it walked on those tentacles and its spines were on its back (as in the photograph of the fossil). These are the kinds of fundamental problems that continue to be asked about Cambrian organisms.

Another place that has provoked visual desperation is the deep ocean. The deep-sea angler (figure 38) is weird but not incomprehensible: it has a large flattened nose, sharp teeth, and a lure growing from its forehead. The lure shines and wiggles, tempting fish closer to the angler's mouth. It is a monstrous fish, even though I can understand its body well enough. But it is a *conceptually* difficult animal. When it mates, the male attaches itself to the female and eats into her until their bloodstreams mingle. (In the photograph two small males who have mated dangle behind the female's tail, and the drawing shows another case with one male attached.) The result is not the same as it is with some spiders and allegedly with praying mantises, where the female simply eats the male. Deep-sea anglers become a composite organism, with their bloodstreams mixed together and their bodies distinct but inseparable. It is not an easy state to comprehend because there is no ready analogy. The closest is probably parasites or parasitic twins (partly formed limbs and torsos that are sometimes attached to people), though those are so disturbing and incomprehensible that they were once the stock-in-trade of freak shows. (On the other hand, the anglerfish could provide a perfect analogy for some marriages, where the husband becomes the wife's appendage.)

• • •

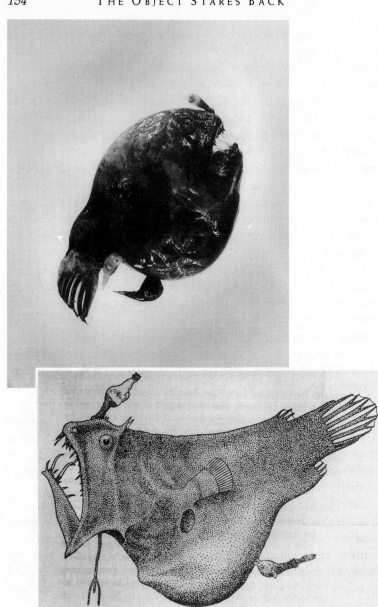

■ FIGURE 38

T H E most difficult bodies to understand and the ones that have provoked the most desperate analogies are microscopic. A myriad of microscopic animals are startlingly close to ordinary animals, so that they are ready-made for analogic seeing. The tardigrade is commonly called water bear; it is a transparent microscopic animal that lives in gutters and in rotting leaf piles. It has a few too many legs and no fur, but its lumbering look is inescapably bearlike, and amateur microscopists have long been content to call it a water bear. Another organism, even smaller, has a petal-shaped body and a long snaking neck. Ever since it was discovered it has been called the swan animalcule, even though its version of a swan is frenzied and nerve-racking: it whips and lashes its "neck" and spins around more like a top than a swan.

Most of the problems with microscopic animals arose shortly after the microscope was first invented, when people saw for the first time what was happening inside drops of water. The discoverers of the new world were dumbfounded. Could it be that protozoa have bodies without limbs or organs? Are they trunks or fragments? Some animalcules looked like eyes or fingers. But can an arm or a finger be alive, function as a body? Can a small chunk of an animal live on its own? And what about the ancient difference between the visible outside and the invisible inside? Can a body lie open and transparent to investigation?

Microscopy showed horrors far worse than the miraculous births, fanciful animals, and Hyperboreans of ancient and Renaissance lore. There did not seem to be a limit on the monstrosity of protozoa. Can the nine orifices known to medieval medicine (ears, mouth, nostrils, anus, urethra, eyes) be multiplied indefinitely? Can a body include fifty stomachs migrating freely in an unstructured interior? Can it be only mouth and stomach, with no tissues to nourish? Can a hundred eggs live together with a heart in a transparent body, itself living inside a coffee louse? Can a body exist without a brain to guide it? And if there is no brain, what is the protoplasm that guides an animal? Can tissues guide an animal without the help of a soul or even a brain?

Other questions concerned metamorphosis. When is an arm really a paddle or a fin? Does a ciliated protozoan have a thousand tiny arms, or are they mechanical helpmates like oars? The amoeba—it was once called blind Proteus after the god who changed his shape —spills its "arms" into its "legs" continuously, churns its "stomachs" into "bladders," and moves its anus to any spot on its body. Rösel von Rosenhof, the amoeba's discoverer, waited patiently for "a head, feet, or even a tail." When the amoeba happened to look like a turtle, he quickly drew it in that position, as if to imply that it was passing through a turtle stage. A moment later the turtle sprouted antlers, and then its head became its anus . . . and the analogy broke down. Another microscopist watched a blind Proteus decapitate itself and then put forth a "wheel-like Piece of Machinery." The early investigators thrashed about for analogies. One called microscopic animals fish and gave them names like "Gold and Silver Bagpipe," "Turtle" (he said it was a "fish" with horns "like a stag"), and "Water Caterpillar." One day he found a "perfect Mask" that had six "legs," a "tail," and a "singular coiffure" (figure 39, bottom).

Gradually, microscopists quenched their visual desperation by finding better analogies and by giving their creatures new names. Contemporary microbiology copes with these oddities by burying them under a heavy weight of neologisms. Current textbooks give scientific names and talk about mitochondria, organelles, and flagella. The immediate problem of seeing has been solved, and the work of biology can go forward. But the conceptual problems remain: the creatures are still bizarre. Isn't a flagellum still like an oar? Isn't a semiautonomous organelle such as a mitochondrion still like an independent organism, somehow "living" inside a cell? Analogic seeing helps construct bodies and bring visual objects into focus, but it cannot solve the problem of strangeness.

V I S U A L desperation is rare outside of dreams, microscopy, the abyss, and prehistory. Sometimes it happens when we can't quite make out what we're looking at—for instance, when we're outside at night or watching a horror movie. In this book it may also be provoked by some images of birth defects and monstrosities. But its rarity shows how resourceful we are and how easily we find the similarities that help us make sense of bodies we encounter. An analogy is almost always on the side of the intellectual appreciation

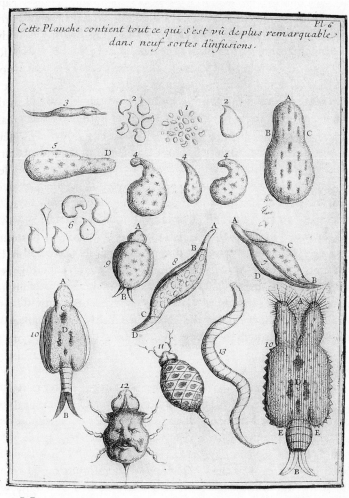

Cette Planche contient tout ce qui s'est vû de plus remarquable dans neuf sortes d'infusions.

Pl. 6

■ FIGURE 39

of the body and detached from the empathic sense of the feel of its body. It is next to impossible to feel anything for a body as heavily analogized as the amoeba. I have tried, watching amoebas crawl along on a microscope slide, to sense something of their bodies, how they hold themselves together, how they roll over themselves. But their body is very strange, very distant from mine, and my mind is clotted with analogies: the amoeba reaches out "arms," it rolls over itself like a tractor tread. I cannot experience the amoeba except through mechanical and biological metaphors.

There is a lesson in this for responding to people who are ill. As a sick person succumbs to her illness, she recedes from us and becomes more a part of the apparatus of life support. The body, in effect, becomes an analogic machine. Eating becomes a matter of intravenous drip, and breathing becomes the oxygen mask. In some intensive care wards, the body disappears in favor of its signs, which appear on electronic screens in another room. In one room there is a small part of a face, surrounded by sheets, hidden under an oxygen mask, crowded in by machines. In another room there is a monitor where everything essential about that person appears as colored lines and numbers. For a visitor, the feeling of the body's suffering becomes diffused; it loses its anchor in the body itself and grows into a general abstract awareness. At last, the body becomes invisible as such: literally hidden under the sheets and behind the mask and accessible only through disembodied metaphors.

A T the end of Kafka's "Metamorphosis," Gregor's sister goes out for a walk with the family. She must be relieved and elated after her monstrous brother has finally disappeared, and Kafka imagines her stretching her "young body." Meanwhile, Gregor's rotting diseased carcass is in the grave, a bug being eaten by worms. Which body is easier to see, Gregor or his sister? Gregor's transformation (another painless metamorphosis) has been elaborately studied, and Vladimir Nabokov has insisted that it is entomologically ambiguous. Is Gregor a beetle? Not exactly, since his shell is so soft an apple can stick in it. Is he a cockroach? Kafka never says so, and there is no exactitude in his anatomical description. That first morning Gregor's legs "flimmer" in his face; the word expresses the revulsion that any insect might produce. Gregor is an obvious, gigantic metaphor, a bugperson, and at the same time he is nearly invisible. "The Metamorphosis" has been illustrated, but the pictures don't look right because the body is not a visible object. Gregor's sister, on the other hand, is entirely visible even though she is scarcely described. She must be thin and pale after all those months worrying, and we can imagine her wearing a poor person's worn dress. Any face will do.

Some bodies can never be seen, and others are forced upon us even though we cannot understand what we're seeing. Gregor's body cannot be seen, even with the mind's eye, but the microscopic creatures appeared unasked in all their disturbing complexity. Some bodies are impossible, and yet they exist; others need to be seen, even though they may never appear. When we do not have bodies in front of us, we hallucinate them, and when we do, we try to control them by covering them with language.

I am occasionally aware of how the eye prefers smoothly bounded objects that are more like bodies to shattered collections of things that cannot be thought of as bodies. It also occurs to me at times that my seeing is heavily dependent on my various concepts of the body and its parts: its weights and heights, its inside and outside, its limbs and head, its many metaphors. But all of this is uncognized. Bodies are woven so deeply and tightly into our thought that we have to work to see how little we would understand without them.

Five

WHAT IS A FACE?

IMAGINE a game played by two very young children, just at that age when they think they have discovered what games are and how they work. The object is to define things, and then to talk back and forth until everything is clear. Since they're children, they think of simple things to define. One says, "What is a face?"

And the other replies, "A face is a thing on top of the body."

And the first one—let's say she's a puzzler by nature, always ready with an annoying answer—says, "What about Spot? Spot has a tail on top."

"Okay," says her friend, who really doesn't understand the point but also doesn't want to lose, "a face is where there's a nose, and a mouth, and ears, and two eyes, and cheeks, and a chin, and hair, all together in one place, on top of the body."

There is a long silence, filled with a sense of premature triumph. Then the first one says, "Birds don't have ears, and they don't have hair, and they don't have cheeks."

There is an even longer silence, filled with intense thought. "Okay, I know, and so a face is a place with two eyes, and a mouth *or a beak,* and maybe a nose." At this point she is beginning to discover why some adults find games so annoying. Of course the first one already has her answer:

"What about spiders? They have eight eyes. And what about people with an eye patch or people with no eyes at all?"—the two of them pause for a moment of exhilarating horror—"and what about worms?"

As she says this, she screws her face into an awful grimace meant to condense the combined horror of a man with no eyes and a worm with no face at all. Her friend becomes frightened, and then, just when everything seems lost, she covers her face with her hands and sticks her tongue out between her fingers, winning the game with a truly magnificent unclassifiable face.

T H A T , I think, is about as far as anyone has ever gotten in defining faces. As adults, we are usually complacent and secure enough to define faces as we see them—I see you, and I know which part of you is your face. But of course that is not defining a face; it is identifying one. It's an odd situation we find ourselves in, not being able to say for sure what faces are, because faces must be among the most important objects that can be seen. They are indispensable for relations of any kind, and our own faces (and people's reactions to them) tell us what kind of people we are.

Often it doesn't pay to spend time on questions this deeply immersed in uncognized thought, this inaccessible to reasoning. But I think some things can be said about faces in general—as opposed to specific faces or famous faces—by asking the kinds of questions that are latent in the children's game. In particular I want to know what counts as a face, other than how many orifices it has or its position on the body. And then I want to ask what is on the border between a face and something that is not a face, and what kind of thing is definitely not a face. Along the way I'll be reviewing several learned theories, and in the end, I'll have an answer of my own.

A large part of the problem is that we already know faces—

undoubtedly too well to easily step back and say what they are in any crisp analytic fashion. It's said that anyone could distinguish all the faces in the world, one from another, and most of us have no difficulty separating the several hundred people we may know or recognize. There are also a few faces we know very well, in many ways better than we know our own face: they belong to the people we love. I can understand many things my wife thinks before she says a word, and I can guess at her mood from changes so slight that I imagine no one else could see them. This ability of mine is so subtle and it runs so deep that I can sometimes tell her she's anxious or tired before she has even realized it herself. "You look sad," I'll say, and she'll say something like, "Am I? Oh yes, I suppose I am." It's a beautiful kind of knowledge, since it brings us closer to each other, and as the years go by, her face says more and more to me. When I first met her, it was almost a mask, and I saw only its main lines. Now it almost never stops speaking to me, even when she is asleep.

But this is also a strange knowledge, since I can't clearly imagine her entire face, as a picture, when she's not there. If I see a photo of her, especially if I don't expect to—if I pull one out of a drawer when I'm searching for something else—I may be overwhelmed for a moment and stare at it, thinking about nothing in particular but filled with thoughts. Then it seems as if I must know her face thoroughly and completely and be connected to it at every point. But I cannot close my eyes and conjure her face in my mind's eye. Sometimes when I'm drifting asleep her face will appear to me (occasionally along with a startling facsimile of her voice), but I don't plan those moments and I cannot control them. She fades then as quickly as she appeared. If I think of her face—if I close my eyes and concentrate, trying to inventory the shapes and colors one by one—then my mind gives me a powerful but incomplete impression: a sense of the face, a memory of what it was like to look at her, and perhaps some details like the thought of black eyelashes or the smoothness of the skin of her cheek . . . but it's not a picture, and I would not be able to draw her face from memory. Of course when I see her, I recognize everything: the almost invisible white down where her eyebrow fades into her temple, the pursed wrinkles in her lower lip, the tight folds of her ear and the tint and size of each tooth. But I do not know how those parts come together into her face; if I did, I think I would be able to draw it when I was not looking at her. When she is away, all I have is this odd, shifting thing that we have to call a memory but that is really the memory of the feeling of seeing, together with momentary remembrances of color or warmth.

What is a face, I wonder, that can be known and loved and memorized so completely and yet can't be called to mind? What is the memory of a face? When we are separated from someone we love, what is it that remains with us? And when someone we love dies, what is it that we keep with us, that fades a little each year but never entirely disappears? Or does it really fade? Perhaps it changes, coming together into something simpler and farther away, like a smaller face or an outline of a face, until finally, when we are old and the person has been dead many years, it becomes nothing more than a little sketch. I think it would be sadder if the faces we can never see again really did fade like old photographs, because then we would know when they would disappear once and for all. But memory is more diaphanous than that. I have lost one person I loved, and I remember him fitfully. His face changes and moves in my memory —one day it is a sound, and then again it is a single eye, and then a certain way he turned his head, and then again it is nothing more than his name. What do we see in faces, and what do we forget?

Words don't give us faces, I think; the best they can do is recall for us what it is like to try to remember a face. If I read a close description of a face and attend to it very carefully and try to construct it in my mind, I end up with something monstrous. If I read, "Your parted lips behind your veil are like a pomegranate cut open" (from the Song of Songs), I imagine a pomegranate with its wet white seeds and their deep red pulp, and then I think of small teeth gleaming in red gums—the picture is a little nauseating, since pomegranate seeds are too small to be teeth, and if teeth were jumbled like pomegranate seeds the mouth would be frightening. So I know not to think that closely but to extract a more poetic image of sweet wetness and smooth whiteness and to leave it at that. But then there are also the words themselves—"a pomegranate cut open";

they are also there, haunting my mental picture, sometimes as if they were stamped on the picture itself, interfering with the wordless image. In English, the word "pomegranate" is work for the mouth, and pronouncing it makes me think of eating. But "cut open": that's another sensation altogether, and it conjures the cut and torn skin of the pomegranate, the way that it can be cut a little and then torn apart; and it's a strange image to evoke when I'm thinking of a mouth, which opens and smiles without tearing. Did the author of the Song of Songs secretly hate the woman he was describing? Could he open her mouth with his fingers while thinking of ripping a pomegranate? Could he look at her and see pomegranate teeth in juicy red gums? "A pomegranate cut open"—the words interfere with my picture as much as they help create it. They have distracting sounds and associations, and even distracting sensations when I speak them, as if my mouth were full of letters.

Written descriptions of faces have to be taken much more loosely and nonvisually. Otherwise they can only be jarring. To read about a face is to set yourself a specific task, and it involves forgetting what is visual and remembering only ideas. I love the image of a pomegranate cut open only if I can stop myself from *seeing* it and think of rich succulence instead. Reading the verse from the Song of Songs, I put a veil between it and my mind's eye, and I let the image remain faint while I entertain the metaphors. That is why I think that written desciptions of faces cannot conjure pictures of faces and why they can only help us recall what it's like to try to remember a face. Rereading the verse, I begin to remember how I picture faces to myself and how fragmentary that picturing is. At one moment, a mouth is a redness, and then again it is a sweetness or a rounded shape—they are all condensed in the pomegranate, but they are also ruined by the pomegranate. As the images come, one after another—"your hair is like a flock of goats," the Song says, "your teeth are like a flock of ewes that come up fresh from the dipping"—they jostle one another, pushing images into my mind, shoving words into my thoughts, until the face is a ruin: but when it works, that ruin is exactly the ruin of remembrance that I know as the face of the woman I love.

•   •   •

S o what is a face, apart from words? What is a face, for example, that I have never seen? What does Moses look like? Since I can never see Moses—no pictures of him were made, and no one who saw him described his face—I have only my own ideas to go on. I think of him as a fatherly figure, and that notion is mixed in my mind with second-rate images like Charlton Heston and first-rate images like Michelangelo's sculpture in Rome. But even as that thought crosses my mind, I know how wrong it must be: it is so insistent, it rushes in so quickly, that there must be a vacuum here. The best idea of Moses' face would be to have no idea at all, if that were possible—if it were possible to read the story of Exodus without thinking of a face at all. That Moses, which I cannot manage, would be pure words: he would have no face, and when he spoke, his speech would appear directly as text. Like Kafka's Gregor, Moses is a monster when he appears as an image, and he belongs in words. But it is not possible to comprehend such a Moses: I have to form some rudimentary concept of his appearance in order to make sense of the biblical account, and it is nearly impossible to stop the flood of kitsch Moseses from supplying the required face.

Michelangelo gave Moses horns, following a tradition that said that Moses "became horned" when he descended from Mount Sinai. But others have thought that the odd word in that verse meant that Moses was glorified or that his skin shone, and painters have also represented him with silver beams of light shining from his temples. Recently a scholar has reviewed the entire literature—over two thousand years of commentaries and translations—with the kind of dispassionate eye that is possible for someone who knows that the text is the only evidence we have left, and he has concluded that the mysterious word must mean Moses was literally hardened by the Lord. His face "hardened like horn," perhaps with "some kind of light or heat burn." His skin became tough; he had keratosis or severe sunburn; he blistered; he was covered with "bumps comparable to budding horns." In short, he was terrifying to see, but also immune to the sight of the Lord—or at least, immune to the sight of the back of the Lord, since that is what he was allowed to glimpse. It's a wonderful theory, made even better by the way it changes Moses from someone we can never know, whose face we can never see, into something even more mysterious. The burn disfigures

Moses and makes him nearly unrecognizable: but we do not know what he looked like to begin with, and so the metamorphosis is a mystery in an enigma, an unknown face toughened into an unknown mask. At the same time, knowing about the "burn" gives the words a face and makes it that much harder to conceive a purely linguistic Moses.

It's tempting, of course, to go on imagining a bearded man with a bad sunburn—to think of Michelangelo's statue with puffy cheeks. I see there is nothing to think about, or rather there is a nothing inside another nothing, but in the end I cannot resist the need for a face, and so I create one to fill the void. My Moses is in between a person (with a whole catalogue of faces, none of them at all adequate to the task) and an absence (an incomprehensible disfiguration of an unknowable face, hidden in a faceless text). This Moses oscillates between those two poles. When my reading is strong, I can let the faceless words stand in for Moses, and when it is weaker, I have to let a kitschy picture help me make sense of the story.

If words are no help, the absence of a face is intolerable. I have a friend, a doctor, who works on burn victims. He describes how difficult it is to simply *talk* to someone whose face has disappeared. I can only imagine that, though I've seen some of his photographs. The effect is an overwhelming, massive *erasure* of the face, a barrage of horrifying evidence that the face has gone, and all there is to see and think about is the red swelling flesh, the corrugated scar tissue . . . and most awful of all, it is that scar tissue that *speaks,* that tries to show feelings and reactions. Perhaps, in talking to someone like that, we could imagine a face and begin to think of how it would be smiling or frowning in response to what we say to it—but any act of imagination would be silenced by the brute presence of the dead tissue. Who could imagine a face so efficiently, so persistently, that they could keep thinking of it while they looked point-blank at the wall of burned skin? I imagine the burn would make it impossible to think of a face, and without a face, talking—as my friend reports—becomes almost impossible. We expect our thoughts to be mirrored in the other's face, and when there is no response, we usually cannot go on.

That need for reactions is one of the reasons acting is not as easy as it seems. In a reaction shot, an actor has to speak without anyone there to speak to. The actor has to keep up the appearance of communication without seeing anyone and without anyone seeing him except the camera and the people on the set. Michael Caine suggests the way to do that is to "make love" to the camera: be intensely aware of it, "play to it" wherever it is, as if it were someone you wanted to seduce without even a glance. It may take an artificial fantasy this strong to sustain the task of reacting to nothing, and I think the problem is only more difficult when there is a person present but not a working face.

These problems also occur in ordinary life: for example, I know someone who habitually doesn't respond and stares back at me with a blank, vacant look. Sometimes that stare can go on for the length of a conversation, and as the minutes pass by it seems to change from a neutral expression (a face that seems to say, "I'm a little distracted today; impress me if you can") to an expression of disapproval (as if to say, "I'm finding this whole conversation incredibly tedious"). (The feeling that an expression is changing when it is actually remaining static was verified in an experiment performed at the Moscow film academy in 1917, where a film was made that alternated shots of a single face with scenes meant to evoke different emotions. The audiences thought they saw the face react to each scene in turn, smiling or frowning a little, and they were surprised to learn that the face had not moved.) Even though I've known this particular person for years, he still makes me uncomfortable. At first I tried to tell jokes or be especially animated, in hopes of provoking a response; but even when I got to know him better, after a few minutes I would notice I was becoming slightly anxious or nervous or embarrassed at nothing in particular. What I missed was a moving face: something that would return my gaze and echo my thoughts and words. Speaking is like making ripples in a pool of water, and a face is like the wall that sends the ripples back. If we speak forcefully, we send waves out toward the other face, and in a moment we can expect to feel the response. Faces move in this way even when they are not speaking. If I am looking at my wife and not saying a word—even if I'm hardly breathing—I am sending very gentle motions, faint undulations in the pool, and each one comes back to me as quickly as I send it. The two of us are like the two sides of a bowl, and the water between shimmers with an intricate pattern of crossing waves. Some of the most important moments in my life have been spent looking into her face as she looks back into mine and watching the liquid motions of her eyes as they make their silent points. In comparison to that kind of communication, everything else is crass.

So perhaps this is what a face is, and all that matters is that the face can be seen and that it works as a face. A memory would not be enough, or rather it would be something different, not a face at all. A face that I can never see would also not be a face, and neither would a face that does not respond. A face would be something that waves, that moves when my face moves, that is neither still nor absent.

But as I think about this I'm not so sure. Doesn't a body respond the same way? If I speak to someone, our bodies shift in quiet dialogue. Those motions are called body English, but the phrase is far too coarse and literal minded to ever explain how much can be said without words—and my body's motions are also linked to my words and my face, so that neither my expressions nor my speech would make full sense without them. (This is a well-known problem for people who have to transcribe speeches, since the gestures and subtler movements can often seem indispensable to the meaning.) No, it's not enough to say a face is something that responds in kind, that is present before my eyes and looks back at me. Faces are like that, but so are many other things—especially bowls of water, waves, and even the ocean itself. If my notion were an adequate description of a face, I would have to admit that every time I stand in the ocean and splash my arms in the water, I am saying something into the waves, and that the beach and the sea walls and the sea floor are an impossibly enormous face that is responding to my little splash in indescribably subtle ways, from the moment I make the gesture on into the incomprehensible future. The ocean would be carrying my little splash away in thousands of echoes that will diminish and be lost among the undulating waves throughout the world. It's a poetic idea, perhaps, but it doesn't help me understand faces.

• • •

ANOTHER way to define faces is as centers of power, things
that punctuate our world with little circles of meaning when everything else is less important. On a weekday afternoon in the city
where I work, the streets are jammed and the sidewalks are filled
with shoppers and businessmen. People are selling jewelry and asking
for donations, and the shop windows are hung with glaring fluorescent signs. Out of all this chaos, I single out faces for first inspection:
as I scan the street in front of me to make sure I'm not going to
bump into someone, I look first at faces. Naturally I have no time to
stare, and I see each face for only the smallest fraction of a second—
but it is not wrong to say that the chaos of the street is composed
of a constellation of moving faces. I see bodies, cars and trucks,
miscellaneous obstacles, and curbs I might trip over, and I have time
to take note of street signs and shop windows, but faces have a special
place in my field of vision. They punctuate the scene. Without them
much that I see would seem empty. When I think what it is about a
big city that keys me up and gives me an adrenaline rush, it is the
anxiety and haste I see on faces, more than the noise or the bustle of
traffic.

And that is when I'm outside, with distractions all around. In the
office, the few faces that I see attract my attention immediately.
Everything else is rather dull: the carpet and the books, the desks
and chairs, even the pictures and calendars. A face may be a center
of power, a moment of concentrated meaning against the backdrop
of everyday objects. To the extent that this is true, it holds good for
all kinds of faces, even for nonhuman faces and fortuitous faces.
Outside the house where I grew up, on the garden side away from
the road, there is a birch tree, which leans toward the house and
gives it some shade. About four feet up it suffered some ancient
injury, and the bark is knotted in several coils of dark parchment.
To me those coils form a perfect face, old and sad looking, with
broad cheekbones and a heavy mouth. I remember when I first
noticed that our house had a silent companion—it was when I was
about four feet tall and I could walk outside and look straight into
its wooden eyes. For me the entire feeling of that garden and the
hidden back side of the house is colored by that face, and even today
it is still there, growing older in its nonhuman way (the eyes are

getting larger, like Raymond Burr's, and the whole face is slowly blurring). A few years ago I found out that the rest of my family had never noticed the face, and I was surprised to think how differently they must picture that garden without the burden of strange sadness that I always felt: once I had seen it (or, as it felt at the time, once it had seen me), the garden was never the same. The rest of the bark has patterns too, but they seem uninteresting, as if the meaning had been washed out of them. The tree has a full crown, tangled and old, but I scarcely notice it.

Here's another insect example, but this time it's a fortuitous face —a face that the insect did not "mean" to grow, that may not be seen as a face by anyone except humans. It's on the abdomen of a trap-door spider, a species that uses its plug-shaped abdomen as a door (figure 40). It crawls into its burrow and stops up the opening with its rear end to discourage ants from attacking. It is an odd thing, this abdomen that is also a door—I can't think of any other animals whose bodies include doors. But even stranger, the door has a face on it—or rather, it *is* a face. And what a face! It has big button eyes with lopsided point-pupils, a broad classical nose, and a pouting, saturnine mouth like a pessimistic philosopher or a disgruntled politician. And all around there are branching rays like a radial fingerprint, expanding out to a piecrust rim studded with spikes. It's a tremendous face, and if I saw it in my house I'd be transfixed: I would not take my eyes off it for a moment. As long as that face stared at me, I would have to look back. If I were a fly, I'd be doomed by that face, and even now, seeing it again in a photograph, I am captivated. (This is a human reaction; there's no evidence that the "face" means anything to insects.) The blurry, horror-movie body that looms behind is only an extra. The face is more than enough to pin me to the spot.

So is a face a source of power? Something that transfixes, or petrifies? Something that gives us orders not to move? That entices us to follow? Is it the unanswerable engine of seduction or destruction? Certainly it is, and it must also be more. A face is a terrifying thing, perhaps *the* terrifying thing—the very idea of terror itself, as Roger Caillois would say. Anything I can think of that's scary is a face or has a face. All the usual horror-movie creatures have faces, and the exceptions only prove the rule—the headless horseman,

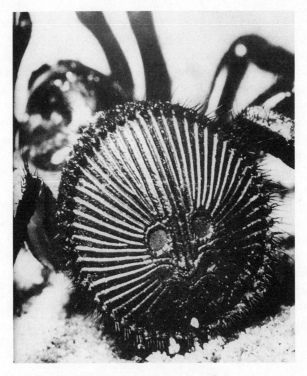

■ FIGURE 40

Jason with his hockey mask, the phantom of the opera, malevolent spirits that hide in the shadows. They all hide their faces, and horror movies work up to the moment when the lights go up and the mask comes off. The terrified victim hesitates just a moment—time enough to scream, but not enough to think of running—and then the victim is killed or carried off to be ravished. The many variations on this scenario account for what tension there is in horror movies, so that sometimes the face is multiple (like the nested jaws in *Alien*), or has surprises inside it (like the protuberances in *Scanners*), or never appears at all (like Jason), or appears over and over, until its normalcy becomes sickening (like the *Elephant Man*). But the face is the indispensable object.

One of Freud's best theories—best because it is most outrageous and unexpected, and yet somehow right—is that Medusa, the prototype of all horrifying faces, is really the female genitals. She turns men to stone—which means, in the code of the unconscious, that she mesmerizes them and takes away their power. A man becomes a statue in front of a woman. He is rigid, hard as stone—but he is also immobile, unable to take a step away from what he sees. In some Greek versions of the story, Medusa was hideous, with huge teeth and a protruding tongue. In other Greek accounts she was exceptionally beautiful, and only her snaky locks were hideous. But that only reinforces Freud's intuition, because after all a woman's genitals can also be imagined as the absolute ideal of beauty, more compelling than any other female form. Either way, the identification works. Freud's fable about Medusa says something to me about the origin of the power of faces: perhaps it is sexual force, and faces are signs for sexuality.

That would be reason enough to be compelled by faces, if they were the conduits of sexuality, but it plays down the idea of terror. It's tempting to follow Freud and see sexuality as the double root of horror and pleasure, but I would rather think of horror in its own terms. A rhesus monkey makes a good example of a fearsome face (figure 41). This is a fear grimace, which is given by a subordinate monkey who is intimidated by a higher-ranking member of the group, so it expresses fear as opposed to confident aggression. (The aggression face is different; the monkey opens its mouth into an O-shape). But could it be that the fear grimace also threatens the adversary? To a human it looks ferocious, and it certainly shows off the incisors and canines. It seems to be a good example of a face that belongs to the world of combat rather than overt sexuality. But here again, Freud may be right. The fear grimace is very close to the copulation grimace: in fact, the only difference between them is that monkeys hold the fear grimace longer. An adult male will make a copulation grimace several times as he mates, and the same expression, frozen in place, serves to show fear or submission in the presence of a superior male. So this face is aggression, fear, and sexuality all in one, and there is no clear way to distinguish them except by observing the context.

| Original | Right-right chimera | Left-left chimera |

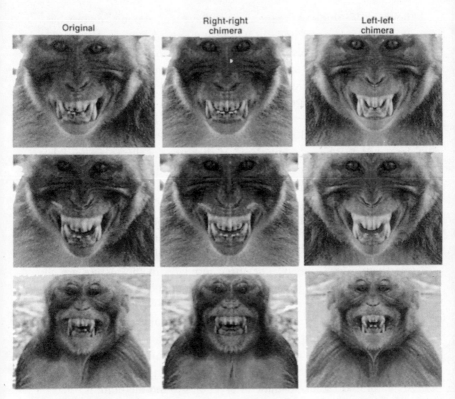

■ FIGURE 41

Faces are powerful in all these confusing ways, and they are also unsurpassably subtle. It may be that I could distinguish all the billions of people in the world, except perhaps for identical twins. We take that kind of ability for granted (imagine how difficult life would be if we could not be sure who was the boss and who was the secretary), but it is not a general property of vision. It applies only to faces. If I could see five billion bodies, I doubt I could distinguish them. Many thousands of men and women would look the same. And I wonder how many hands or feet I could distinguish. I'd like to think I could tell my own feet apart from anyone else's, but I know that's probably not true. If I think of the men's feet I have seen at pools and beaches, they can look quite similar. Of course the smaller the body part, the harder it will be to distinguish. What about parts of feet? Could I tell the arch of my own foot from anyone elses? And could we really tell the bodies of our loved ones from other people's bodies?

Animals' bodies are even more difficult to tell apart. There is a novel by Günter Grass about a young boy who has such sensitive eyes that he can tell the individuals in a flock of starlings. When I first read the book I wondered if that were really so impossible: maybe if I could get close enough, I could tell one from the other. But of course the birds don't have to be that close: they can see and hear one another well enough to know who is who. To human eyes, herds of animals and flocks of birds—not to mention schools of fish and clusters of bacteria—are just faceless mobs. It takes a biologist to sit down with a group of mountain gorillas to begin to see them as individuals. The three monkeys in the picture are all different, even though I cannot see any difference at all between the one in the top row and the one in the middle. The right-right and left-left chimeras are composite photos that double the right and left sides of the face, and the idea is that when a face is composed of two left sides it is perceived as more expressive, because emotions inhabit the left side of the face more strongly than the right. Those chimeras are a common stock-in-trade in psychology, and the point is usually made that they do not look like real faces: that we need some asymmetry to see a face. But that is also a function of our superior sensitivity to the human face, since I have no problem seeing the chimeras as plausible monkey faces.

Still, we aren't infinitely sensitive to faces. I know from experience that identical twins present problems (figure 42). Twins can be identical even down to their freckles: when they're sixty years old, if one twin gets a liver spot the other might get one at the exact same place. Most people distinguish twins by their dress or their hairstyle or by small features that are not identical. I am not secure looking at twins until I can fix on a difference, no matter how trivial it might be: it's as if my mind refuses to engage, refuses to start building my understanding of the two individuals, until I can present it with something that makes sense. Unresolved twins are like a nonsensical

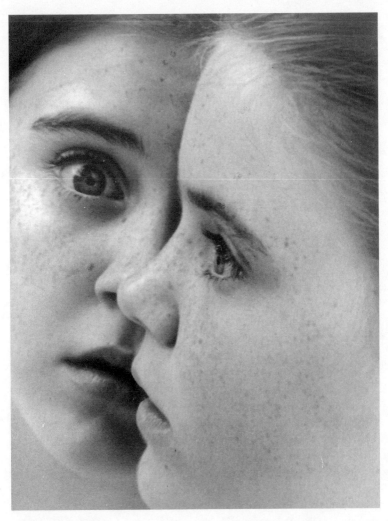

■ FIGURE 42

proposition in mathematics: $1 + 1 = 1$. I cannot begin to think about mathematics until I know that $1 + 1 = 2$. Once I have found that displaced freckle or that hair out of place and I begin to think, I am still haunted: it's not that there might be better choices for distinguishing marks (choices that are not so trivial, so unimportant for character and personality); it's that there must be many more points of similarity than there are differences. Perhaps $1 + 1 = 1$ after all.

And what if there were more than two identical faces? What if twins came in flocks, like starlings? If I rake a pile of maple leaves and I look at them one by one, each seems different. I can line them up side by side according to color or the sharpness of their serrations, and it might begin to seem as if I could tell every leaf apart from every other. But after a few minutes I come across two leaves that are identical twins. To tell one from the other I have to look for some telling detail—a little bite that some caterpillar took, a spot of mold, a slight curvature. That is not the kind of seeing that helps me tell one face from another, since with faces I do that automatically without thinking. Soon the game of distinguishing leaves becomes a tedious exercise in memorizing arbitrary marks and signs. I need to remember to look for a small spot on one leaf and at a slightly elongated stem on another, just as I need to recall the one freckle on the twin's cheek. The whole business is more like a game of concentration than the fluid inventory of faces that I perform so easily. And what if they were pine needles instead of maple leaves? Heidegger said that two pine needles can be distinguished only because I know I am holding one in my right hand and the other in my left hand—and that's not seeing; that's philosophizing.

The face is definitely the object I see best. I see the most in it: in fact I see far more than I am aware of seeing, more than I could ever describe or list. It is the site of the most nuanced looking of which I am capable, and I am lucky if I see anything else in the world with a tenth of the concentration that I train on faces.

A face is also like a machine, one that produces effects peculiar to itself that no other machine can make. A body has its own mechanisms, and a face is something that is attached to it. Bodies can spin and twist; they can propel themselves through space; but a face is like a console or a diagram planted on the body. All its parts work together to produce its special effects. If I begin thinking about the face as a machine that specializes in certain signals, then I also lose sight of it as the great index of individuality. I would no longer think of my face as *my* face but as a location on my body that obeys different laws and follows its own purposes. All faces, I could say, are examples of a single kind of machine—what the philosophers Gilles Deleuze and Félix Guattari call the "abstract machine of faciality." Ultimately, it's relatively simple: a blank surface punctured by apertures. The "white wall" and the "black holes" of the face form a system, a machinelike collaboration, that produces the effects we think of as faces. Sometimes everything works well and the system operates smoothly, producing expressions and moods, sounds and tears. Other times something goes wrong, and the face begins to break down. Even a little tic at the corner of my eye might be a sign of revolt, as some part tries to break free of the despotic rule of the faciality machine. The face bears down on the tic and tries to force it back in line.

If a face is this kind of machine instead of a bearer of individuality, then many things can be faces. There is a curious moment in the development of an embryo, sometime around the fifth week, when it suddenly becomes visible as a face (figure 43). The eyespot is just barely visible (just below the letter *A* on this model), and the nostril at *B* is starting to invaginate, to burrow into the clean surface of the face. As it grows, the embryo is continuously folding and infolding: cavities open and others close as the faciality machine constructs itself out of the "white wall" and the "black holes." Here the future bridge of the nose is to the right of the single nostril, and the future sides of the nose are to the left (*C* and *D*). They will rearrange themselves several more times and divide again into a working nose. The mouth is beginning to form itself between the upper and lower jaws (*E* and *F*), but it is not yet a hole, and the nose has not connected with the mouth as it is at the back of our throats. For that to happen, a membrane has to break: a sheet has to be transformed into a branching hole. The eyespot does not yet see—the little dimple

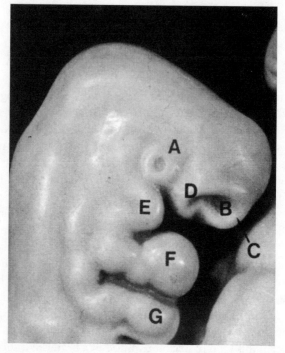

that is forming here is the optic placode, and it will become the lens of the eye—and there is no duct to connect it to the brain. At the moment it is more like a ripple on the surface of the face. It cannot yet breathe, or cry, or see. But it is a face, and it cannot be anything else. When I look at this image, I see it as a cartoony face, since I read *F* and *G* as lips: but the mouth is up above that, in the cleft between *E* and *F*. Still, it's a face as soon as it contains a few holes and swellings, and this is how faces build themselves: sending out projections and waves of flesh and then infolding, piercing holes and penetrating the interior of the body. The abstract machine of faciality is rooted in the body, and parts of it are repeated, strewn across the body's surface. The anus, the urethra, and the vagina were once called the "other face": an appropriate name for mock eyes, noses, and mouths. The armpits are blind, failed faces, and the navel is a partial face.

Parts of the machine can exist anywhere. A face does not need membranes or living flesh. A geometric diagram with black spots for points and intersecting lines can function as a face: the spots can be holes or apertures cutting into the white page, and the lines can show how the whole thing works, how the spots are related to the sheet. Even a simple triangle can be a faciality machine, with its lowest vertex for a mouth and the upper ones for eyes. As I look up from my computer with thoughts of faces in my mind, I see a wall with a single thumbtack and, a few feet farther down, a light switch. The thumbtack is off by itself, above and to the left, and the light switch is near the edge of the wall. But the machine is insistent, and I can see it as a partial face: a single glassy eye and a mouthlike fixture with a single tooth pointing upward. Both the thumbtack and the switch penetrate the wall, and one is connected to its insides: like a human face, the ensemble is rooted in a bodily thickness.

All this is fanciful only if I believe that these objects *are* faces or that it's reasonable to look at a geometric diagram or a thumbtack and think of a face. After a few moments, I admit that the wall is better thought of as a wall than a face in the process of building itself. But those moments are very interesting. As long as the wall is a face, I see it differently than I see anything else in the room. It has compelling, unanswerable attraction: it *works;* it says something. When it lapses back into a wall, it also falls silent. The machinery stops moving, and it takes on the uninteresting look of an abstract form. Even so, the faciality machine is intensely powerful, and a little echo of the face remains, teasing me into looking up one more time.

T H E R E is yet another way of thinking about faces, and it is my favorite. It has to do with the sequence in which we see faces: when we look at a face, our eyes move in a particular fashion. They travel over the surface, seeing one thing and then another, and they never stop. They inspect, assess, and monitor. This is assuming that we are allowed to look as we please; usually, in social situations we are not

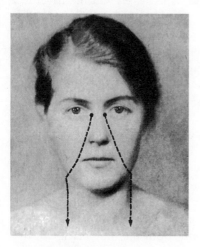

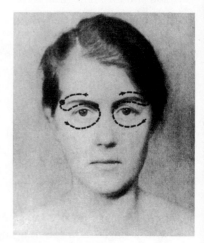

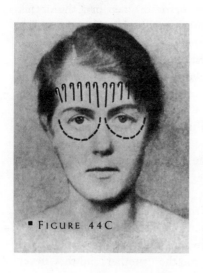

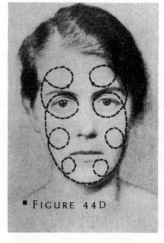

■ FIGURE 44A

■ FIGURE 44B

■ FIGURE 44C

■ FIGURE 44D

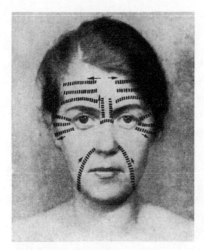

■ FIGURE 44E

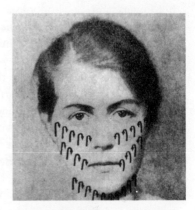

■ FIGURE 44F

allowed to do more than look from eye to eye with a furtive glance at the lips or the cheeks. But if we can look freely, we do, and we look around and around: up and down the nose, over the curve of the eyelid, across the lips with a pause at the corner, around a cheek and up toward the ear. Faces, I think, invite this special kind of seeing. They are like maps with all the roads erased—but we know where to go anyway.

These illustrations (figures 44A–F) from a Polish book on cosmetics are intended to show the ways of putting on makeup, but they are also literal realizations of the invisible maps. The dotted lines and arrows are examples of the ways that my eyes move or *feel like* moving. The woman's fingers will actually trace those lines, and so she will be miming the motions of our eyes. As she puts on makeup, she gives herself a special kind of massage: one that follows the natural habits of seeing. I may never look in these exact curlicue paths, but I often *feel* as if I want to. In this way of looking at it, a face is a place where looking and feeling are very closely allied. There are invisible paths of looking, which want to become visible paths of touching. As the woman massages her face, she sees with her fingers, and she also looks at herself in a strongly tactile way: she has fingers in her eyes and on her face.

There is also an impetus to make those paths permanently visible. That is what the cosmetologist who wrote this book did, by drawing on photographs. And these are the same patterns that can be seen in African, Melanesian, and Maori tattoos, circling and recircling the face until they realize all its hidden pathways. This seeing that is also touching is also writing. The face is like a blank sheet that cries out for a design. As I look at a face, I also sense a desire to somehow *complete* it, by seeing it as intensely as I can, or by touching it, or by decorating it. So I would say that in this last definition, a face is something that is incomplete: a work in progress that stands in continuous need of being seen or touched or written upon. And maybe that is a fundamental reason for our fascination with faces: like the personalities they express and the ideas they communicate, faces need to be used because they are not finished images.

PROBABLY this game of interpreting faces and stacking up theories could be continued ad infinitum, and that may in itself be a trait of faces. But when I get tired of thinking of models and metaphors it is not because there could be so many more: it is because there is another way of thinking about faces that works at a deeper level than any of these theories. For me it is a way of bringing the concepts of faces together and tying them in to some ideas that at first seem very different: the concept of style, as in artistic style, and the concept of coherence, or unity. This way of thinking involves a journey from faces that we can recognize and understand to objects that are at the end of the face, where faces give way to illegible objects.

The best place to start is with a universally acceptable face, one that poses no problems and causes considerable pleasure. I am thinking of a face such as Rembrandt's portrait of his friend Jan Six (figure 45). Jan is a meditative, gentle, obviously intellectual young man. I would say that he was in the middle of a moment of quiet reflection, the kind that sometimes comes over us just as we're busily doing

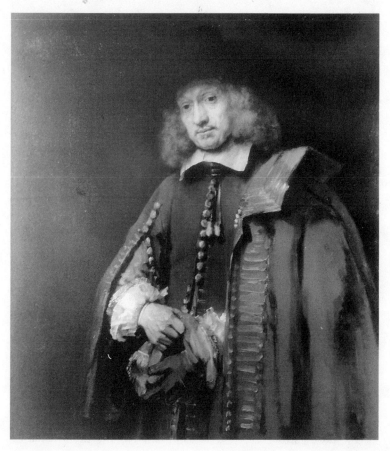

■ FIGURE 45

something else. He had been putting on his gloves, and then the thought occurred to him, and he stopped. It is a sad thought, but he must have thought it before, since he is composed or perhaps reconciled.

This is the kind of writing, by the way, that art historians hate: it's too speculative and it's not based on any kind of evidence. I am thinking along with the painted figure, imagining myself in his place, and so my thoughts become entangled with what the picture proposes—which is really very little. Perhaps Jan is not thinking at all and this is only a representation of a young man dressing. Or perhaps I have misread the point entirely, and this is a portrait of a rich nobleman, intended only to show his aristocratic features and his wealth. There are many possibilities, but as we all know paintings such as this one are valued precisely because they open the way to vague ruminations about the psychology of their subjects. If I lived in Amsterdam, where this painting is, I would probably want to visit it regularly. It takes months or even years of looking to form an impression of what might be going on in Jan's mind or in Rembrandt's. The dialogue can continue endlessly. Is he melancholy? And what other kinds of thoughts could provoke that pause? Normally this kind of speculation goes on as I look at the painting, and it does not find its way into words. I do not even formulate the questions to myself; instead, the mood I see in the figure filters into my mind, and the figure seems to answer back, thinking in its own way . . . the whole experience is illusory, of course, and there is only me, standing in front of the painting.

No matter what we choose to say or think about the painting, we continue to believe that it has a mood and that the mood is especially rich or nuanced. Art historians would normally want to leave it at that and let viewers have whatever inner monologues they choose. I have spelled out a little of it in order to emphasize that this is a face that seems to give privileged access to the motions of the mind. The sitter's and the observer's soul are commingled, they are meshed in some silent meditation. The painted face, in short, is a window on the soul. That is the usual case with psychological portraits and with interesting faces in real life.

In actual fact, I know nothing about this person. I cannot trust my feelings at all: Jan Six may have been a mass murderer, or Rembrandt may have painted the portrait as a joke. It's possible that Rembrandt figured out how to make faces that look as if they have psychological depth, and then went on to mass-produce them. He may even have taught his assistants how to do it, since it seems easy enough to fake. But years ago, I was sure enough about what is happening here to fall in love with the portrait, to see it as a kind of confirmation of what I was feeling at that time. As the years passed, I drifted away from it, and I no longer think it's such an ideal thing to stand in a dark room and meditate in a gentle sad way while wearing fancy clothes. But I am still just as sure that the portrait means those things.

I would say this is a face that is fully functional. Every smear of paint works to communicate *something,* whatever it might be. It is undependable, and even after years of intermittent looking the best I could do would be to compare it to other portraits of the same decade—but that would not make my conclusion any more secure. Still, no matter what kind of person Jan was, and no matter what Rembrandt may have intended, the face *works:* it is fully expressive —a fully functioning faciality machine. There are also faces that are entirely broken, completely unreliable. In the condition known as hydranencephaly, an infant may look normal, feed, and even smile. But if the baby is laid down in front of a bright light, the light will shine straight through, illuminating the cranium like a paper lantern (figure 46). The globe of the skull will light up, and if the light is put directly behind the head, the pupils will send out flashlight beams. Hydranencephalic infants have only a brain stem, and in place

■ FIGURE 46

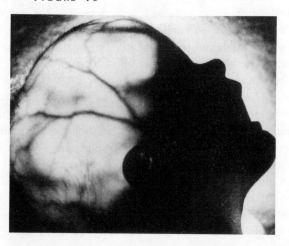

of the upper brain there is nothing but fluid. Such children usually die of infections, and so they do not live long enough to develop a larger repertoire of facial expressions. But what do their expressions mean? When such a child smiles, what is it smiling at? Does it make sense to call it a smile at all, when it may mean nothing? Presumably, only rudimentary expressions having to do with hunger or fear could have meaning, since the brain stem is directing the face. If a smile is something that can come from the brain stem, indicating an uncognized emotion, then how are we to think of the smiles of normal people? Do I sometimes smile as vacantly as this infant, with no thought in my mind, not even realizing I am smiling? And when that happens, is it right to call my expression a smile?

It seems to me that we have no choice but to continue to assume that expressions are intentional, even when we have evidence that is not so. In everyday life we assume that each shift in facial musculature expresses something and shows a state of the soul. Even the facial tic does that by expressing some tension or exhaustion. In the end I may not know if Jan Six was a murderer or not, but even if I learned he was, I would interpret his face as a consummate acting job, a perfect cover-up—in other words, as an intentional mask. His face would still be busy expressing, and I might be even more intrigued, knowing how devious it was. But the hydranencephalic child is a separate case. It raises the possibility that the face may sometimes break down and that its connections to the soul might be severed. In that case we would still go on reading the face. I assume that it is impossible not to go on thinking such a baby has a mind, even when it screams in the peculiar, high-pitched cry that is a telltale sign of the defect.

This also happens when there *is* a mind. The odd deformations of the cloverleaf syndrome force the body and cranium into shapes that are generally incompatible with life. The skull sometimes resembles a cloverleaf, and other times a stepped pyramid—hence the syndrome's other name, tower head. Some cloverleaf infants look surprised. Others look as if they would disintegrate in an excess of pain. I know of one photograph where the infant stares wildly and screams, as if it had been born into a nightmare. It is too strong even for the images in this book, more like an acid than an image: it burns into the retina, as someone who saw it told me, and it remains there. Its strength is due to its expression, which seems to record pain that is so searing that it cannot be withstood even for a moment. But can we say that? Is it right to look at such a picture and be overcome with a wave of empathy? I cannot help myself, and when I see the image I begin to feel uncomfortable—a little prickly or hot—as my body recoils from what it takes to be the presence of intense pain. At the same time, however, I know that I may very well be wrong. The cloverleaf infants that appear surprised probably look that way because their eyes are forced out slightly by the deformations in the cranium behind. Those who appear sleepy look that way because the cheeks are pressed outward more than a normal baby's. If I examine the image more closely, I see that the stretch lines around the mouth cannot be the result only of opening it as widely as possible in order to scream: the mouth was partly formed in that shape. And the veins that bulge in the temple not only are swollen from crying but were also prominent at birth. The eyes are not only bloodshot from crying; they are naturally discolored (ulcerated). They do not look wildly outward; they are naturally strabismic. In this way I can gradually convince myself that I ought not to feel anything in particular except sadness that a child was born this way. But that conviction is rational, and the face exerts a much more powerful force. I know it is an arrangement of features that cannot be read, but I can *see* that it is a face, and therefore it must be read.

There is no difference in dependability between the Rembrandt painting and a photograph of an infant wracked by the cloverleaf syndrome. I want to look at Jan Six much longer than I can stand to look at a cloverleaf deformity. I feel pleasure at the one and revulsion at the other. But I have to disallow that distinction, because I can easily imagine people who would hate the Rembrandt or be bored by it, and there are many people who would not feel revulsion at the cloverleaf deformity. What if I were a conceptual artist like Joseph Kosuth, uninterested in and disdainful of old master painting? What if I were a masochist and I loved torturing myself with the photograph? What if I were a doctor, and I cared equally for either image? No, these distinctions ultimately have no force. What binds the two pictures together and makes them examples of the same phenomenon is that we *cannot help* reading them as signs of emotions and we *cannot help* being certain that we are reading them right. Beneath the dissimilarities there is the underlying desire we have to see contentment, melancholy, pain, or any sign of life beneath the patterns of light and shade.

That impulse has been critiqued at least since the eighteenth century, when a hunchbacked author refused to allow his body to be understood as an expression of his soul. Georg Christoph Lichtenberg railed against the physiognomists, the perpetrators of the science of reading faces, saying that character is illegible in the face and that the soul is hidden inside. Eventually physiognomy died out as a science, largely because there is no reliable way to determine mood from facial expression—but we continue to believe just as deeply that the mind plays across the face.

M O S T of us have considered the odd effect caused by minor changes in a face. Nose jobs are usually thought of as simple substitutions: a nice nose for an ugly one. But after a nose job, something of a person's character is gone, permanently traded for a feature that may seem at first to belong to another body. It is not always easy to get used to the new face, because the new nose is not merely beautiful; it is also *different*. We have to get used to reading the person's character into the new nose, so that we can see how our idea of their character can fit with the new addition. That is sometimes difficult: if the person has a sharp, witty character, like someone I knew who had a nose job, then the blunt new nose might not seem right. And that is not the only problem, since we also have to adapt our sense of the person so it coincides as nearly as possible with whatever associations we *already have* about that new feature. A beautiful nose is commonly described as just that: something without any particular meaning or expressive value aside from an entirely neutral and ideal beauty. But plastic surgeons' cosmetic nose jobs have specific references. They remind me of movie stars and of a kind of popular-culture idea of beauty that began in the 1920s. Before then, other shapes of noses were "simply beautiful." So I have to find a way of imagining how Hollywood and *Vogue* magazine are related to the personality I thought I knew. A nose job trades one complex set of half-understood feelings (my idea of the person's old nose, and her whole personality, which was literally attached to it) for another (my idea of the kinds of people who thought noses like the one the surgeon made are merely beautiful).

Even in this common case, there are difficulties when it comes to interpreting the face. The same thing happens whenever the face changes, after an accident or even just with acne. With these examples I am starting again to move down the road that leads to the end of the face, but this time thinking of adult faces. Next would be the more serious cases, where there is widespread illness or deformation but where we can see that the person is still in control of the face. A person who is suffering badly will not be likely to laugh much, and his face will probably show the strain of fighting the malady (figure 47). This patient was suffering from syphilis and mercury poisoning (mercury was given as a treatment for syphilis), and he would have been in pain; and in addition, he would have known his life would not get better and that he would probably die. Those thoughts are evident even in this somewhat unskilled lithograph. We may be seeing those thoughts on his face, and it may be right to say that his face still expresses everything very clearly. But it is also possible that the illness has gotten a grip on his mind: he may have become somewhat distracted, or unresponsive, or violent—and in that case, what we see is not an expressive face or a face that expresses an entire intact mind but a face that communicates a mind *and also* an illness. The illness begins to speak through the face, just as, in the other example, the Hollywood nose speaks alongside the original face. Part of this face is a man suffering and part is a bacterium and a chemical element interfering with the mind and taking over the face.

As things get worse the pathology can end up doing most of the speaking. The affliction can become expressive in its own right, reminding an observer of a character that may not exist in the patient. The patient's own thoughts may also be crowded out in the effort of fighting the condition, so that what little is expressed may not be reliable. That is graphically illustrated in an old plate of a woman with a facial tumor (figure 48). It looks as if the healthy side of her face is contemplating the unhealthy side, trying to stare it

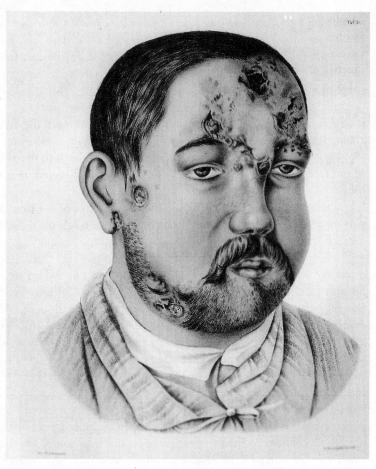

■ FIGURE 47

down or lamenting over it. The deformity is balloonlike—a monstrous adversary, a literally embodied form of the struggle that must be going on in her mind. So much has happened to this face, and so little remains undisturbed, that it is difficult to be sure if we should read the patient's expression at all: perhaps her eye is turned toward her monstrous side by the pressure of the tumor rather than intentionally. Even if we can trust that sad stare, it is hard not to believe that her mental state has been invaded in a way analogous to the way the tumor has invaded the face, so that whatever expression is left is effectively meaningless.

I could go further and think again about the burn victims whose

■ FIGURE 48

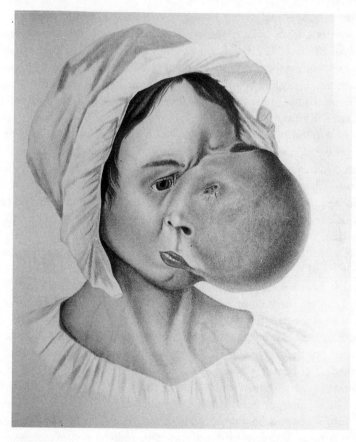

faces have been entirely erased or the hydranencephalic child whose face is so incomprehensible. But my reason for this grisly trip is not to think again about what happens when there is no face but to explore something about the last moments of the face, when it is still partly functioning. There is a kind of blind desperation to our desire to see faces and to read them as expressive of mental states. It persists even when a pathology has rearranged or cramped the face, or where massive deformations have left only a shell of a body twisted into the semblance of expression. Even then we read the wholeness and expressiveness of the face. And that word "wholeness" is the key to what is happening here. Whenever we believe we are receiving expressions from a face, we are imagining a single, whole mind behind the face. If it is a Rembrandt, I might prefer to say a single character or personality, and if it is an infant, I would probably rather say mind. The older word "soul" also seems right when someone is suffering badly. But every case is the same: to read a face, to get a message from it, to see it *as a face,* we need to posit that it exists with a whole mind. That is what makes these last few examples so troubling: we don't know if the mind is whole or if it has been partly torn down by the illness. Who is speaking here, the woman's original sense of herself? A new sense, weighed down by the illness? Or a mindless invasion of tissue or chemicals? If we doubt the answers to those questions, I think we step back and try to stop understanding the face.

It seems to me this is a bedrock assumption that we make about people and faces, and also about all kinds of things that seem expressive. It happens exactly the same way when we look at a work of art: I can see the Rembrandt painting as something that is expressive, because it seems whole. It comes from a single mind; it was created more or less all at once, at one time, by a person with one intention. It does not fight against itself. No part of it is random or damaged or ruined. It coheres, *in exactly the same way as a personality coheres.* If I cannot understand how a friend of mine behaves, I cease to think of him as a coherent personality. I need to know that he is a single person: I need to be able to make a mental picture of the kind of person he is, and it must be a coherent, unified picture, or else I cannot understand him. The same is true when I look at his face, and the same is true when I look at a painting. If part of the Rembrandt portrait were restored by some later artist, I would not look at that portion in the same way that I look at the undamaged portions. Instead I would consider the restoration as the product of a different personality—almost as a separate painting parasitically attached to the original. In effect I would try to ignore it and hope that enough of the original remained so that I could form an idea of what it meant.

I n the Middle Ages, cathedrals sometimes took so long to build that different parts ended up being made in different styles. Chartres cathedral (figure 49) was under construction for more than a century, and it was not finished until four centuries after it had been begun. The spire on the right in this photograph was completed about A.D. 1142, and the other was not finished until the sixteenth century. The result is a lopsided church, at least from the west end. Medieval worshipers do not seem to have cared about this, but that was before the modern sense of styles had developed. To a post-Renaissance observer this may be one cathedral, but it needs to be looked at in parts. The right spire has the blocky, architectonic feel of Romanesque architecture: it is simple and solid. The other spire was begun in 1194 in a more ornate, Gothic style and not completed until four centuries later. To an architect or a historian, these speak with entirely different voices: one is sober and the other is almost flamboyant. I can see the cathedral as a whole, but only by refusing to think about it in any detail. To understand how it functions as an expressive artwork I have to see it piece by piece.

This situation is exactly the same as the picture of the woman with the tumor: the two are identical problems. We need to assume that a face or an artwork is the product of a single imagination or a single mind in order to comprehend it as a face or as an artwork. This is not to say that we can ever know we're right or even anywhere near the mark. The object might have been made at random, by nature, or it may not have any expressive purpose (like the thumbtack and the light switch). And the force of our expectations and our habits of reading might lead us badly astray, so that we see

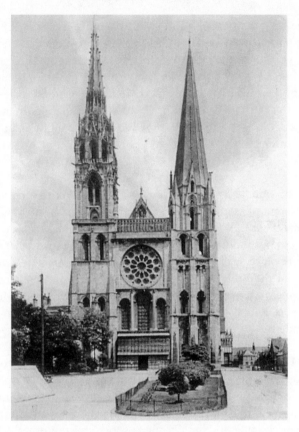

■ FIGURE 49

an intriguing personality in the face of a murderer. But all that is ancillary to the irreducible moment when we decide, instantly and intuitively, that we can sense a coherent personality or mind or intention or style, so that we can set about trying to understand what is being communicated.

In this way the idea of the face has deep connections with art in general. I agree with the historian E. H. Gombrich, who has proposed that the habits we have of reading faces determine how we read artworks. He argues it this way: we put together a picture of what a person is like by assembling individual interpretations of the mouth, the eyes, the hairstyle, and so forth. We tend to assume that each trait is part of a unified character, and we adjust our sense of that character as we see each new feature in turn. The same happens with art styles: we recognize that something is Gothic by certain features, and eventually we come to think all the features express a single, coherent Gothic style. As Gombrich knows, that is is a dangerous way to reason, since the various parts may not fit together: one may be later than another, or damaged, or restored, just as in a face. But all this happens so quickly we do not notice it, and it happens without words or conscious thought. In fact it seems to happen before we even begin to see the object: no sooner do I catch sight of someone's face than I know (or I think I know) what kind of person she might be. I can't even begin to study a Gothic cathedral until I have already seen that it is Gothic and formed a rough idea of what it might mean and how it might go together as a whole.

This is a theory that makes excellent sense. It explains why faces are so difficult to understand and describe: because they are at the very beginning of our understanding of unity and coherence. And it makes sense of the fact that it is so hard to talk sensibly about artistic styles, because it explains styles as secondary applications of principles that originally pertain to the way we see faces. Everything turns on my inbuilt notion of what a coherent personality is, and that is something that is almost beyond my ability to think about directly. I know that I can understand all my friends as coherent personalities: I have ways of thinking about them that help explain their behavior and their character. I know, as we tend to say without thinking about it, what they are "like"—that is, I can come up with some story or image that encapsulates them, ties them together, and shows how they fit. There are also people I don't understand, and I cannot explain them to myself. I have no sense of how some people fit together—I don't think I understand Pollock, or Raphael, or Busoni, or Stravinsky, or Nietzsche, or Goethe, or Celan, or Homer, or Beckett. There are many interesting people who elude me, not because I haven't read their books or listened to their music or seen their artworks, but because they sometimes do things in ways I can

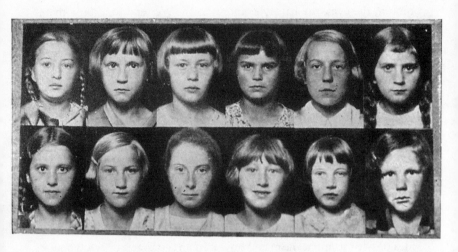

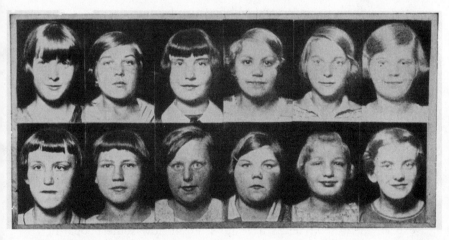

■ FIGURE 50A

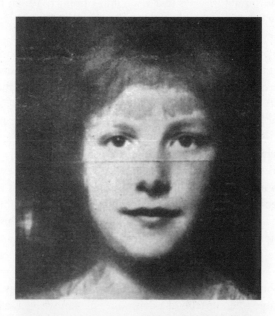

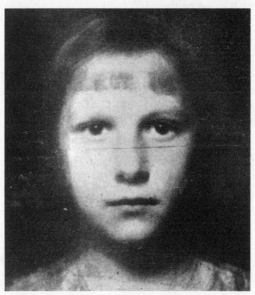

■ FIGURE 50B

understand and other times they seem to care about things I cannot understand, or act in ways that I wouldn't predict. When that happens, they have just moved off the scale of personality as I understand it, and they effectively splinter into several personalities.

Figure 50A shows a group of primary school girls who were fed only meat for a month and another group who were fed only vegetables. There doesn't seem to be any common trait among them; they are twenty-four individuals, each one strongly marked and easily recognizable. Figure 50B shows two composite photographs of all the meat-eating girls and all the vegetarian girls. Those two faces look remarkably similar, almost like twins. They both have ghostly bangs and the same full mouths, broad noses, and placid eyes. (And they both look uncannily like the *Mona Lisa,* which makes me wonder if Leonardo was thinking of making a composite of various beautiful faces when he composed his painting or if his famous smoky light is the result of blurring features.) But assuming the composite pictures could actually capture the idiosyncrasies of each girl's face, what would they look like? If I had known all those girls and had formed a good impression of what each one was like, would I also be able to comprehend a composite person who has all of their traits and yet is none of them? Would I be able to understand that person? Would she be something like a ruler, who seems to personify a country? Or would she be forever an enigma, a multiple personality, a collage of a person? (Perhaps this is part of the reason we are so fascinated with rulers: they are composites of the nation's people and yet somehow, paradoxically, they must also be individuals themselves.)

And what about a partial face, a fragment of a person? Could I understand *that* as a whole? Figure 51 is a very odd face—it's monstrous or strange, and yet somehow familiar. If you look at it for a few minutes, you may be able to see why: actually it's a very famous face (try it yourself before you read the next sentence). The photograph is a composite of the left and right thirds of the *Mona Lisa*— hold your hand over half the picture and you'll see how it works. This is a facial fragment, and yet it clearly functions as a face. What is the relation between this face and the Mona Lisa? Can I use this face to help think about the *Mona Lisa,* or do I need more of the

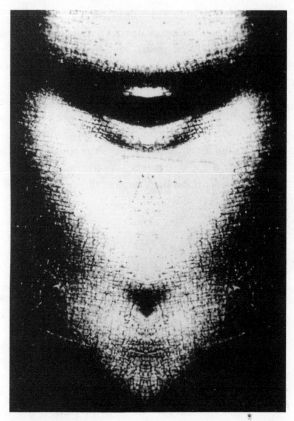

■ FIGURE 51

original? Is there enough left to make this a version of the *Mona Lisa,* or is it something new? And what does the compression add to my sense of the Mona Lisa? How will I look at the painting differently next time I see it in Paris?

Part of the challenge of complicated personalities is trying to expand my sense of a unified personality to encompass each character trait—or, in the case of partial faces, to retract my sense of personality into a fragment of a face. When I do that, I don't come to a better understanding of unity or coherence itself. I think about what makes someone hang together and what fragments them, but I never think directly about what it means to "hang together" or be "fragmented." Coherence itself remains unanalyzable. For that reason I also have no hope that I will ever be able to explain why I think that one face is the expression of a single mind and why another is hard to figure out, and I am sure that historians are not about to be able to explain the concept of artistic styles in any rational fashion. But thinking about the face in this way helps me to see the reasons why I will never know those things: because they depend on my innate sense of what a whole mind is. A face, in the end, is the place where the coherent mind becomes an image.

Six

BLINDNESS

L E T us pause a moment and take stock of what we have seen in the last five chapters. Vision, I have argued, is not the simple thing it is imagined to be. It has to do with desire and possessiveness more than mechanical navigation, and it entangles us in a skein of changing relations with objects and people. In particular, vision helps us to know what we are like: we watch versions of ourselves in people and objects, and by attending to them we adjust our sense of what we are. Because we cannot see what we do not understand or use or identify with, we see very little of the world—only the small pieces that are useful and harmless. Each act of vision mingles seeing with not seeing, so that vision can become less a way of gathering information than avoiding it.

Vision is immensely troubled, far more than a neurophysiological experiment or a psychoanalytic meditation could ever uncover. In the last two chapters I have charted two subjects of vision, the body and the face. In neither case do we see the whole object, or see without gaps, or understand completely what we see, and in both cases our vision overspills and we see other kinds of objects in terms of faces and bodies. Many forms that the world presents can be comprehended only because they seem to have to do with bodies or faces, and a multitude of things remains incomprehensible because they do not draw near enough to bodies or faces. Those observations reveal a crucial quality of our failure to see: human sight is not merely partial blindness or selective seeing but a determinate trading of blindnesses and insights. In this final chapter I want to look as carefully as possible at how and where vision fails and why that failure is intimately connected to seeing itself.

N A T U R A L L Y at first it seems that blindness is the opposite of seeing. When I try to imagine blindness, I can only say it is something outside my experience. Blindness belongs in the future of illness and death. In my case, I know I will be thinking more about blindness before too many years have passed, since my eyes express the gene for glaucoma. My mother, who has glaucoma, has experienced partial blindness, and she has thought a great deal about losing her sight. But for me that is for later. The gradual dimming of the world and the amblyopic extinction of light are more figures of speech than realities. I don't think of blindness routinely when I see, because sight and blindness are like white and black or on and off: they are opposites, and when sight is working, blindness is not present.

Yet if blindness belongs to old age, it also belongs to infancy. We cannot remember seeing as infants, and so in a sense we all began blind and remained that way for several years. How did I see as an infant, and what did I see? One of the reasons I cannot answer those questions is that memory is necessary for vision. Everything from the first few years of my life is lost to me, partly because I was not old enough to *remember* seeing, to think of seeing while it was happening. In this most elementary way, seeing and memory go together, and the blindness of my infancy was a time when sight and memory were not yet linked. As soon as I became aware that I was seeing and began to form ideas about myself and my experiences, I passed out of the blindness of infancy and began to see and remember at the same time. For some people the blindness of infancy continues on into childhood. I am one of those people who can hardly recall anything from the first five or six years of my life, and up until high school the images I can bring to mind are spotty and random. In a very real sense I was blind as an infant, and I continued in partial blindness up through adolescence. Now I am better at recalling what I have seen, but there are still days and even months that I forget altogether—they produced no images; they are blind spots in my past. This infantile blindness is not physical blindness, but it is more than just a metaphor. If I have no visual memory whatsoever from those first years, in what sense was I not blind? I am not the child who saw his family and toys at age two, and no one could have those memories except me. Those years and that world are lost to me, just as my current world would be lost if I were blind.

Since seeing can be dependent on memory, and blindness on forgetfulness, it is not extravagant to find the same relations in collective memory—in history—as there are in individual memory. Blindness in this sense overtakes much of history. Entire cultures have disappeared into blindness because they let themselves be forgotten—they left no images of themselves or what they made. The Khazars were once a major power in the area around the Caspian Sea, and now there is virtually nothing left of them. No one knows what language they spoke, few artifacts survive, and even their cities have vanished. This most incurable form of blindness is brought home to me by this photograph (figure 52). It is among the things handed down in our family, but for decades it went unnoticed, and now there is no one left to ask who these people might be. All of the surviving members of my family recognized one face the moment they saw the photograph: my grandfather, now long dead, is the little boy sitting at the lower right. I knew his skeptical expression, which he must have carried with him his entire life, emigrating from Russia to New York and into his old age, when I knew him. The other faces in the photograph, which was taken in some anonymous studio in Russia, look as strange to me as they might to any reader of this book. These are my vanished ancestors, and everything they saw in their lives has disappeared along with them. It is

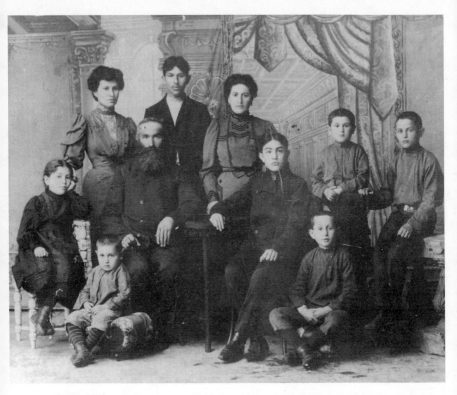

■ FIGURE 52

possible that they descended from the Khazars, since they came from the same part of the world—but there will probably never be a way to find out. They fell into their eyes, as the poet W. S. Merwin says.

These are huge blindnesses: the calamity of impeding blindness and death, the amnesia of childhood, the gradual forgetting of all history. Blindness seems to hem in vision from front and back, leaving us very little time to see. In return I have the small comfort of thinking there is a domain of normal seeing where blindness is excluded. For several decades in the middle of my life I expect to see reasonably well. As children, we used to play a game that involved trying to read a book outside after sunset. Several of us would take turns reading passages as the twilight became full night, and the best players—I was not among them—would continue the game by taking the book into the woods to shade themselves from the moonlight. I remember standing in a field outside the woods and hearing their disembodied voices crying out the words they managed to see. I don't think it would have occurred to me that my slightly poorer night vision might be the first faint hint of vision problems that would grow along with me as I got older. And I never thought that the game itself was a way of beating blindness, a childish boast that the whole world was visible. Then as now, I do not often think about blindness.

But blindness is a strange, insidious thing. The more we watch for it, the more it creeps in, until it seems that blindness also happens alongside seeing—that is, it happens *while* we are seeing. Blindness is like a weed that grows in the very center of vision, and its roots are everywhere. There are things we do not see and things we cannot see and things we refuse to see, and there are also things we can't make out, puzzling things and sickening things that make us wince. There are things too boring to see, too normal or unremarkable to ever catch the eye, things that fall through the cracks of vision, things so odd we never figure them out, blurs, confusions, smudges, and smears. There are things emptied of meaning because they have no use, they answer to no desire, they cannot be owned or moved or enjoyed. There are flickering things we can't quite catch in the corner of our eye, movements that are gone when we turn our head. There are things too brilliant to see, that sear the retina, and things too dangerous to see, charged with frightening emotional power. There are sexual things we might love to see but can't make ourselves look at, and there are beautiful faces we would love to explore but propriety tells us we shouldn't. There are things we don't see because we don't know their names, things we overlook every day of our lives and will continue to miss as long as we live, things that try to get our attention and fail, and things that hide, camouflaged and secretive things, little things hidden and forgotten among other things.

In that sense this whole book has been about blindness. In every chapter I have been talking as much about what is not seen as what is. Why do we continue to see so little even when we want to see so much? Why should a single glittering thing in a store blind us to everything else that is on sale, to everyone standing around us, to the entire store, and even to ourselves? The field of vision appears to be seamless, but it is shot through with holes. I look at a naked body and I fail to see entire limbs. I look at a landscape and I do not notice whole mountains. Perhaps ordinary vision is less like a brightly lit sky with one blinding spot in it than like the night sky filled with stars. Maybe we see only little spots against a field of darkness. Once in a great while there may be a flash of lightning and we see everything, but then the darkness returns. My vision, even at its most acute, is probably not much better than the points of the stars against their invisible field of black.

A fair amount of ordinary seeing is really just glancing. We glance at bright reflections and at deep shadows where there's "nothing" to be seen. A glance can mean strong emotion or no emotion at all. I may glance at someone I know intimately and then give the same glance to a person I will never see again. At a restaurant I glance at the person who is with me, and then I glance at the waiter. I may love the person I'm with, but probably I hardly even notice what the waiter looks like. Either way, it is an attempt to see as little as possible. I do not care about the waiter, and I also don't want to see him (I just need him so I can pay the check). It's the opposite with the person I know well, because the glance is meant to be seen: it's coy, since by refusing to see the person clearly, I mean to invite her to look at me again, to initiate a longer series of looks. Intense interest and intense disinterest both result in quick looks that see relatively little.

Glances can be even closer to blindness when fear is involved. We glance at dangerous-looking people when we're scared. We glance at strangers as we approach them on the street—a brief look, and then we avert our eyes. That's a way of *not* seeing, an urban strategy for avoiding eye contact. On the street I don't want to see people clearly, and really I don't want to see them at all. (I'm always taken aback when I'm out walking in a small town and people meet my

eyes and smile. For someone living in a city, it seems normal to try
not to see people on the street.) People also glance at extremely
violent art or art they think is perverted. A great deal of glancing was
done at a recent show of homoerotic photography, and there was
both glancing and wincing at an AIDS exhibit. Visitors walked
through the galleries trying hard to look at neutral patches of white
drywall or at other visitors' clothing or at the wood floor. Some
people glance at scary movies or right-to-life placards of aborted
fetuses, and you may have chosen to glance at some pictures in this
book. The same kind of thing happens in museums. If you're not
happy with Christianity, you may have just glanced at the *Icon with
the Fiery Eye* (figure 3). If you're uncomfortable or offended by
pornography, you may glance at it as you walk by the newsstand—
but by the same token another person might glance at it because he
finds himself too much attracted.

The opposite of a glance, by the way, is a glimpse: because in a
glance, we see only for a second, and in a glimpse, the object shows
itself only for a second. When an object appears coy—say, a bird
disappearing in foliage—it is because glimpsing something is like
glancing at it. In both cases, we see only for a moment. Perhaps a
glimpse is the glance of an object—it is the way an object glances
at us.

Glancing is a strategy in the arsenal of blindness, a way of skipping
over the surface of the world and taking in almost nothing. But even
in more normal kinds of seeing—I suppose the word "looking" is
as good as any for average, everyday seeing—blindness is right there
in the act of seeing itself, working to ensure that some things are not
seen. If you are talking to someone, you will look away every few
moments. But why look away at all? Why not look straight into the
person's eyes, or watch her mouth or her gestures, so you don't miss
anything? Perhaps it's to avoid too much intimacy or to express a
certain level of interest—as if to say, I'm interested but I'm not
fascinated. Or maybe looking away is something we do to rest our
eyes and give them a moment of relaxation by letting them focus on
a chair or a table. Ophthalmologists say that eyes have to be in more
or less constant motion, and when they fix on an object without
blinking and without turning aside, they cease to function. (I should

say that I have never been able to make that experiment work for myself. After a minute or so of fixing my eyes on a single point, things start to shimmer, and my eyes tear up and I blink. But apparently it is possible to resist blinking or moving and end up seeing nothing.) In one experiment, people stood watching perfectly smooth white walls. They were deprived of all visual information: they could not tell how far away the wall was, and there was no form to look at except the sides of their own noses. The lighting was perfectly uniform so there was no shadow or gradient to help the eye find a purchase. (The experiment has been replicated by cutting table tennis balls in half and using them in place of eyeglasses.) The subjects experienced a kind of blindness: they reported seeing gray clouds or hazy darkness. If the wall was lit with a bright color, after a few minutes the observers would think the color had been turned off, and they would insist there was nothing present but gray. So it may be that we look from place to place in order to keep our eyes working. As every child knows, if you stare directly at someone without looking away, you will start to laugh. (I've always wondered why the game works that way. Why does it end in laughter? Why not crying, for example, or sleepiness? And what happens when adults play? Do they laugh, or do they get bored? Are faces less interesting to us as we grow older?)

There are plenty of reasons why we do not look steadily at some-one while we're talking—I might almost say there are too many reasons, and it is suspicious that we would need so many reasons. I don't really like any of the reasons, and I do not have a good way of explaining to myself why ordinary, everyday looking should always also be looking away. Part of my experience of talking to a friend is *not* looking at that friend. We spend a fair amount of time failing to see the person we intend to communicate with, and in an obscure way those moments of blindness are necessary in order to look at a person at all.

What about more determined kinds of seeing, where it becomes important that my eyes function well and show me as much as possible? I think of a stare as a constant, unnaturally motionless or persistent look. A stare is an intense look: it usually means there is none of the turning away that accompanies ordinary looking, none of the flightiness of glances and glimpses. People stare at things that are inexplicable or unusual but not overly disturbing. Sometimes we stare at interesting people in crowds or at some problem in our complexion. If a part is broken in my car or my mechanical pencil, I may stare at it for several minutes at a time. We stare at the TV, but that's different, since its images are always changing, and so it's as if we were looking from place to place or glimpsing things in rapid succession (we don't stare at the snow or the color bars after a station goes off the air). And we also stare when we're tired and we're not really seeing anything. Students stare at teachers that way during long lectures, and then their eyes roll up and they fall asleep. We also stare at artworks, and that's one of the curious things about them, since it puts them in the same category with faces we spot in crowds, car engines, and mechanical pencils. Staring is an unusual kind of seeing, and there's usually something odd going on when I find myself staring. Perhaps staring is a sign that an artwork has malfunctioned: it has arrested my thinking, slowed me down, paralyzed me so I can barely move.

Each of these forms of staring has its accompanying blindnesses. If I'm staring at a person, I have probably forgotten everything except that person, and blank, exhausted staring is very close to total blindness. Staring is very tiring, as people who stare at static computer screens know, and the intensity it demands fades into a kind of blank oblivion. Many times I have caught myself staring without seeing anything at all, thinking of something else. That, I think, is as close to literal blindness as I have gotten, because I don't see what's in front of me (or anything else, for that matter) and I also don't see the mental images of the daydream, because they're canceled by the daylight that continues to flood into my eyes. It is a kind of blindness caused by an excess of images.

Art history has recently become enamored of another word for seeing, and that is gazing. "The male gaze" is a notion used to describe the way that women in Western paintings are traditionally arranged to give male viewers pleasure. Such pictures are set up for a certain kind of viewer (a heterosexual white male over the age of puberty), and they can be hard to see for other people. I'm not so sure this use of the word "gaze" fits in with what I'm describing here, because the male viewers might look or stare or glance; but the ideal viewer would look with a particular thirsty intensity, and that is a good way to think about gazing. Often enough the women in these pictures gaze back, as if to say to the viewer, "Go ahead, gaze at me." In life a gaze challenges, it inquires, it takes pleasure, and it asks for a response. When we gaze at a lover, we are communicating without using words. Every once in a while I gaze at the moon or a sunset, and I become rapt: my attention is riveted and I begin to forget other things that are happening around me.

At the same time, the male gaze is really more like a male stare because a gaze is not focused on a single point. It's not the lover's eyes or her beauty spot that I focus on but the lover as a whole, the entire moment, the scene and her body together. A sunset is something we see all at once—we don't look at one cloud or another, but we remain aware of the encompassing scene and how we are part of it. That's how I would distinguish a stare or a glance from a gaze: stares and glances are focused on details. As I gaze at a sunset or a woman's face, I also glance from place to place, but my impression is of the wholeness of it. Though it may seem that gazing is as close to pure seeing as it is possible to get, I think it's closer to blindness. Gazing is unfocused awareness, and a gazer does not see anything very well. Hollywood directors still use soft-focus lenses to mimic that state of fuzzy appreciation that sometimes accompanies love. Of course we don't usually let our eyes slip out of focus (though that's an interesting ability that some painters use to assess the overall appearance of an image), but in its awkward way the soft-focus lens shows how gazing is also poor seeing.

THE paradox of seeing is that the more forcefully I try to see, the more blind I become. A really piercing stare is its own kind of blindness, and it even causes blindness in people who receive it. The painter Franz von Lenbach (figure 53) is an interesting case, because his normal way of looking seems to have been a rather harsh stare. In picture after picture and even in his self-portrait paintings, he has this same faintly ridiculous pompous stare. It may have been an accustomed squint or an affectation—as if to say, I am a great and

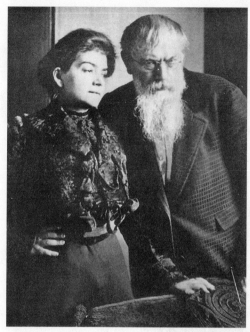

■ FIGURE 53

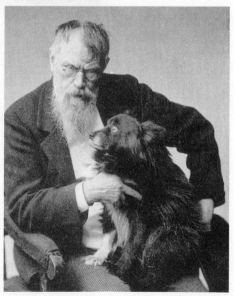

■ FIGURE 54

penetrating artist—but I almost prefer to think it was the symptom of a concentrated effort to see. (He wasn't a first-rate painter, and I also wonder if he might have been hampered by the very intensity of his stare. Perhaps he looked so hard that he crushed everything under his gaze, so that there wasn't much left to see.)

In this photograph, he fails to impress his wife, and in another (figure 54), he scares his dog. There is something in common between Franz's face and a penis: his face steals the show in every photograph (and there are many more of them). If Franz's face is around, whatever is nearby is either reacting to it or fading into the background. When one of Franz's friends painted a double portrait of the two of them, he was smart enough to throw Franz into a deep shadow. Here Franz's wife has an interesting strong and tired expression, but it is difficult to keep looking at her when Franz is glowering. Even the dog has a tough time attracting our attention away from its master. Looking at these pictures—perhaps staring back at them without realizing it, my eyes widening in unconscious mimicry—I remember the matted hair, the pinched eye, and the crooked elbow, but I fail to see other things. I don't remember the background, the chairs, parts of the clothing, other hands and legs. Franz's stare is an act of blindness, and it blinds us in return.

Piercing stares can be even more blinding when they come in crowds. Anyone who has stood on stage in front of a hostile audience knows the paralysis that can cause. In the realm of art, Picasso's *Women of Avignon* (figure 55) is one of the rare pictures that can be intimidating to look at simply because so many people in the picture are staring back at us as intensely as they can. Leo Steinberg has written some brilliant pages on this painting. "The picture is a tidal wave of female aggression," he says. "No modern painting engages you with such brutal immediacy. Of the five figures depicted, one holds back a curtain to make you see; one intrudes from the rear; the remaining three stare you down." The heart of the picture, he thinks, is the "startled" awareness "of a viewer who sees himself seen." Yet these are curiously empty eyes. Though they stare with "unsparing directness," they are not trying to capture our attention, as Franz von Lenbach tried to do. "They are simply alerted, responding to an alerting attentiveness on our side."

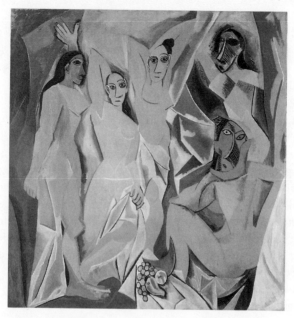

■ FIGURE 55

The stares are hypnotic—I want to say deafening. There are pictures with larger crowds than this, but numbers alone may not have this effect. When a whole crowd turns around to see *us,* we are rooted in place. (Imagine a painting of heaven with everyone, from Jesus to the smallest soul, staring right at you.) I cannot treat Picasso's painting as an occasion for harmless reverie. I do not think to myself, How would it be if I wandered around inside this painting? Where would I go? Is it a pleasant place? For one thing, there's almost no room in it, because the figures are pressing out at me so insistently. The proto-cubist curtains don't entice me with thoughts of what lies beyond. They're flat, hot, claustrophobic. But the real problem is that wall of eyes. They impel me to stand rooted in place as if I were a painted figure myself: like zombies, they turn me into one of their own. I cannot forget myself, I cannot move, I cannot turn away. I am seen with such intensity that I go partially blind, and I use all my energy returning the stares. Afterward, when I have left the picture, its eyes continue to follow me, and at those moments I again become a little blind. The blindness is like an infection that I carry with me, or like the reverberating deafness hours after a loud concert or a jet at an airport.

What happens to me here? My freedom is taken away, and my body hardens into a plank. I can't stroll back and forth in front of the picture or walk up to it and inspect some detail. I can't laugh or sigh or turn around and look at something behind me. I am riveted as the painting's power comes streaming out from those gazes. The history of art has many examples of pictures that gently push viewers toward preferred viewing positions, herding them into little imaginary enclosures where they can best see the image. Pictures with strong perspectives can do that, and so can large landscapes. That feeling is not unpleasant. This is different: I am frozen to no good purpose, my feet latched to the floor and my eyes fixed on the surface of the canvas. The stares of those five women make it difficult to go anywhere, or think of anything, or see anything but the eyes that see me.

By this logic I must conclude that the wildest stares mean the least. This photograph (figure 56) is even more powerful, I think, than Picasso's stares. It is from a German anthropological textbook printed about the time of the *Women of Avignon,* and it is one of a series of Aborigine portraits: that is, specimen photographs of typical Aborigines made in order to enable anthropologists back in Berlin to take measurements of typical Aborigine proportions. Some of the sitters in the collection obviously hated the photographer, and others were terrified or just angry and impatient. The very strongest stares, like this one, are nearly illegibile. Does this woman despise her photographer? Or is she mostly terrified? The combination of the photographic process and the woman's dark irises turns her eyes black, making them even harder to read. As a result, the stare has a shrill intensity but is nearly meaningless. Like the wild mask face at the lower right of Picasso's painting, there is no longer any expression here—just the blank force of the stare. Staring is sometimes this way, bordering on blindness. It makes us blind in turn because we cannot know how to return the look, what to think, or what we are expected to do.

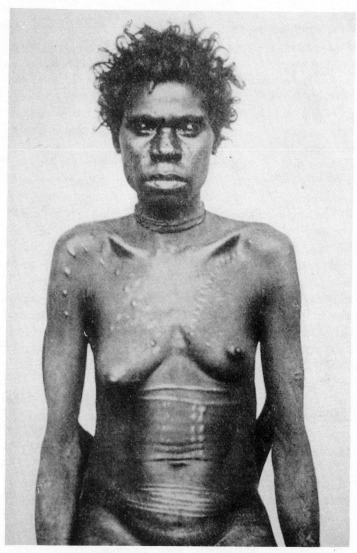

■ FIGURE 56

• • •

I N medicine, too, blindness is not an all-or-nothing proposition but a constant accompaniment of sight. The most common visual problems are not total blindness but ordinary nearsightedness, astigmatism, and other difficulties we have bringing the world into focus. Each of them is both a medical condition and a way of seeing, so that we speak of people who are nearsighted or farsighted without meaning they are literally so. Such people concentrate on nearby objects or on distant ones and ignore the middle ground. In that sense the medical conditions of myopia and hyperopia are only the literal forms of common habits of seeing. And the parallel may be extended into a metaphor, since some people also *think* as if they were nearsighted or farsighted: they comprehend only the most immediate problems or the most distant abstractions, and they remain oblivious to the bulk of the world. Astigmatism and other aberrations are also analogues of problems people have seeing things correctly—some people distort everything they think about, like the idiosyncratic flaws in an astigmatic's eyes, and others see the world with halos of light, the way it appears through lenses with chromatic aberrations.

More serious problems with vision also have parallels in ways that we ordinarily see and think about the world. Glaucoma can create a narrowing tunnel with blackness all around. Eventually it can close down like the iris in a camera. It is the analogy for all obsessive staring—we say a person who stares has blinkers on, or has tunnel vision—with an essential difference: when the eyes are not working right, the person is constantly aware of that fact. If I stare at a trinket in a store, I am happily unconscious of the fact that I have blotted out most of the world. Someone with glaucoma may not see more than I do at that moment, but he will also be aware of what he does not see. In medical blindness, the subject is not blind to the blindness itself—or to put it in philosophic terms, the blindness is visible, it is there to be seen. The blind area may be physically visible as a gray region, rather than unthought and unseen as a pure absence of sight. Ordinary obsessive staring is a double blindness, since the person who stares has no idea that he is partially blind.

The same thing happens, for example, with a Freudian slip. If I misspeak, I don't notice my error. I am both mistaken and blind to my mistake, until someone points out what happened—and only then will I realize that my speech was not a seamless expression of my intention but something interrupted without my knowledge. An idea from the unconscious, as Freud would say, had punctured a hole into consciousness. But the Freudian slip enfolds itself, covering both the rent in my awareness and the act of covering. Freudian slips are so uncomfortable, even for unbelievers in Freud, because they imply there are other gaps in my thought. The sheet of my consciousness may be largely in tatters, but it is in the nature of things that I can see only a few rents, and so I continue to act as if it were mostly smooth and whole. Entire theories of psychology and of literature have been built around the idea that we all have inescapable moments of blindness that we fail to notice, and the original model for those theories may come from vision—and if *that* is so, then the theorists might learn about new blindnesses by studying what happens with vision.

Cataracts and macular degeneration can cause the opposite phenomenon to glaucoma: they can create black spots directly where we want to look, which can grow larger until they cover the entire visual field. (Cataracts can also make the entire visual field hazy, like the effect of a soft-focus gaze.) Cataracts that cause dark spots at the center of vision also mimic a kind of seeing that happens in everyday life, when an object is too painful or too desirable to be seen and the vision is deflected onto nearby objects. Bataille's examples may still be the best, though the same happens with much more ordinary objects that are just distasteful, exhibitionistic, or nauseating. In each case the object on which the eye is trained is what disappears. It's also an apposite metaphor for the way some people think, intending to attack one thing and tilting at everything else instead. An exhibition called *Seeing Without Sight* drew attention to visual disabilities by passing out partially masked eyeglasses and by illustrating the effects of some common disabilities (figure 57). These photographs are intended to be literal embodiments of conditions that are normally subjective, but they cannot begin to evoke the oppressive presence of a cloud at the very center of the eye. Still, they serve to

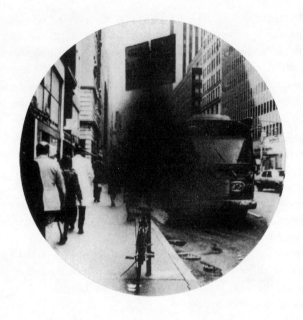

■ FIGURE 57

show how medical blindness, as opposed to its analogues in ordinary seeing, is visible to the blind person: in fact, here it is hard to look at anything *but* the blind spot.

And of course we all have a blind spot built into each eye. Both eyes together will usually cover for each other, but not always. The blind spot is easy to locate by covering one eye, fixing the open eye on a dark spot, and slowly looking in the direction of your nose. In a flash the spot will disappear, and in its place—and this is the interesting thing—there is *nothing*. It appears that the eye has automatically filled in the missing place with whatever color or texture is in the field of vision. Try the experiment on a checkerboard or put an object on a Persian carpet and you will see how resourceful the eye is in letting us think that we still see everything.

Even this quick survey shows that vision is far stranger than the generic blindnesses or the male gazes that preoccupy philosophers and art historians. All of the common pathologies of vision correspond to habits in ordinary seeing. Some might even be correctives to theories about metaphorical blindnesses. According to experimental psychology, the eye does not fill in the blind spot but tricks us into thinking that it has been filled. If you look at a yellow wall with one eye closed, you will see seamless yellow in all directions, but that does not mean the blind spot has painted itself yellow; instead, it means that the blind spot is pure absence of vision and cannot be experienced at all. To the critic Paul de Man, blindnesses are necessary in any self-reflexive thought, so that no theory can know itself entirely. The blind spot is a way of thinking about that more precisely, since it is neither a visible absence (a darkness) nor a constructed absence (a hole papered over by extrapolating from visible objects) but an invisible absence: an absence whose invisibility is itself invisible. This is not the dark gray annoyance that is suffered in actual partial blindness, nor is it the oblivion of the fixed stare, but something different, another kind of blindness, where we believe we see but do not.

This illusion of sight has interesting consequences. If I look at an artwork with one eye closed, there will always be a portion of it I do not see—and who am I to "fill in" for Raphael or Picasso? We all have an ongoing unawareness of the blind spot: as you look at this page, if you close your right eye, you will not be seeing something off to the left—but no matter how hard you think about it, you won't be able to decide what's missing. Anytime you look at the world through one eye, part of your field of vision is lacking. According to Helmholtz, there is not a single blind spot but many, scattered throughout the field of vision. Each person has defective spots in his retinas (negative scotomas) and defective neurons in his visual cortex, so that we are more or less blind in spots without ever knowing it: an exact analogy to our intermittent awareness of the visual field. There are objects in every scene that we don't see— both psychologically and also physiologically.

THE less common pathologies of vision do not lend themselves as easily to metaphoric parallels, but they also reveal new facets of vision. Achromatopsia, for instance, is a kind of color blindness in which patients also forget the *names* of colors and even what colors are. It is as if colors had never existed, either as sensations (as most of us know them) or even as empty words (as the congenitally blind experience them). Telling an achromatopsic patient about colors would be even more senseless than insisting we all live upside down or that we each have invisible twins. In achromatopsia color is absolutely absent from thought in a way that is impossible to understand. The fact that such a condition can exist (even though I can hardly begin to understand it) indicates that vision reaches deeply into the mind. This is no ordinary blindness, in which a patient knows what he cannot see, and it is not the same as the analogies I have been pursuing in ordinary vision, where the observer can become instantly aware of what he has been missing. The blind spot can be located by a simple experiment, even though it is unlocatable without that experiment (that is, if you simply stare straight ahead and try to guess what you're not seeing). But achromatopsia can *never* be located in consciousness, and if it is demonstrated, the demonstration is meaningless. It runs much deeper than the figurative blind spot in critical thinking; in this book, it would correspond to the inability of generations of viewers to comprehend what Renaissance painters were trying to show them about Christ.

Chromatopsia (as opposed to achromatopsia) is the illusion of color where there is none, and it can produce an especially strange condition: a few patients see nothing but color, and so they try to identify everything by color. Samir Seki, the researcher who first named this condition, says that patients may become baffled attempting to distinguish objects and end up doing things like misidentifying "all blue objects as 'ocean.'" Like achromatopsia, this is absolute visual amnesia, the permanent erasure of ideas from the eye and from the mind itself. If it has its analogies in my own vision, I can never know them.

Akinetopsia is a condition in which patients cannot understand motion: they see only things that stay still, and objects that move seem to vanish. It has interesting resonance for painting, since it is often inconceivable that painted figures should ever move—in a sense, if they did move, they would cease to exist. Painting is an art based on inherently motionless figures, which are very different from

frozen figures that are captured by the camera. I can imagine a figure
in a photograph coming alive, like a still scene being released into
motion, but I cannot imagine a painted figure moving and talking,
unless I am willing to settle for some comic travesty. If the Venus in
Botticelli's painting walked out of her canvas, as she does in an
episode of *Monty Python,* she would be a silly mannekin. If I am
more serious about painting, I have to acknowledge that motion is
not just absent but inconceivable. I am tempted to say the same
about any object that is ordinarily inert. In the age of cartoons and
computer animation, practically anything might come alive, but the
moment it does so it becomes a comedy (or a horror movie). If I am
unwilling to imagine surrealistic transformations, nightmare resur-
rections, or cartoon animations, then I have to admit that moving
versions of inanimate objects are inconceivable. Akinetopsic patients
have the opposite malady to a dog's vision, since a dog is not good
at seeing things that keep still. There may be a fundamental choice
here, made at the lowest levels of image processing. There are motion detectors in the retina, and so, in neurological terms, motion is
distinct from stasis at the very beginning of vision. In ordinary seeing
things are more complicated, but akinetopsia reminds us how motion is sometimes merely patched onto shape.

Pathologies like these tell us that concepts like color, shape, name,
and motion are far more entangled than we might otherwise believe.
Shape is not something that contains color the way a bucket contains
paint, and motion is sometimes entirely detached from the object
that is moving. The name of a color or a shape is not just tacked
onto an object like a label but is linked in a much more intimate
way. A figure is not something that sits on a ground, in the way that
painters speak of figures and backgrounds, but it is linked by the
curious, unnatural outline that artists sometimes represent as a dark
line. Our retinas have specialized cells for each of these elements of
vision, and we have only a very slight knowledge of how they work
together. Space perception is also stranger than it once seemed to
artists and philosophers. It has been proposed that if a person is facing
away from us, we assume that his head is whole and that the person
has a normal kind of face—but we don't think about it too actively,
and another scientist says our minds use a "two-and-a-half-

dimensional sketch" to fill in the missing volume. What are the shapes of the backs of things? Is the world forced into three dimensions when it becomes visible, in the way it used to be thought that mother bears would give birth to formless cubs and then lick them into shape? Are things flat cutouts until we think them into shape?

These issues are still the domain of neurobiologists and experimental psychologists, but they are provocative antidotes to the building-block theories of vision that are used to teach art. Of all these conditions the most spectacular and confusing is blindsight. Blindsight patients think they are partially or entirely blind, but if they are asked to follow moving objects or name shapes or colors, they sometimes can. They imagine they are guessing, the way we would if we closed our eyes and tried to point to things, and they are amazed when they are told they are correct. What kind of seeing is this? The neurological explanation is that a large part of vision is not available to the conscious mind and that we become aware of only certain aspects of vision. As Zeki puts it, "blindsight patients are people who 'see' but do not 'understand.' Because they are unaware of what they have seen, they have not acquired any knowledge." Researchers are currently debating the exact mechanism that is responsible: Does the residual vision bypass the visual cortex entirely, involving areas of the brain that are not thought to be connected to vision? Or is the visual cortex still responsible, but in ways that are disconnected from conscious awareness? Either way, blindsight shows it is possible to see without understanding what we see or even *that* we see—a truly strange thought. Vision seems to be a kind of model of conscious thought: we think of it as something we control, and we are sure we see everything we look at. Francis Crick, the codiscoverer of the double helix, has chosen visual consciousness as a way to investigate consciousness itself. But blindsight is a reminder that a great deal happens before we are given the final image. Vision is largely unconscious, and we get only the final result.

Figure 58 is a picture of a person in the act of seeing. He is a healthy, whole human volunteer, whose brain has been painlessly sectioned by a magnetic-resonance imaging device. The small irregular areas toward the bottom of the cross section show where the

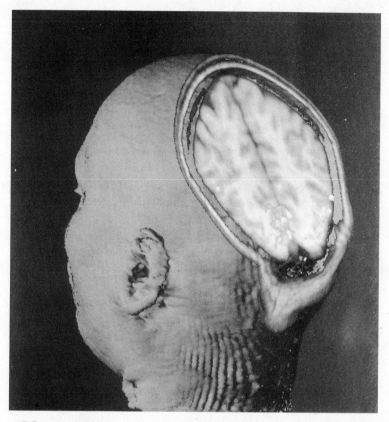

■ FIGURE 58

brain is especially active—it is the visual cortex in the back of the brain. The subject was fitted with a visor that showed him flashing lights, and his head was fixed in place with a padded clamp so that he wouldn't move and blur the image (hence the flattened ears). So this is a picture of seeing itself: the neuronal activity that accompanies all seeing takes place in part at the back of our heads, invisible and unthought.

• • •

ONE of the deepest currents here is the connection between seeing, blindness, and thinking. Each of the blindnesses I have mentioned so far is also a way of seeing the world and a way of thinking about it. The more I think about blindness, the more it seems to be a failure of thinking as much as vision. Since the Greeks, thinking and seeing have begun together, at the same moment in imagination. If I think about something, I reflect on it: that is, I imagine myself and the thought reflecting each other. It seems that thinking is imagining—and as the word suggests, the imagination is a place inhabited by images. All the principal metaphors for thinking, knowledge, and truth itself have to do with seeing: notions such as illuminating, casting light on a problem, being enlightened, insightful, clear, distinct, or brilliant are only the symptoms of this relation, which has become as deeply ingrained as thinking itself.

In the West, this has always presented itself (the phrase is another visual metaphor) as an opportunity to think about thinking and to say how thinking begins with seeing. Hegel, who loved to wrestle with these almost unthinkable thoughts, said that anything that exists —any being, which means also any thought—must be something that can be luminous or illuminated, so that it can be *seen* in the mind's eye. Nothing can exist, he thought, without the possibility that it be visible to the mind. But must truth always have to do with unveiling, revealing, and illuminating? It is an issue that continues to vex contemporary philosophers, who have been attempting to find other ways of thinking about thought that do not depend on seeing.

When philosophers think about these problems they are usually out to explain thinking rather than seeing. Philosophers do not start out asking how they can account for seeing and then bring in thinking as a source of metaphors. But that is an interesting possibility to contemplate. What if thinking were not the basic motion of our minds? What would the world be like if we could *start* from seeing and find our way toward thinking? What if reflecting, illuminating, imagining, and all the rest were fundamental, and thinking were only a figure of speech that could sometimes help explain them? What if blindness held the keys to both thought and vision?

I am entranced by these thoughts, partly because they are a little too extravagant to believe and partly because they have the power to invert our habitual ways of understanding thinking and seeing. For example, I might entertain the idea that there are two kinds of seeing, instead of the single equation that says seeing equals thinking. The first would have to do with expressions such as "illuminating a problem" or "shedding light on an idea." When it's put that way, then thought is the illumination, and the truth is what needs to be lit by thought. On the other hand, when I say I'm "reflecting" on a problem or something has just "dawned on me," then it's as if the truth is already luminous and my thought merely collects the light.

According to the first model, thought takes place in darkness. Ideas and things and selves must be in a primordial darkness until thought sends out its beams to reveal them. But if I reflect on something, then I exist along with various objects in the world, all bathed in a light that comes from somewhere else. In the first model blindness is all around: it is the condition of the world, and a thought is like a flashlight that temporarily reveals some local object. In the second there is no place for blindness, except in my own mind. If I fail to reflect, if I decline to try to understand the world, then I become blind, or rather I give way to the blindness that is already within me. The second model, where the world is bright and suffused with thought, really has no place for catastrophic, ongoing blindness. If I live in such a world and I choose not to see, then I suffer a momentary blindness—it might be a slip, an error, a blunder, or a mistake, or in visual terms a blind spot, a moment or a day of hysterical blindness, amnesia about a trauma, or just a misapprehension, something I overlook, something I fail to notice. No matter how serious those blindnesses are, I can recover from them: I can become aware of my mistake; I can look again and see better. In the first model, where the world is dark and only thought can illuminate it, blindness is more permanent, and I may not be able to recover from it at all. That kind of blindness would include ingrained prejudices, permanent gaps in my thought, failures of imagination, psychotic breaks, fanaticisms and dogmas, and in visual terms, all the things I cannot see or that I refuse to see. Blindness would be all around. Every image would be a light in the darkness, and seeing or thinking would take place against a backdrop of blindness. In this way of setting the problem, blindness is the precondition and constant accompaniment of vision. It cannot be fully seen, but it must always be present wherever there is seeing.

I would be more content to think of the world as it looks each day, filled with light. The sparse shadows and dark spots that remain would be like the few gaps in my sight—the blind spot in each eye, for instance. If I choose to think this way, thought is beautiful and easy. All we have to do is conceive of an idea and it appears in front of us, bathed in the light of thought, clear and distinct in all its details. And sometimes this happens: if we know an issue very well, we can call it to mind and see all its contours, everything that is involved in it, without effort and in great clarity. But there are many other moments when the other model seems more true. If we do not understand a problem very well, then we cannot form a mental image of it. It seems dark, and thinking about it requires great effort. Even if we think hard, we may illuminate only a small portion of it, and the light we throw may make it look distorted. In that case we might say we can't see the problem very well, that we cannot generate enough light to illuminate its outlines. It is sadder, but it strikes me that this is much closer to the truth: like seeing, thinking is intermittent, unreliable, and difficult. Both take place in darkness and both depend on light. Blindness is their constant accompaniment, the precondition of both thought and sight.

MAKING a drawing is a wonderful way to experience the varieties of blindness. Because it depends on touch, all picture making is in some degree blind. There is the light contact of the pencil on paper, the wet friction of the brush against canvas, the hard push of the engraving needle cutting into copper. When an artist is concentrating, trying to feel the exact pressure of the lead and even the texture of the paper as the pencil skips across its surface, then vision is occluded. It can take a lifetime of practice even to begin to control the delicate or forceful meeting of pencil and paper, the stickiness and weight of a paintbrushful of color, or the sensitive motions of an ink brush. Drawing is strongly tactile, both in the way it is made and in the way it is seen.

The lines of a drawing record the pressure of the fingers on the pencil that made it, the speed and ease of the marks, and their impatience, control, or anxiety. Some styles of drawing will slowly force the hand into a state of exhausting muscular tension, and that creeping paralysis shows in the marks. In other styles the grip is normally loose, and it is tempting to draw too quickly or thoughtlessly. The marks may turn violent or febrile, and the drawing may become unstrung. Any drawing is an archive of its maker's muscles, and some of the best drawings force that awareness so strongly on viewers that they may feel their hands tightening in response. Both making and looking are strongly tactile, bodily experiences, and to the extent that drawing pertains to touch, it loses contact with vision. When I think of a drawing, my mind is occupied with a mixture of thoughts: in part I'm remembering the look of the drawing as best I can; and in part I'm remembering its *feeling:* I am sensing the size of it, recalling whether I stooped to see it, whether I was looking up or down. In ways so subtle I can scarcely become aware of them, my body is rehearsing its response to the picture at the same time as my mind's eye is redrawing the image itself. The two responses are one.

Yet we are habitually oblivious to these meeting places of mind and musculature. Only artists routinely look at pictures with eyes sharpened for these nuances. After a few years practicing drawing, the sight of a drawing becomes an exquisite reminder of the act of drawing. For that reason it is easy to tell an artist from an art historian by the way she responds to a drawing. A historian, trained with books and color slides, will stand at a respectful distance and look without moving. An artist, at home with gestures, will want to move a hand over the drawing, repeating the gentleness of the marks that made it, reliving the drag of the brush or the push of the pencil. The drawing has *become* its bodily response, and the body moves in blind obedience to what it senses on the page.

Some beautiful and simple experiments have been done on these ideas. An invisible line was drawn on the back of a person's hand by tracing lightly with a fingernail (figure 59, top left). The subject reports that he feels a straight line and "immediately visualizes a black ink line." The tactile imagination evokes a visual image, and the two are slightly different: the lower part of the mental image is blurred, but the lower part of the tactile sensation is crisp. In a few

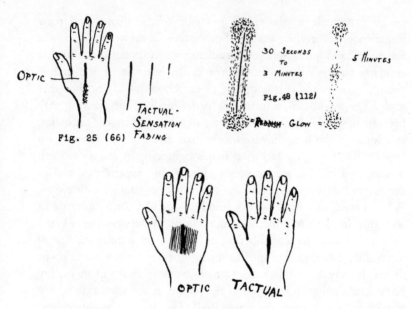

• FIGURE 59

moments, the tactual image—the remembered shape of the drawing, still felt on the back of the hand—begins to disappear from the bottom upwards. Was it following the visual image? Or was the defect in the visual image a presentiment of a hidden defect in the sensation? The experimenters also trace lines and then turn the subjects around to find out if the images are influenced by motions of the body. (It appears they are, and tactual memories as well as mental pictures will slip out of place as the body moves.) One of their subjects is abnormal and has hypersensitive skin that forms a small reddish area whenever it is touched. They trace a line on his abdomen and watch as the skin reddens into a dumbbell shape, the same as an ink brush line would make with its two thickened ends (figure 59, top right). After five minutes the line fades, but it leaves its endpoints and a string of isolated points. The neurology of the retina ensures that we always look with special attention at the endpoints of lines, and some drawing media such as ink brush painting reproduce that unequal seeing. Could it be that the same emphasis is built into tactile sensation, or even that it is strengthened by tactile experience? Another subject is asked to describe the effects of imagining that a line is being drawn on the back of his hand (figure 59, bottom). At first he sees a hand holding a pencil, but he cannot make it contact his hand, and there is no touching sensation. Instead he feels the fingertips gripping the pencil. On the next try he succeeds —he sees the line and at the same moment feels a faint sensation. The optical image is stronger than the tactual image, but it begins to multiply: instead of one line, he now sees many. The tactual image remains single, but he feels the middle of it best; and then it too begins to multiply, but only in its middle section. In other experiments there is no tactual image, and the subjects are asked just to imagine the lines. In general those mental images are much less stable. One person thinks of a white line against a black background, but when he tries to keep his eye on it, it rolls up like a carpet. Another person thinks of a horizontal line on a blackboard, but it breaks up and the parts begin drifting independently of one another, and some of them even lose contact with the blackboard. A third person pictures a line and watches as it spreads and glows. The experimenters conclude with a rather profound thought, that the very act of imagining distorts the visual field. It is a curious idea, that the pressure of thought transforms images. There are many other unsubstantiated assertions in their work, but it is mostly an exploration of the intricate and idiosyncratic relation between what they call optic and tactual images. The two go together, but neither one goes first. Sometimes a tactual image helps stabilize a visual image, and in other cases they help each other melt away.

No one knows quite what to do with this blind bodily aspect of pictures. Some writers, like Robert Vischer thinking of empathic response, stress individual experiences—a melting sensation in front of one picture, a neckache in front of another—and that is probably the most sensible thing to do. If I remain alert to myself while I look, I can fight the tendency to ignore my bodily sensations. Still, there will be some things that I am aware of and others that I may have repressed too effectively to be able to sense them. Here is one of my favorite pictures (figure 60). It was drawn by a Viennese chimpanzee named Jonny in 1957. When artists are shown this, they often say it looks like a picture by the artist Cy Twombly—but really it doesn't, and as the scientist who published it points out, it's also unlike a child's drawing, since it is more rhythmically sophisticated. It is

■ FIGURE 60

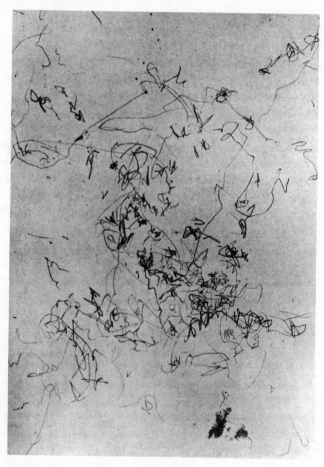

always possible to distinguish apes' drawings from children's drawings and the intentional scribblings of artists—but that is another story. What is interesting here is that as Jonny drew, he became sexually excited. Both the biologist and the zookeeper noticed his increasing fervor—they must have been watching his erection while he was watching the paper.

People who studied primate drawing and painting in the 1960s were concerned to find primitive versions of what they called aesthetic sense. They were on the lookout for apes who would try to produce balanced, harmonious compositions, and they tended to design their experiments so that they seemed to get what they were after. Many primate artists will either throw the pencil down (or throw it at the keeper) or else draw until the page is entirely covered; and so in order to have a composition to exhibit, the scientists had to take the pages away when they were still in the process of being drawn. Most ape artists begin in the center of a blank page, and that was consistently interpreted as a rudimentary sense of composition —but it might be better to say that apes, like people, want to see coherent forms instead of scattered chaos. The centered scribbles might be evidence of the search for bodies or faces, even though they do not seem representational to us. Figure 60 does not look like a body, and because of our experience with abstract painting we would be apt to associate it with the kind of gestural abstraction that fragments and disperses references to the body. But how could we possibly be sure? Jonny might have been excited because he was absorbed in the creation of a body or just in thoughts of touching. Like other chimpanzees and gorillas who paint, Jonny spent a fair amount of time doing *other* corporeal things with his brushes and pencils—rolling them across the page, stabbing them into the paper, biting them, throwing them down. Other apes who will not play along still show some interest in the media. The same biologist who writes about Jonny reports that his mate, Fanny, had a destructive and vexed disposition. She would not usually draw but she would grab at the paper in order to rip or bite it. Eventually she had to be separated from Jonny in order to let him get on with his favorite activity. And then one day she was handed a small ink brush. She fell quiet, studied the brush, and then made a small drawing (figure

61). Afterward she handed the brush and the paper back to the biologist. It was one of her few pictures.

The engagement with the tools of drawing is not an intellectual one, and it has connection to the full range of the body's functions. We do not need to imagine that Jonny was thinking of Fanny (or some other chimpanzee) when he made his passionate scribbles, and we certainly don't need to suppose he was trying to *represent* a chimpanzee. Jonny and Fanny did not look at anything except the paper when they drew. It is enough that the body is at work when the picture appears. Jonny's and Fanny's drawings are a kind of love story: they are evidence of Jonny's nameless sexual passion, of Fanny's hatred or jealousy, and of her one concession—a gift, which she gave to the keeper but which may also have been for Jonny, or *of* Jonny.

■ FIGURE 61

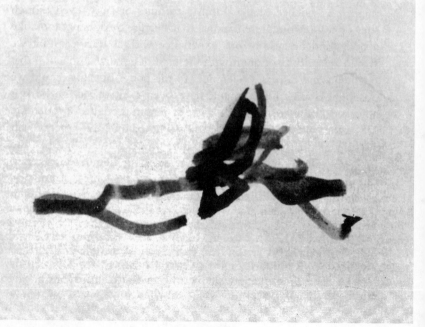

Of course Jonny's erection did not fit in with the theories of the day, since sexual perversion was the last thing the scientists would have wanted to connect with the search for aesthetic harmonious composition. Desmond Morris, the author of *The Naked Ape* and just the person you'd think would know what to do with Jonny, just says the phenomenon is "most intriguing" and "worthy of further investigation." At first blush it might seem best just to let this remain an isolated instance, like the more recent signing female gorilla who masturbated while looking at *Playgirl* magazine. (After a while her keepers decided that might not be the best idea, and they took the magazine away.) But can we be so sure that there is no deep connection between drawing and sexual excitement? How exactly would we go about arguing that there could be no such connection? It is much easier to argue the other way. Most artists may not be aroused by the act of painting or the sight of an ordinary picture, but seeing can be absorbing and arresting, hypnotic, even stupefying . . . and what are those, if not emotions associated with desire?

S o I would say drawings are blind and they are about blindness, because they deeply involve the body. A drawing also begins in blindness, with a pure white sheet. At the moment when the artist sets pencil to paper there is nothing to see, and the first mark is made in isolation and framed by emptiness. As the pencil travels along the page, it always moves into blindness, leaving behind a narrow path of vision. Unless the entire page is covered with marks (and in the history of drawing, it is rare to find an image that is principally marks, where the marks have won out against the blank page), the drawing exists mostly in blindness. A small fraction of the sheet will be marked out, like paths through a wilderness, and the remainder will be a trackless surface. A drawing is an expression of a dialogue with blindness, and the most beautiful drawings are beautiful because they show it is sometimes possible to win that battle and produce a form out of nothing. Fanny's drawing has this quality for me, although I harbor no illusions about what it might have meant to Fanny. (I suspect it meant nothing at all and was of use only as something to give her keeper. A recent sociological survey finds that the principal use of pictures in people's living rooms is as tokens of friendship. Pictures start conversations, and they symbolize welcoming homes. In that way it does not matter what they represent, or how interesting they are, or what kind of composition they have, or what they might symbolize—it only matters that they can function as signs of intimacy.) For me, Fanny's drawing is eloquent in its own way: it has the kind of spareness that I have learned to associate with the struggle—in the end, often a hopeless struggle—with the white page. It doesn't represent anything I can understand, and it doesn't have human balance or harmony, but it still speaks about the hand's encounter with the blindness of the white page.

There is also a blindness in the drawing implement itself, since the pencil does not have an eye to guide it along the paper. The pencil, its lead and its shank, and the hand that holds it are all blind, and seeing takes place only farther away, where the artist watches the drawing emerge. Artists do not look directly at their pencils or their hands but at the marks on the paper, and even then there is blindness because each look at the paper is also a look away from the model. At the instant a drawing is begun, the artist is often looking at the paper, so that, as one philosopher says, there is a double blindness— the artist sees neither the model nor the drawing that does not yet exist.

Even the image in imagination is gradually erased by the drawing as it appears. Any actual configuration of lines is more forceful than even the clearest mental image, and as the drawing progresses the image will change to fit what is happening on the page. If I imagine a certain figure, and then my drawing begins to reveal something different, the thought of the figure weakens. It may rearrange itself in my mind in an attempt to conform to the emerging drawing, but soon it will begin to fade. The actions of my hand will also urge on the dissolution of the mental image, since layers of sensation and thoughts of the drawing as it feels to my fingers and wrist will be sweeping over the once-clear mental image. As the drawing grows, the mental image is erased, and each gesture creates something on paper and effaces something in my mind.

A mark is born in blindness, and as pictures are drawn they slowly emerge from blindness without ever leaving it behind. There is a partial blindness in every drawing as the image hovers between the real and the imaginary, and a finished drawing preserves that balance. All pictures are fossils of the original blindness that went into their making. Looking at visual art, we see the product of blind touching and the memory of it. An artist looking at a drawing will be aware of all of this in some way, even though it rarely needs to find its way into words. And the moral I would draw is this: pictures stand in their own way for seeing in general, for the processes of sight, and the motions of the eye. Jonny's drawing is a map of the habitual movements of my eyes, of the amount that I see out of a full field of vision, and of the ways my body responds. His tight scribbles and expansive wobbling lines are analogues to the ways I tense and relax as I scan the world. His anxiety and even his excitement are models of my visual dialogue with what I see. And Fanny's small drawing is another mode of seeing, one that belongs with a different mood and different purposes.

I am not proposing pictures as skeleton keys to the ways we see, and a picture has no clear correspondence with sight. But drawings are a place to observe the exchange between seeing and blindness and to meditate on the ways that blindness threads its way through vision. As I turn my eye, I trace out narrow paths and points of attention, bright places in the darkness of what is not seen. Blindness holds my hand and guides me. I know very little about what happens, where I am going, or what I am doing. That is seeing.

Envoi

T H I S book could have been five hundred pages long or five thousand. Vision is inexhaustible once it reveals itself as more than a machinery for the efficient processing of light. My principal argument has been that vision is forever incomplete and uncontrollable because it is used to shape our sense of what we are. Objects molt and alter in accord with what we need them to be, and we change ourselves by the mere act of seeing. Early in his career, Ludwig Wittgenstein was fascinated by pictures and by the very idea of a picture. He thought, for instance, that pictures were a kind of underlying support for meaning itself. "Picture" to him meant a view of the world, or a sentence, or a mathematical relation: anything that had rational sense. In later years he abandoned the hope that pictures could give us the logic of the world, and he began to think about how pictures change depending on what we want of them and how we choose to talk about them. "A picture held us captive," he wrote, remembering his early ideas. These days, the later Wittgenstein is the one who is seriously debated and widely accepted, and the early Wittgenstein is studied more by historians of philosophy. But there is good reason to hold on to some of each view. What we see fundamentally remakes us, until sentences like "the observer looks at the object" no longer hold—an idea that is in accord with Wittgenstein's later opinion. For that reason a book like this can only show what the possibilities are, and it can never be a manual of vision. But the other view also has its claim on truth, because in any given moment, as I witness something in the world, I am held captive by it, and for that instant I am held in a frozen trance.

Wittgenstein had a dream about a dazzling Oriental carpet with an enthralling incomprehensible pattern: a puzzle that could never be solved because it would never change or reveal anything more than what it was. The poet Wallace Stevens was entranced by "mere being," by pictures that simply exist without sense or plan, and he wrote a poem about a beautiful bird sitting motionless in a palm tree, singing meaninglessly. The static traps of vision complement the evanescence of observers and objects, so that vision is both change and paralysis. And in that spirit, I will bring this book to an end with a parable about a gorgeous sight, full of motion and meaninglessness.

C O N S I D E R the blue peacock, a bird nearly ruined by centuries of bad poems (figure 62). Peacocks' tails are said to have all the colors of the rainbow, but even a first look at a living peacock shows that is not true and demonstrates how much our ability to see peacocks has been trampled by clichés. Peacocks certainly are not absolutely beautiful, since they hide their wings, bellies, and rump feathers, which are mud or leaf colored. In an Arabic poem, the peacock complains it is marred by "ill feet," and together with its leathery legs, the uninteresting back half of the peacock makes a dull pedestal that keeps our eyes on the tail and the deep blue that spreads slowly downward from its throat to its breast. The tail is not the constellation of stars that it is often said to be: in fact its plumage is sparse, and if a peacock displays against a bright light, the effect is threadbare. Even with perfect illumination, as in this photograph, the hollow white shafts are at least as prominent as the famous feathers. Some of the longest feathers look like hollow vegetable stalks and have no eyespots at all.

All those uglinesses are built in, and they serve the central purpose of drawing the eye inward and downward. The purple front half of the body does the same, sliding the eye down and back to the hidden half body behind. The white feather ribs are like arrows, all pointing in the same direction. The eyespots themselves play that game with great precision: they loom on the upper margin as if to trap the eye, and then they fall toward the body, getting smaller as they go. As they approach the peacock's back, they cluster and imbricate, form-

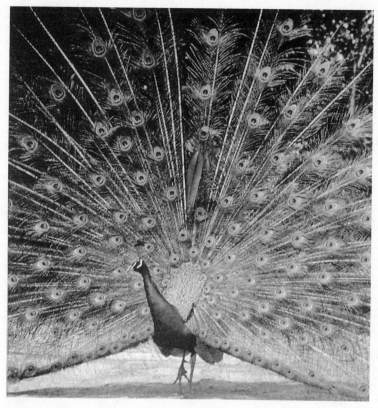

■ FIGURE 62

ing a fish-scale pattern of overlapping eyes that continues to grow in density, seamlessly flowing together, and then diving *into* the bird's blue back. Eyespots also gather along the bottom margins, as if they had fallen there, and they are gathered up off the ground and pulled in toward the flanks. The eyespots are not randomly scattered across the tail but arrayed in flamelike arcs, so our eyes can also begin at the apex of an arc and swoop down and away from the bird before being turned and brought inward to the body. Continuous circling and falling motions are crucial to the hypnotic effect, and as the peacock shakes its feathers, the whole assembly seems to tremble and collapse, as if the eyespots were dew sliding on a spider's web.

And the eyespots are definitely eyes. They all look in, toward the body: the large ones on top look down with a surprised expression, and the ones on the lower margins look up as they ascend the trailing edge. Their irises even reflect the deep blue neck, so that the peacock is surrounded by dozens of reflections of itself. Together they are almost two hundred eyes transfixed on the place where the visible breast becomes the hidden belly. It is essential to see that the eyes do not focus attention on the peacock's head but on the iridescent neck and the incomprehensible place where it widens and the body is cut in half by the root of the tail.

In this galaxy of seeing, notice how much remains unseen. Not only the bulk of the bird, including the "ill feet," the actual wings, and the genitals themselves—the point of the whole display—but especially the peacock's real eyes, which are small and camouflaged between yellow stripes. It is as if the hen could never be attracted if it felt itself being seen. All eyes have to be trained on the male, and especially his purple neck. The appropriately named Argus pheasant, *Argusianus argus* (figure 63), a native of Borneo, sometimes actually hides its head by folding its neck back behind a wing and peering out through its feathers like a spy between the wings of a folding screen. Unlike the blue peacock's scattered offering, the Argus pheasant's feathers are an impenetrable shining wall of bronze-colored eyes, row after row of mesmerizing dark irises, a stunning apparition of a body that sees itself, that is nothing but vision—interrupted, in the very middle, by a small, naked, wrinkled bluish head with rangy black hairs. It may be the most elaborate misdirection in the animal kingdom: the female imagines itself possessed by a luminous host of golden feathers, until the ugly head pops out. Blue peacocks have a simpler strategy: instead of trying to hide their eyes, they disguise them with protective coloration. Peacocks become decapitated necks, and Argus pheasants turn into a cascade of disembodied feathers.

And there is one other part of the blue peacock that is not seen, even though it is in the very center of the display: the four large copper-colored feathers that emerge in the middle of the fan. They

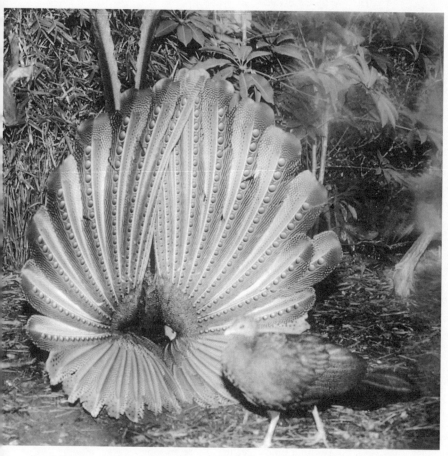

■ FIGURE 63

cross slightly, forming a mandorla, and it is larger and more opaque than anything else in the latticework of the tail. In a sense they are nothing other than the blind spot of the peacock's image, the interruption that makes it possible for the entire effect to work. They are the one place where vision shuts down entirely: they are not half hidden like the body or camouflaged like the eyes but simply absent from mind. I take those few copper feathers as an emblem of the impossibility of seeing the whole, and at least for my human eyes, they are the center of power of the whole composition. Once I see them and fix my eyes on them, the pattern begins to swirl, and the white ribs—especially the eyeless ones—shoot upward like sparklers. That is the moment I am most helpless, most transfixed, and it is also the moment I cease to see the peacock's body. It would be interesting to know if peacocks could attract hens without those four brown feathers.

Blue peacocks are vision made visible. Everything I have been saying in this book circles around these themes of objects that stare back, of webs and traps of vision, and of things that are overlooked or hidden or impossible to see. Peacocks are maps of seeing, and their patterns apply universally. We are not free to see as we please. Some things reshape us as we see them, and others hold us utterly captive until they drain us out of ourselves.

This is the place where Stevens's poem fits most perfectly, because palm trees are another radiant shape that hypnotizes, another eye, and another place where thought comes to an end in the snares of vision.

> The palm at the end of the mind,
> Beyond the last thought, rises
> In the bronze decor,
>
> A gold-feathered bird
> Sings in the palm, without human meaning,
> Without human feeling, a foreign song.
>
> You know then that it is not the reason
> That makes us happy or unhappy.
> The bird sings. Its feathers shine.
>
> The palm stands on the edge of space.
> The wind moves slowly through its branches.
> The bird's fire-fangled feathers dangle down.

For Further Reading

This list names some texts that lead further into these issues. Be sure to check the Photo Credits; if a citation is given there, I have not repeated it here.

Introduction

Decompartmentalization: Erwin Panofsky, *Renaissance and Renascences in Western Art* (New York: Harper and Row, 1972).

Hawking's science and his popular science: Quentin Smith, "Stephen Hawking's Cosmology and Theism," *Analysis* 54, no. 4 (1994): 236–43.

One: "Just Looking"

Disinterested interest: Immanuel Kant, *Critique of Judgment,* trans. Werner Pluhar (Indianapolis: Hackett, 1987).

Salpêtrière: *Iconographie de la Salpêtrière* and *Nouvelle Iconographie de la Salpêtrière* (1867–1908).

Hysteria: Georges Didi-Huberman, *Invention de l'hysterie: Charcot et Piconographie de la Salpêtrière* (Paris: Macula, 1982).

Eunuchs: See further R. Millant, *Les Eunuques à travers les âges* (Paris: Vigot, 1908); P. Sainton, "Statue d'eunuchoide infibulé," *Nouvelle Iconographie de la Salpêtrière* 21 (1908): 295–96; F. T. Camiz, "The *Castrato* Singer: From Informal to Formal Portraiture," *Artibus Asiæ* 18 (1988): 171–86.

"Dissolve the skin": Harold Brodkey, "A Story in an Almost Classical Mode," *Stories in an Almost Classical Mode* (New York, 1988), 236.

Seeing in strings of moments: John W. McClurkin et al., "Concurrent

Processing and Complexity of Temporally Encoded Neuronal Messages in Visual Perception," *Science* 253 (August 9, 1991): 675–77.

Pecham: *Perspectiva communis,* trans. David C. Lindberg (Madison: University of Wisconsin Press, 1970), Proposition 43, 126–27.

Mermaids: *Fake? The Art of Deception,* ed. by Mark Jones *et al.* (London: British Museum, 1990).

Eighteenth-century philosophers: Denis Diderot, *Lettre sur les aveugles,* in *œuvres philosophiques,* ed. P. Vernière (Paris: Garnier, 1964); Etienne Bonnotde Condillac, *Essai sur l'origine des connaissances humaines,* with Jacques Derrida, *L'archaeologie du frivole* (Paris: Galilee, 1973).

Hearing versus sight: A. J. Hudspeth, "The Cellular Basis of Hearing: The Biophysics of Hair Cells," *Science* 230, no. 4727 (November 15, 1985): 445–52, esp. 750.

A picture as the sum of many memories: J. Elkins, "On Monstrously Ambiguous Paintings," *History and Theory* 32, no. 3 (1993): 227–47, esp. 239; Thomas Nagel, "The Mind Wins!" review of John Searle, *The Rediscovery of Mind* (Cambridge: MIT Press, 1992), in *The New York Review of Books* 40, no. 5 (March 4, 1993), 39–40.

The plastic baby-doll Jesus: David Freedberg, *The Power of Images: Studies in the History and Theory of Response* (Chicago: University of Chicago Press, 1989).

Anecdote of the Michelangelo sculpture: Michael Camille, review of Hans Belting, *Bild und Kunst: Eine Geschichte des Bildes vor dem Zeitalter der Kunst* (Munich: Beck, 1990), in *The Art Bulletin* 74, no. 3 (1992): 514.

Between man and thing: Martin Heidegger, *What is a Thing?* (Chicago: Henry Regnery, 1967), 243. See also Kenneth Liberman, "The Economy of Central Australian Aboriginal Expression: An Inspection from the Vantage Point of Merleau-Ponty and Derrida," *Semiotica* 40, no. 3–4 (1982): 267–346, esp. 271.

The lost "I": *Who Comes After the Subject?* edited by Eduardo Cadava *et al.* (New York: Routledge, 1991).

Two: The Object Stares Back

Hunting spiders at night: B. J. Kaston, *How to Know the Spiders* (Dubuque, Iowa: Wm. C. Brown, 1953), 10.

The earth's shadow: A. Meinel and M. Meinel, *Sunsets, Twilights, and Evening Skies* (Cambridge: Cambridge University Press, 1983);

P. Gruner and H. Kleinert, *Die Dämmerungserscheinungen* (Hamburg: Henri Grand, 1927).

Halos: M. Minnaert, *Light and Color in the Open Air,* abr. ed., trans. H. M. Kremer-Priest (New York: Dover, 1954).

Carlo Ginzburg: C. Ginzburg, "Morelli, Freud, and Sherlock Holmes: Clues and Scientific Method," in *History Workshop* 1 (1980): 5–36.

Poe: Edgar Allen Poe, *The Purloined Letter* (London: Ulysses, 1931); and *The Purloined Poe: Lacan, Derrida, and Psychoanalytic Reading,* edited by John Muller *et al.* (Baltimore: Johns Hopkins, 1988).

Lightning: E. H. Gombrich, *Art and Illusion* (Princeton: Princeton University Press, 1984), 271.

Bees' purple: H. Rossotti, *Why the World Isn't Grey* (Princeton: Princeton University Press, 1983).

Grue and bleen: Nelson Goodman, *Languages of Art* (Indianapolis: Hackett, 1974).

Flounder vision: Adolf Portmann, *Animal Camouflage* (Ann Arbor: University of Michigan Press, 1959).

Radar imaging: Dean L. Mensa, "Radar Imaging," *International Journal of Imaging Systems and Technology* 4 (1992): 148–63, citing F. Jay, *IEEE Standard Dictionary of Electrical and Electronic Terms* (New York: IEEE, 1977), 361.

Extromission theories: David Lindberg, *Theories of Vision from al-Kindi to Kepler* (Chicago: University of Chicago Press, 1976).

Jacques Lacan: J. Lacan, *Le séminaire, livre XI: Les quatre concepts fondamentaux de la psychanalyse* (Paris, 1975), 79–107; and *Reading Seminar XI: Lacan's Four Fundamental Concepts of Psychoanalysis,* edited by Richard Feldstein *et al.* (Albany: State University of New York Press, 1995).

Mirrors: Jean Paris, *Miroirs, sommeil, soleil, espaces* (Paris: Editions Galilée, 1973), 24, cited by Anne-Marie Virot, "Réflexions sur le regard dans les *Caprices* et les *Peintures noires,*" in *Goya: regards et lectures,* Actes du colloque tenu à Aix-en-Provence les 11 et 12 décembre 1981 (Aix-en-Provence: Université de Provence, 1982), 79–91, esp. 81–82.

Lacan's harshness: Mikkel Borch-Jakobsen, *Lacan, The Absolute Master,* trans. Douglas Brick (Stanford: Stanford University Press, 1991).

Gleam on the coffee cup: E. H. Gombrich, "The Heritage of Apelles," in *The Heritage of Apelles* (Ithaca: Cornell University Press, 1976).

The sun, metaphor for all eyes: Jacques Derrida, "White Mythology:

Metaphor in the Text of Philosophy," in *Writing and Difference,* trans. Alan Bass (Chicago: University of Chicago Press, 1978).

Eyes in butterfly wings: H. F. Nijhout, *The Development and Evolution of Butterfly Wing Patterns* (Washington: Smithsonian Institution Press, 1991); Sean B. Carroll et al., "Pattern Formation and Eyespot Determination in Butterfly Wings," *Science 265* (July 1, 1994): 109–114.

Lantern fly: Roger Caillois, *The Mask of Medusa,* trans. George Ordish (New York: Clarkson N. Potter, 1964), 127.

Porcelain dachsund: Edward B. Poulton's correspondence, in *Proceedings of the Entomological Society of London* (1924), xlviii.

Fashionable insects: Antonio Berlese, *Vita e costumi . . ., Gli Insetti . . .* vol. 2 of (Milan: Società Editrice Libraria, 1925), 401, fig. 402; Paul Vignon, *Introduction à la biologie expérimentale,* in *Encyclopédie biologique,* vol. 8 (Paris: P. Lechevalier, 1930), 411.

Three: Looking Away, and Seeing Too Much

Prisons, etc.: Elaine Scarry, *The Body in Pain: The Making and Unmaking of the World* (Oxford: Oxford University Press, 1987).

Varieties of pornography: Catherine Mackinnon,

Blind spots in seeing: Rosalind Krauss, "Antivision," *October* 36 (1986): 150.

Peripheral vision: Hermann von Helmholtz, *The Perceptions of Vision,* vol. 3 of *Treatise on Physiological Optics,* trans. James P. C. Southall (New York: The Optical Society of America, 1925).

Piero della Francesca: J. Elkins, *The Poetics of Perspective* (Ithaca: Cornell University Press, 1994).

UFOs, flying machines: Ron Miller, *The Dream Machines: An Illustrated History of the Spaceship in Art, Science, and Literature* (Melbourne, Fla.: Krieger, 1993).

Visualizing the invisible: Barbara Stafford, "From 'Brilliant Ideas' to 'Fitful Thoughts': Conjecturing the unseen in Late-Eighteenth-Century Art," *Zeitschrift für Kunstgeschichte* vol. 48, no. 1 (1985): 329–363.

Georges Bataille: Bataille, *Œuvres complètes,* ed. (Paris, 1970), vol. 1, 187, and "Histoire de l'œil," vol. 1, 30–85. Bataille on rapture: *Tears of Eros,* trans. Peter Connor (San Francisco: City Lights Books, 1989), 20.

Courbet's *Origin of the World:* Linda Nochlin, "Courbet's *L'origine du monde:* The Origin Without an Original," *October* 37 (Summer 1986): 77–86.

Scientific accounts of sex: Desmond Morris, *The Naked Ape* (New York: McGraw Hill, 1967).

Death by division: R. Heindl, "Strafrechtstheorie und Praxis," *Lehrbuch der Charakterologie,* vol. 1, ed. E. Utitz (1924): 137.

Forbidden images: Thomas McEvilley, "Who Told Thee That Thou Was't Naked?" *Artforum* 25 (1987): 102–108.

Leo Steinberg: Steinberg, *The Sexuality of Christ in Renaissance Art and in Modern Oblivion* (New York: Pantheon, 1983).

Optical unconscious: The term is Walter Benjamin's; see Rosalind Krauss, *The Optical Unconscious* (Cambridge: MIT Press, 1993).

Images that fall apart: Georges Didi-Huberman, *Devant l'image* (Paris: Editions de Minuit, 1990).

Details: Daniel Arasse, *Le détail* (Paris: Flammarion, 1992).

Four: Seeing Bodies

Psychoneurology: Philip Kelman and Thomas Shipley, "Perceiving Objects Across Gaps in Space and Time," *Current Directions in Psychological Science* 1 (1992): 193–99; Kelman and Shipley, "A Theory of Visual Interpolation in Object Perception," *Cognitive Psychology* 23 (1991): 141–221; K. Nakayama and S. Shimojo, "Experiencing and Perceiving Visual Surfaces," *Science* 257 (1992): 1357–63.

Quilting points: Jacques Lacan, *The Psychoses: 1955–1956,* translated by Russell Grigg (New York: W. W. Norton, 1993).

The egg, or zoocyte: Freud, *Beyond the Pleasure Principle,* trans. James Strachey, in *The Standard Edition of the Works of Sigmund Freud* (London: Hogarth Press, 1955), vol. 18, pp. 7–64; Gilles Deleuze, "How to Make a Body Without Organs," in *A Thousand Plateaus,* trans. Brian Massumi (Minneapolis: University of Minnesota Press, 1987).

Smoothed contours: G. Kanisza, "Subjective Countours," *Scientific American* 234, no. 4 (1976): 48 ff.

Twisted bodies: David Summers, "Contrapposto . . ." *The Art Bulletin* 59 (1977): 336–61 "Maniera and Movement: The *Figura Serpentinata,*" *Art Quarterly* 35 (1972): 269–71.

Mapmaking compromises: Ulrich Graf, "Pathologische Perspektiven," *Jahresbericht der deutschen Mathematiker-Vereinigung* 50, Abt. 2, vol. 2 (1940): 35–53.

Lyapunov space: Mario Markus, "Chaos in Maps with Continuous and Discontinuous Maxima," *Computers in Physics* 4 (September/October

1990): 481–93, summarized in A. K. Dewdney, "Leaping into Lya-punov Space," *Scientific American* (September 1991), 178–180.

Proprioception: Oliver Sacks, *The Man who Mistook His Wife for a Hat* (New York: Summit, 1985).

Empathy: Robert Vischer, *Das optische Formgefühl* (1872), in *Drei Schriften zum ästhetischen Formproblem* (Halle, 1927); C. E. Gauss, "Empathy," in *Dictionary of the History of Ideas,* vol. 2, ed. P. P. Wiener (New York: Scribner, 1973); Theodor Lipps, *Ästhetik,* 2 vols. (Hamburg and Leipzig, 1903–06); *Empathy, Form, and Space: Problems in German Aesthetics 1873–1893,* edited by Harry Francis Mulgrave et al. (Santa Monica, California: Getty Center for the History of Art and Humanities, 1994).

Medical illustration: J. Elkins, "Two Conceptions of the Human Form: Bernard Siegfried Albinus and Andreas Vesalius," *Artibus et Historiæ* 14 (1986): 91–106.

Museo della Specola: B. Lanza et al., *Le Cere Anatomiche della Specola* (Florence, 1979).

Bidloo: Mario Perniola, "Between Clothing and Nudity," trans. Roger Friedman, in *Fragments for a History of the Human Body,* vol. 2, ed. Michel Feher (Cambridge, Mass., 1989), 236–65.

Visual desperation: J. Elkins, "On Visual Desperation and the Bodies of Protozoa," *Representations* 40 (1992): 33–56.

Hallucigenia: Rick Gore, "The Cambrian Period Explosion of Life," *National Geographic* 184, no. 4 (October 1993): 120–36, esp. 126–27.

Abyssal bodies: Bruce C. Heezen and Charles D. Hollister, *The Face of the Deep* (New York: Oxford University Press, 1971).

Five: What Is a Face?

Song of songs: Song of Songs 6:5–7.

Moses: William H. Propp, "The Skin of Moses' Face—Transfigured or Disfigured?" *The Catholic Biblical Quarterly* 49 (1987): 375–86. Moses sees God in Exodus 33:18–23; the "mysterious word" is *qāran,* Exodus 34:29.

Russian film experiment: Cited in Rosalind Krauss, "Cindy Sherman's Gravity: A Critical Fable," *Artforum* 32, no. 1 (1993): 163–64, 206, esp. 163.

Medusa: Robert Graves, *The Greek Myths* (Harmondsworth: Penguin, 1974), 127.

Twins: Mary Ruth Yoe, "Twin Peeks," *University of Chicago Magazine* 82, no. 4 (1990): 22–25.

Pine needles: Martin Heidegger, *What Is a Thing?* trans. by W. B. Barton, Jr. *et al.* (Chicago: H. Regnery, 1967).

Faciality machine: Gilles Deleuze and Félix Guattari, *A Thousand Plateaus, Capitalism and Schizophrenia,* trans. Brian Massumi (Minneapolis: University of Minnesota Press, 1987), 167–91.

Rembrandt: Svetlana Alpers, *Rembrandt's Enterprise: The Studio and the Market* (Chicago: University of Chicago Press, 1988).

Hydranencephaly: A. P. Norman, *Congenital Abnormalities in Infancy* (Oxford and Edinburgh, 1971).

Cloverleaf syndrome: H. A. Gathmann and R. D. Meyer, *Der Kleeblattschädel* (New York, 1977); the photo is in Richard Merle Goodman and Robert J. Gorlin, *Atlas of the Face in Genetic Disorders,* 2nd. ed. (Saint Louis: C. V. Mosby, 1963), Fig. 2.25, p. 74.

Physiognomy: Georg Christoph Lichtenberg, *Über Physiognomik, wider die Physiognomen* . . . (Steinbach: Anabas Verlag Günter Kämpf, 1970); J. C. Lavater, *Physiognomische Fragmente,* trans. T. Holcroft as *Essays on Physiognomy: For the Promotion of the Knowledge and the Love of Mankind* (London, 1804).

Mercury poisoning: J. Hermann, *Ueber die Wirkung des Quecksilbers auf den menschlichen Organismus* (Berlin, c. 1850).

Style: E. H. Gombrich, *The Sense of Order* (Ithaca, New York: Cornell University Press, 1984), 200. See also J. Elkins, "Style," *MacMillan Encyclopedia of Art* (New York: MacMillan).

Meat-eating girls: David Katz, *Animals and Men* (London, 1937).

Six: Blindness

W. S. Merwin: "He was old he will have fallen into his eyes," from "The River of Bees," *The Lice* (New York: Atheneum, 1974), 32.

Experiments with white walls: W. Metzger, "Optische Untersuchungen am Ganzfeld. II. Zur Phänomenologie des homogenen Ganzfelds," *Psychologische Forschung* 13 (1930), 6–29; J. E. Hochberg, W. Triebel, and G. Seaman, "Color Adaptation under Conditions of Homogeneous Visual Stimulation (Ganzfeld)," *Journal of Experimental Psychology* 41 (1951): 153–59.

The male gaze: Laura Mulvey, "Visual Pleasure and Narrative Cinema," in B. Wallis, ed. *Art After Modernism: Rethinking Representation*

(New York, 1984); E. Snow, "Theorizing the Male Gaze: Some Problems," *Representations* 25 (1989): 30–41.

Gazing as overall seeing: Norman Bryson, *Vision and Painting, The Logic of the Gaze* (Cambridge: Cambridge University Press, 1984), esp. chapter 5.

Franz's stare: Siegfried Wichmann, *Franz von Lenbach und seine Zeit* (Cologne: M. DuMont Schauberg, 1973).

Steinberg on Picasso: Leo Steinberg, "The Philosophical Brothel," *October* 44 (Spring 1988): 12, 14, 15.

Rooted in place, returning stares: Alois Reigl, *Das holländische Gruppenporträt* (Vienna, 1931); Jonathan Crary, *Techniques of the Observer: On Vision and Modernity in the Nineteenth Century* (Cambridge: MIT Press, 1990).

Paul de Man: *Blindness and Insight: Essays in the Rhetoric of Contemporary Criticism* (Minneapolis: University of Minnesota Press, 1971), esp. 102 ff.

Chromatopsia: Semir Zeki, "The Visual Image in Mind and Brain," *Scientific American* 267, no. 3 (September 1992): 73.

Retinal outline and image detectors: David Marr, *Vision* (San Francisco: W. H. Freeman, 1982).

Awareness of three dimensions: Ray Jackendoff, *Consciousness and the Computational Mind* (Cambridge and MIT Press and Bradford Books, 1987); Francis Crick and Christof Koch, "The Problem of Consciousness," *Scientific American* 267, no. 3 (September 1992): 154.

Blindsight: L. Weiskrantz, *Blindsight: A Case Study and Implications* (Oxford: Oxford University Press, 1986); Petra Stoerig, "Sources of Blindsight," *Science* 261 (July 23, 1993): 493; Ray Jayawardhana, "Unraveling the Dark Paradox of 'Blindsight,'" *Science* 258 (November 27, 1992): 1438–39; Robert Friedrich et al., "Residual Vision in a Scotoma: Implications for Blindsight," ibid., 1489–91.

Crick on consciousness: Crick and Koch, op. cit., 153.

Picture of a man thinking: J. W. Belliveau et al., "Functional Mapping of the Human Visual Cortex by Magnetic Resonance Imaging," *Science* 254 (November 1, 1991): 716–19.

Metaphysics of thinking: Plato, *The Republic,* Book 5; Mikkel Borch-Jakobsen, *Lacan, The Absolute Master,* esp. 52 ff.

Truth as unveiling: Martin Heidegger, *An Introduction to Metaphysics,* trans. Ralph Manheim (New York: Yale University Press, 1959),

102; Philippe Lacoue-Labarthe, *Typography: Mimesis, Philosophy, Politics,* ed. Christopher Fynsk, with an introduction by Jacques Derrida (Cambridge: Harvard University Press, 1989), esp. 81 ff.

Hysterical blindness: H. Kron, "Ueber hysterische Blindheit," *Neurologisches Centralblatt* 14 (July 16, 1902): 649–60.

Experiments on tactual images: See also Leo Kanner and Paul Schilder, "Movements of Optic Images and the Optic Imagination of Movements," *The Journal of Nervous and Mental Diseases* 72, no. 5 (November 1930): 489–517.

Chimpanzee picture: See also Desmond Morris, *The Biology of Art, A Study in the Picture-Making Behaviour of the Great Apes and Its Relationship to Human Art* (New York: Alfred A. Knopf, 1962), esp. 30–31; and Bernhard Rensch, "Malversuche mit Affen," *Zeitschrift für Tierpsychologie* 18 (1961): 347–64.

Pictures as signs of intimacy: Mihaly Csikszentmihalyi and Eugene Rochberg-Halton, *The Meaning of Things, Domestic Symbols and the Self* (Cambridge: Cambridge University Press, 1981).

Double blindness: Jacques Derrida, *Mémoires d'aveugle, l'autoportrait et autres ruines,* Exhibition Catalogue, Louvre, October 26, 1990-January 21, 1991 (Paris, 1990), trans. Michael Naas and Pascale-Anne Brault as *Memoirs of the Blind* (Chicago: University of Chicago Press, 1993).

Envoi

Wittgenstein's picture theory: P. M. S. Hacker, "The Rise and Fall of the Picture Theory," *Perspectives on the Philosophy of Wittgenstein,* ed. Irving Block (Cambridge: MIT Press, 1981), 85–109: Max Black, *A Companion to Wittgenstein's* Tractatus (Ithaca: Cornell University Press, 1964); J. Elkins, "Torturing Paintings in Wittgenstein's *Tractatus,*" *Visible Language,* forthcoming.

Ill feet: Farid-Uddin Attar, *The Bird Parliament,* trans. Edward Fitzgerald (Boston: L. C. Page, 1899), 132.

Argus peacock: G. W. H. Davison, "Sexual Selection and the Mating System of *Argusianus argus* (Aves: Phasianidæ)," *Biological Journal of the Linnean Society* 15 (1981): 91–104.

Wallace Stevens: "Of Mere Being," in *Opus Posthumous,* ed. by Milton Bates (New York: Knopf, 1989), 141.

Photo Credits

1. A eunuch. From A. Marie, "Eunuchisme et érotisme," *Nouvelle Iconographie de la Salpêtrière* 19 (1906):472–474, plate 68.
2. A mermaid. Photo: author.
3. *Icon with the Fiery Eye*. (1340s). Moscow, Cathedral of the Dormition, Inv. no. 956.
4. Universe of eyes. From Thomas Wright, *An Original Theory or New Hypothesis of the Universe* [1750] (New York: Elsevier, 1971). Photo from Edward Harrison, *Darkness at Night: A Riddle of the Universe* (Cambridge,: Harvard University Press, 1987), fig. 9.3, 106.
5. Ice halos in Alaska. Photo by Takeshi Ohtake. From R. Greeler, *Rainbows, Halos, and Glories* (Cambridge: Cambridge University Press, 1980), color plate 2.21.
6. Top: Fourier transform of GaAs hologram with box indicating sideband used to reconstruct modulus and phase image. Lower left: modulus of GaAs image wave. Bottom right: phase of GaAs image wave. From M. Gajdardziska-Josifovska et al., "Accurate Measurements of Mean Inner Potential of Crystal Wedges Using Digital Electron Holograms," *Ultramicroscopy* 50 (1993):285–99, fig. 3.
7. Dr. Shigeyuki Hosoki, the letters NANO-SPACE written on the surface of MoS_2. From François Grey, "STM-Based Nanotechnology: The Japanese Challenge," *Advanced Materials* 5, no. 10 (1993):407–10, fig. 1, 705.
8. Fresco of the Madonna and Child and defect in the wall behind it. Fontecchio (Abruzzo), Italy. Photos by Guiseppe Schirripa Spagnolo. Interferometry image from D. Paoletti and G. Schirripa Spagnolo, "Fiber Optics DSPI for *In Situ* Diagnostics," *Journal of Optics* (Paris) 24, no. 1 (1993): 7–10, fig. 4.

9. Flounders against patterned backgrounds. From W. P. Pycraft, *Camouflage in Nature* (London: Hutchinson & Co., 1925), facing p. 53. Otherwise in Adolf Portmann, *Tarnung im Tierreich,* trans. A. J. Pomerans as *Animal Camouflage* (Ann Arbor: University of Michigan Press, 1959), fig. 96, 91.

10. Radar image of a plane. From Dean L. Mensa, "Radar Imaging," *International Journal of Imaging Systems and Technology* 4, no. 3 (1992): 148–63, fig. 30 (left half).

11. *Pararge aegeria, achine,* and *megera.* From Russero Verity, *Le farfalle diurne d'Italia,* vol. 5 (Florence: Marzocco, 1953), pl. 55, detail.

12. The lantern fly, *Laternaria sp.* From Edward B. Poulton's correspondence, in *Proceedings of the Entomological Society of London* (1924), xliii–xlix, plate A.

13. Scene in the Okefenokee swamp. Photo: author.

14. The nudibranch *Chromadoris vicina.* From Terry Gosliner, *Nudibranchs of Southern Africa, A Guide to Opisthobranch Molluscs of Southern Africa* (Monterey, Calif.: Sea Challengers; Al Cajon, Calif.: Jeff Hamann; and Leiden: E. J. Brill, 1987), fig. 109, 75.

15. The nudibranch *Corambe sp.* From Gosliner, *Nudibranchs,* fig. 166, 95. 16. *Bocidium globulare.* Photo from *The Illustrated London News* (April 5, 1924), 588.

17. Patient at the Salpêtrière. From *Nouvelle Iconographie de la Salpêtrière.*

18. Albrecht Dürer, *Self-Portrait.* (c. 1507). Weimar, Schlossmuseum.

19. Electrical flying machine. From Louis Guillaume de la Folie, *Le philosophe sans prétention ou l'Homme rare . . .* (Paris: Clousier, 1775).

20. Gustave Courbet, *The Origin of the World.* Private collection. Reproduced from Robert Fernier, *La vie et l'oeuvre de Gustave Courbet* (Paris and Lausanne, 1977–78).

21. Chinese execution. (1927). From Sandy Lesberg, *Violence in our Time* (New York: Peebles Press, 1977), 71.

22. Chinese execution. (1927). Ibid.

23. *Ling-tschi,* Chinese execution by division into a thousand parts. From Robert Heindl, "Strafrechtstheorie und Praxis," *Lehrbuch der Charakterologie* 1 (1924): 89–152, plates following.

24. Lucas Cranach, *The Crucifixion.* (1503). Munich, Alte Pinakothek.

25. The Hankel function, altitude chart and relief. From Eugene Jahnke and Fritz Emde, *Tables of Functions with Formulae and Curves,* 4th ed. (New York: Dover, 1945), 132, fig. 72, and 133, fig. 73.

26. Sandro Botticelli, *Adoration of the Magi,* detail and entire. Florence, Uffizi. Alinari/Art Resource, New York.

27. The constellation Microscopium. From Johann Ebert Bode, *Uranographia* (1797–1801); a globe by John Adams (1751–60), Science Museum, London; and Samuel Leigh, *Urania's Mirror* (1820–1842). Photos from John Gustav Delly, "Microscopium—The Celestial Microscope," *The Microscope* 36 (1988):281–92.

28. Common sea dragon. From Fred Bavendam, "You Don't Have to Look Like a Fish to Succeed as One," *Smithsonian Magazine* 23, no. 5 (August 1992):56–61.

29. Mario Markus and Benno Hess, a Lyapunov "jellyfish." From A. K. Dewdney, "Leaping into Lyapunov Space," *Scientific American* (September 1991): 178–80.

30. Benvenuto Cellini, *Perseus and Medusa,* detail of Medusa detached from Perseus. Loggia dei Lanzi, Florence. Photo: David Finn.

31. Matthias Grünewald, study for the Arm of Saint Sebastian, for the Isenheim Altarpiece. (1512–1515). Left: Staatliche Kunstsammlungen Dresden; right: Museum Dahlem, Berlin.

32. Picasso, *Tête de femme souriante.* August 10, 1943.

33. Mattäus Merian, anthropomorphic landscape. Early 17th c. New York, Mrs. Alfred H. Barr Jr. Collection. Photo from *The Arcimboldo Effect* (New York: Abbeville Press, 1987), 197.

34. Extensors of the forearm. From Govard Bidloo, *Anatomia humani corporis* (1685), Tab. 70.

35. Left: torso of a woman who died at term. Right: the same, dissected. From Charles Nicolas Jenty, *Demonstratio uteri praegnantis mulieris cum foetu ad partum maturi* (Nuremberg, 1761).

36. Cerebriform, or cartographic, tongue. From L. Bianchini, "Langue cérébriforme chez un aliéné épileptique, observation sur un cas de tératomorphisme congénital de la langue," *Nouvelle Iconographie de la Salpêtrière* 16 (1903): 252–56, plate 51.

37. The Cambrian organism *Hallucigenia sparsa,* USNM 83935 (holotype) and diagram. Photo courtesy Simon Conway Morris, University of Cambridge. Diagram from Morris, "A New Metazoan from the Cambrian Burgess Shale, British Columbia," *Palaeontology* 20 (1977): 624–640, pl. 73, text-fig. 2.

38. Deep-sea angler *Borophryne apogon,* female, with two parasitic males attached. Inset: the angler *Linophryne argyresca,* showing lures and attached male. Photo by William T. O'Day. Inset from C. Tate

Regan and Ethelwynn Trewavas, *Deep-Sea Angler-Fishes* (Copenhagen: The Carlsberg Foundation, 1932), pl. X, fig. 3.

39. Microscopic "fish." From L. Joblot, *Descriptions et usages de plusieurs nouveaux microscopes . . .* (Paris, 1718), plate 6.

40. Rear view of the trap-door spider *Cyclocosmia truncata.* From Andreas Feininger, *The Anatomy of Nature* (New York: Dover, 1956), 144–45.

41. Three fear grimaces (left column) of rhesus monkeys and six chimeras made by doubling half the face. Photos by Marc D. Hauser.

42. David Teplica, *The Awakening.* 1989. 8' × 10' selenium toned gelatin silver print. Courtesy of the Art Institute of Chicago.

43. Model of the face of a five-week-old embryo. From B. K. B. Berkowitz et al., *Color Atlas and Textbook of Oral Anatomy* (Chicago: Year Book Medical Publishers, 1978), figure 378, 144.

44. Cosmetic diagrams of the face. From Henryk Mierzecki, *Kosmetyka, zars encyklopedyczny kosmetyki lekarskiej, technologicznej i zdobniczej* (Warsaw: Panstwowy Zaklad Wydawnictw Lekarskich, 1960), figs. 83, 87, 89, 98, 106, 109, pp. 377, 381, 383, 392, 400, 402.

45. Rembrandt, *Portrait of Jan Six.* (1654). Amsterdam, Six Collection.

46. Hydranencephaly. From Archibald Percy Norman, *Congenital Abnormalities in Infancy* (Oxford and Edinburgh: Blackwell Scientific, 1963), fig. 2.25, 74.

47. Mercury poisoning in a syphilitic patient. From Josef Hermann, *Ueber die Wirkung des Quecksilbers auf den menschlichen Organismus* (Teschen: Prochaska, 1873), pl. III.

48. Facial tumor. A. Auvert, *Selecta praxis medico-chirurgicæ* (Paris: Plon, 1851), reprinted in Goldschmid, *Entwicklung,* pl. 57.

49. Chartres cathedral, west façade. (12th-16th c.) Alinari/Art Resource, New York.

50. Meat-eating and vegetarian girls. From David Katz, *Psychological Atlas* (New York: Philosophical Library, 1948), figs. 127, 128, 131, 132, pp. 73–74.

51. Roman Cieslewicz, *La Joconde.* (1974). Photomontage. Private collection, New York. From *The Arcimboldo Effect* (New York: Abbeville, 1987), 390.

52. Family photograph. Photo: author.

53. Franz von Lenbach, self-portrait with his wife. From Siegfried Wichmann, *Franz von Lenbach und seine Zeit* (Cologne: M. DuMont Schauberg, 1973), fig. 1.

54. Franz von Lenbach with a dog. Wichmann, *Franz von Lenbach,* fig. 8.

55. Picasso, *Women of Avignon.* (1907). New York, Metropolitan Musem of Art. Acquired through the Lilie P. Bliss Bequest. Photograph © 1995 The Museum of Modern Art, New York.

56. Aboriginal woman. From Carl Heinrich von Stratz, *Naturgeschichte des Menschen* (Stuttgart: Enke, 1904), fig. 35, 89. Used by permission.

58. Simulation of macular degeneration, from the exhibit *Seeing without Sight.* From *Update, 1991–92 Smithsonian Institution Traveling Exhibition Service* (Baltimore: Schneidereith and Sons, 1991), 95.

58. Magnetic resonance image of a man seeing flashing lights. Courtesy John Belliveau, Massachusetts General Hospital NMR center.

59. Experiments in tactual images. From Walter Bromberg and Paul Schildler, "On Tactile Imagination and Tactile After-Effects," *The Journal of Nervous and Mental Disease* 76, no. 1 (July 1932): 1–24, 133–55. Left: plate III, fig. 25. Middle: plate VII, fig. 48. Right: plate II, fig. 10.

60. Drawing by the chimpanzee Jonny. February 27, 1957. From Hermann Goja. "Zeichenversuche mit Menschenaffen," *Zeitschrift für Tierpsychologie* 16 (1959):369–73, fig. 2.

61. Drawing by the chimpanzee Fanny. From Goja, "Zeichenversuche," fig. 3, 373.

62. The blue peacock, *Pavo cristatus.*

63. Argus pheasant, *Argusianus argus.* Photo courtesy Kenneth W. Fink.

Index